P9-DWX-710

GED BASICS

3RD EDITION

Nancy Lawrence

THOMSON
ARCO

Australia • Canada • Mexico • Singapore • Spain • United Kingdom • United States

An ARCO Book

ARCO is a registered trademark of Thomson Learning, Inc., and is used herein under license by Peterson's.

About The Thomson Corporation and Peterson's

With revenues of US$7.2 billion, The Thomson Corporation (www.thomson.com) is a leading global provider of integrated information solutions for business, education, and professional customers. Its Learning businesses and brands (www.thomsonlearning.com) serve the needs of individuals, learning institutions, and corporations with products and services for both traditional and distributed learning.

Peterson's, part of The Thomson Corporation, is one of the nation's most respected providers of lifelong learning online resources, software, reference guides, and books. The Education Supersite^{SM} at www.petersons.com—the Internet's most heavily traveled education resources—has searchable databases and interactive tools for contacting U.S.-accredited institutions and programs. In addition, Peterson's serves more that 105 million education consumers annually.

For more information, contact Peterson's, 2000 Lenox Drive, Lawrenceville, NJ 08648; 800-338-3282; or find us on the World Wide Web at: www.petersons.com/about

Third Edition

ISBN: 0-7689-0987-2

Printed in the United States of America

10 9 8 7 6 5 4 3 2 1   04 03 02

Contents

CHAPTER 1

Using This Guide

ANSWERING YOUR QUESTIONS ABOUT THE GED

What Is the GED?

GED stands for General Educational Development. The GED is designed to be a test of adult basic knowledge in five content areas (Language Arts, Writing; Social Studies; Science; Language Arts, Reading; and Math). The test is an opportunity for you to earn the equivalent of a high school diploma without having to return to a formal school setting. Every state has testing centers that are qualified to administer the test. If the test sites are not listed in your phone book, you can call your state Department of Education or your local superintendent of schools to find the nearest test site location. These contacts can also explain scoring procedures for your state and the cost of taking the test.

What's on the Test?

You will be tested on Writing in a two-part exam. The first part consists of 50 multiple-choice questions dealing with sentence structure, organization, mechanics, and usage. You will be given 1 hour and 15 minutes to complete this part of the test. You will be asked to read several passages of twelve to eighteen sentences each. Each passage is followed by a series of multiple-choice questions that ask you to either find mistakes in the sentences or indicate the best way to rewrite the sentences. Thirty percent of the total number of questions deal with sentence structure; 30 percent test your knowledge of standard usage; 15 percent deal with the organization of ideas; and 25 percent deal with mechanics such as punctuation, proper use of homophones, and capitalization.

The second part of the Language Arts, Writing test is your opportunity to write an essay. You will be given your topic and scratch paper on which to write an outline and draft. You will have 45 minutes to compose an essay of approximately 200 words that clearly states your ideas and is reasonably well organized and free of mechanical errors.

The Social Studies test is made up of 50 multiple-choice questions, and you will have 1 hour and 20 minutes in which to complete it. The five areas this test covers and the percentage of questions for each area are as follows: history (40 percent), economics (20 percent), civics and government (25 percent), and geography (15 percent). The reading material for this test will either be formatted as a single paragraph or as a longer passage. You will be expected to interpret graphics such as graphs, maps, and political cartoons.

The Science test is similar to the Social Studies test in format—you will be asked to read either short paragraphs or longer passages, and you will need to have the ability to understand graphic information. Forty-five percent of the Science test covers life science, 20 percent deals with earth and space science, and 35 percent with chemistry and physics. There are 50 multiple-choice questions on this test, and you will have 1 hour and 20 minutes to finish this component of the GED.

Language Arts, Reading is the fourth component of the exam. The reading selections vary from short poems to longer passages and include contemporary classical literature, poetry, and drama. The prose passages will consist of selections written before 1920, between 1920 and 1960, and after 1960. Although there are only 40 multiple-choice questions in this test, you will be given 1 hour and 5 minutes to complete the test because many of the passages are lengthy. The majority of the test (75 percent) covers popular literature. The remaining 25 percent is non-fiction: reviews, business, and biography. You will be asked not only to comprehend what you are reading, but to analyze the material and apply your knowledge to related topics. Each passage of this section of the GED is headed by a question designed to direct your thoughts to the purpose of the passage. By paying attention to these questions, you will be on the right track for formulating the best possible answer to the multiple-choice questions following the reading selection.

Math is the final test in the battery that makes up the GED. You will have 90 minutes to complete this portion. Each of the 50 questions has five answers from which to choose. Half of the Math test (25 questions) will require you to apply basic operations using whole numbers, fractions, and decimals. You will also be tested on your knowledge of ratios, percents, and measurement. Your skills on computation will be applied to word problems, so your ability to read and comprehend the questions is essential for success. Twenty to thirty percent of the Math test will deal with algebra, and 20 percent to 30 percent will test your basic knowledge of geometry and measurement. The Math test is arranged so that the easier questions will be at the beginning of the test. This is important to remember when pacing yourself during the test.

How Is the Test Scored, and When Do I Know My Results?

Although scoring varies slightly from state to state, generally, you will need to achieve a minimum total score of 225 points or an average of 45 points on each of the five tests. This means that you don't necessarily need a score of 45 points on *each* test as long as the average of the five is 45. A score of *less than* 35 points on any of the components will mean, however, that you will have to repeat that test. In other words, as long as you score a minimum of 35 on one test, you can "make up" points by doing exceptionally well on another test.

Receiving the results of your test will vary depending on the center where you took the test. It is possible that the center will let you know the score immediately, but usually the scores will be mailed to you within eight weeks. Your testing center will be able to let you know its scoring procedures. The center will also be able to explain what fees, if any, are involved with testing in your state and receiving your credential.

After you've received your official scores in the mail, you will be eligible to retest, if necessary, on any or all of the sections of the GED in which you did not meet the standard score for your state. At the time of retesting, you will be given a different version of the test, which means that you will not be tested on the same questions you worked with previously.

The official transcript of your scores that you will receive in the mail is not the GED credential, although it may be used to enter college or as proof for employment purposes that you have achieved a GED. The GED credential, or diploma, is a separate document that is issued by the state in which you live. Some states require that you reach a minimum age before the credential is issued to you, although you will have a transcript of your scores soon after completing the test. It is important to keep the credential in a safe place because a state will issue only one to you. Official copies of your transcript will generally be made available to you through your state for a fee.

Study Tips for Passing the GED

This book is designed to help you study for the GED. Although it is divided into sections corresponding to the test, you will find that the guide has been arranged so that the Language Arts, Reading component is first. Because your ability to read and comprehend what you have read is crucial for the entire test, most of what you learn in this chapter about developing your reading skills will be helpful to you throughout your studies.

Whether you take the GED in one sitting or spread it out over a period of several days, it is a long test. There are some proven strategies that will help to make this a successful experience for you. These strategies are reviewed in general below, and they will be discussed in greater detail in each of the following chapters.

Planning

Your chances of passing the GED on the first try will be improved by determining how much time you will need to thoroughly study for the test and then choosing a realistic target date for testing. You probably already have a good idea of your strengths and weaknesses, in terms of general knowledge, and after briefly reviewing the competencies addressed in each test, you will be able to decide which areas will require more attention than others. You will need to devise a systematic approach to studying—one that works best for you. As a rule, "cramming" is not the best way to tackle studying for the GED. Remember that the GED is not based on recalling facts—your ability to analyze and interpret information is the key to success, and this ability is not learned in an all-night study session.

After deciding the areas to which you will devote the majority of your time, make up a study schedule for yourself. You will ultimately learn more by working on small sections of material than by trying to do everything at once. This might mean that you will only be studying 1 hour each day, or you might choose to spend longer periods of time on a particularly difficult section. The important thing is to devise a plan and then stick to it.

It is also important to find the right place to study. Choose a location that is comfortable for you, but not so comfortable that you get sleepy. Ideally, you should be at a desk or seated at a table with good lighting where you can spread out your materials and have a good writing surface. Make sure there are no distractions, such as a television, in the place you choose.

In working out your study schedule, don't forget to factor in time to periodically go back and review sections you have already completed to refresh your memory and to prepare you for upcoming sections. Even though you might have completed Language Arts, Reading, the reading skills you applied there will also be applicable to Science and Social Studies. You will be asked in these sections to read for the main idea and details, and you will be required to know how to draw conclusions from some of the passages. Analyzing data in the Math section of the book will also be helpful in other sections where you will need to read and decipher maps and charts.

Get a good night's sleep before your test day, and avoid the temptation to "cram" for the test. If you have followed your study schedule, last minute studying won't be necessary and will only confuse you and leave you tired on the day of the test. Although it is natural to be nervous when you are faced with the actual test, if you have prepared yourself well, you won't panic, and after you begin the test, you will be able to relax and concentrate on your task.

Attitude

Your mental outlook will affect your test-taking ability. Everyone has a wide base of knowledge gleaned from just living, and being able to apply this knowledge is what much of the GED is all about. If you have worked in a department store where you have had to apply discounts to the prices of merchandise, you have a working knowledge of decimals, for example. If you have cooked, you are probably experienced in working with fractions. Have you ever used public transportation? If so, you are already familiar with reading charts in the form of timetables to get to your destination. Analyzing your skills and giving yourself credit for what you already know will go a long way in boosting your self-confidence. At this point, achieving your GED might seem like an overwhelming task, but after you scan the topics in this book, you will realize that you already have many of the skills you need for success in this endeavor. Some of the material in this book will be new to you; but generally, you will be learning new ways to apply a great deal of knowledge you already have.

You have already decided to take the GED for your own reasons. You might be planning to attend college, or you might need your GED for promotion in a job or for licensing in a trade, or you might have chosen to pursue your GED for your own personal satisfaction. Whatever your reasons are for taking the GED, you have made a commendable decision that will affect your life in a positive way. Staying focused on your goal will help you to overcome any doubts and frustrations along the way.

Multiple-Choice Questions

With the exception of the essay component, the GED test is formatted with multiple-choice questions that require you to choose the best answer from five possibilities. There are a number of things to keep in mind when you are taking a multiple-choice test:

- **Make sure you understand the question.** Read each question carefully so you know exactly what it is asking. It is often wise to read the question even before you read the passage so you have an idea of what to look for in the passage.

- **Attempt to answer the question in your own words before you even read the choices.** If you can answer the question in your own words, you will simply have to choose the answer that best matches in wording what you already know is correct.

- **Read all the answer choices carefully.** The first answer you see might appear to be the correct one, but by reading further, you might discover that there is a better choice.

- **Eliminate decidedly wrong answers.** Because you already know that there is only one best answer, you can usually eliminate at least one answer that you instinctively know is wrong or illogical.

- **Focus on the main idea of the passage you read.** Generally, the correct answer is embedded in the passage's main idea.

- **Don't waste time on a question that is completely puzzling to you.** Because these are timed tests, you can't afford to spend too much time on one question. You can always go back to the questions that were difficult for you. Sometimes, by proceeding, you will actually be able to get a hint from the questions that follow.

- **When you have completed the test, review your answers.** Reviewing your answers will cut down on the possibility that you knew the correct answer but inadvertently chose the wrong space to fill in on your answer card.

- **Answer every question.** Your score is derived from the number of questions you get right. There is no penalty for answering a question wrong, so your best guess to a difficult question is far better than not to try at all.

The Essay

For many people, the thought of writing a 200-word essay is a scary one. Most of us don't write on a daily basis, so putting ideas down on paper in a logical and clear fashion is something that doesn't come naturally. Making an outline and a first draft of the essay will help you create a good essay. Chapter 3 of this guide will go into greater detail explaining how to write an essay that will pass the scrutiny of the readers. Proofreading for clarity and structure is also covered in Chapter 3.

About This Book

Each of the chapters in this guide deals specifically with one of the elements of the GED. At the beginning of each chapter, you will find study tips for each component that will help you review the material efficiently and prepare for the test. Following the study tips are tutorials for every subsection of the GED. Finally, each subsection includes practice exercises and a mini-test so you can track your progress. The answers to the tests are included in each subsection as well as an explanation of each answer. By testing yourself periodically and fully understanding the answers to the test questions, you will ensure that you are able to answer each type of question that arises on the test. You might find that keeping a notebook handy while you go through the guide is a good idea. Jotting down terms, examples, and definitions as you go along will help you to remember concepts and key points.

CHAPTER 2

Language Arts, Reading

TEST-TAKING TIPS

The Language Arts, Reading test will challenge your ability to read for comprehension. The questions will deal with nonfiction, commentary, fiction, drama, and poetry. You will be reading passages for the main idea, details, and inference.

For each passage presented, there will be a purpose question. It is important that you know what is going to be asked before you start to read the passage. By reading the purpose question, you can focus your interpretation of the material on answering a specific question. If you look at the selections of answers prior to reading the passage, you will be able to concentrate better on the specific information you will need to make a correct choice.

There are 45 items on the Language Arts, Reading portion of the GED, and you will be given 65 minutes in which to complete the test. Budget your time so that you can give each passage the time you need. Often, skimming the passage first will give you a general idea of the content, and then going back and reading it carefully will allow you to zero in on the correct answer.

Look for word clues as you read. The clues will present themselves in the purpose question, in the choices of answers, and in the passages themselves. If you come across an unfamiliar word, you can sometimes determine the meaning of the word by looking at the words around it. Because you can't afford to waste a lot of time figuring out what a word means, you will have to keep reading and settle for a general idea of the meaning of a word.

NONFICTION

Nonfiction is any prose that claims to be true. It can take the form of an essay, a first person narrative, or a longer work.

The main idea of a passage is part of the topic of the passage. While the topic is the subject matter of the passage, the main idea is the most important idea stated about the topic. Frequently, the main idea is stated in the beginning of a passage, and the rest of the sentences are details that further explain the main idea. Or, the main idea could be the last sentence of a paragraph. In this case, the details lead up to the main idea.

The main idea will not necessarily be stated outright in the passage. If it is not directly expressed, the main idea will be implied, and you will be able to find it by looking at the passage as a whole and making an educated guess at what it is. Again, you would ask yourself the questions, "What is the general topic of this passage?" and "What is the most important idea the author is discussing?" By answering these questions, you can make an educated guess as to what the main idea is.

After you have identified the main idea of a passage, look at the supporting details. Each sentence should give you more information about the passage. The details will help you to see the entire picture the author is attempting to paint.

Practice

Choose the *one* best answer to each question.

Items 1–4 refer to the following passage.

All through my childhood I spent much of my time on the shore. It was not so quiet and solitary then as it is today. Those were the days when the mackerel fishing was good, and the shore was dotted with fishing houses. Many of the farmers had a fishing house on the shore field of their farms, with a boat drawn up on the skids below. Grandfather always fished mackerel in the summer, his boat manned by two or three French Canadians, fishing on the shores. Just where the rocks left off and the sandshore began was quite a little colony of fishing houses. The place was called Cawnpore, owing to the fact that on the day and hour when the last nail was being driven into the last house news arrived of the massacre of Cawnpore in the Indian Mutiny. There is not a house left there now.

The men would get up at three or four in the morning and go out fishing. Then we children had to take their breakfast down at eight, later on their dinner, and if the fish "schooled" all day, their supper also. In vacations we would spend most of the day there, and I soon came to know every cove, headland, and rock on that shore. We would watch the boats through the sky-glass, paddle in the water, gather shells and pebbles and mussels, and sit on the rocks and eat dulse, literally, by the yard. The rocks at low tide were covered by millions of snails, as we called them. I think the correct name is periwinkle. We often found great, white, empty "snail" shells, as big as our fists, that had been washed ashore from some distant strand or deep sea haunt. I early learned by heart, Holmes' beautiful lines on "The Chambered Nautilus," and I rather fancied myself sitting dreamily on a big boulder with my bare, wet feet tucked up under my print skirt, holding a huge "snail" shell in my sunburned paw and appealing to my soul to "build thee more stately mansions."

—L.M. Montgomery

1. Which of the following sentences best states the main idea of the whole passage?

    (1) Grandfather loved to fish.

    (2) The author has wonderful childhood memories of the shore.

    (3) The farmers had fishing houses along the shore.

    (4) The author liked to collect snail shells along the shore.

    (5) The children worked hard bringing meals to the fishermen.

2. Which sentence best describes the main idea of the second paragraph?

    (1) The children worked hard bringing meals to the fishermen.

    (2) The author liked to collect snail shells along the shore.

    (3) The author spent her summer days exploring the shore.

    (4) The author liked to daydream.

    (5) The children played well together.

3. Which of the following details supports the main idea of the passage?

    (1) The farmers had fishing houses along the shore.

    (2) The men would fish all day.

    (3) The rocks were covered with snails.

    (4) Cawnpore was named after the massacre of Cawnpore.

    (5) The children would spend all day at the shore.

4. How does the author compare the shore of her childhood to the shore of her adulthood?

    (1) It was less quiet and solitary.

    (2) It was more quiet and solitary.

    (3) It had more snail shells to collect.

    (4) The author no longer spends vacations there.

    (5) There were more boats in her childhood.

Summarizing means to restate the main ideas of the passage in your own words. This can help you better understand the author's intention and enables you to focus on what a paragraph is about. After you have read a passage for the first time, try to think about what the author wrote. Formulate a sentence or two that summarizes the main idea. Then, it will be easier to go back to the passage and select the important details.

Authors often use **comparison and contrast** to express an idea. When an author **compares** two or more things, he or she points out the similarities between the objects or ideas. When **contrast** is used, the differences are pointed out.

Another devise used by writers is cause and effect. In this case, the author will explain both an event or an occurrence and the reason why the event happened. The effect is the event itself, and the cause is the reason it happened. Frequently, the effect is described in the topic sentence. The causes are the details in the rest of the passage that reflect back on the effect.

Choose the *one* best answer to each question.
Items 5–8 refer to the following passage.

In daily life, we assume as certain many things which, on a closer scrutiny, are found to be so full of apparent contradictions that only a great amount of thought enables us to know what it is that we really may believe. In the search for certainty, it is natural to begin with our present experiences, and in some sense, no doubt, knowledge is to be derived from them. But any statement as to what it is that our immediate experiences make us know is very likely to be wrong. It seems to me that I am now sitting in a chair, at a table of a certain shape, on which I see sheets of paper with writing or print. By turning my head I see out of the window buildings and clouds and the sun. I believe that the sun is about ninety-three million miles from the earth; that it is a hot globe many times bigger than the earth; that owing to the earth's rotation, it rises every morning, and will continue to do so for an indefinite time in the future. I believe that, if another normal person comes into my room, he will see the same chairs and table and books and papers as I see, and that the table which I see is the same as the table which I feel pressing against my arm. All this seems to be so evident as to be hardly worth stating, except in answer to a man who doubts whether I know anything. Yet all this may be reasonably doubted, and all of it requires much careful discussion before we can be sure that we have stated it in a form that is wholly true.

To make our difficulties plain, let us concentrate attention on the table. To the eye it is oblong, brown and shiny, to the touch it is smooth and cool and hard, when I tap it, it gives out a wooden sound. Any one else who sees and feels and hears the table will agree with this description, so that it might seem as if no difficulty would arise; but as soon as we try to be more precise our troubles begin. Although I believe that the table is "really" of the same colour all over, the parts that reflect the light look much brighter than the other parts, and some parts look white because of reflected light. I know that, if I move, the parts that reflect the light will be different, so that the apparent distribution of colours on the table will change. It follows that if several people are looking at the table at the same moment, no two of them will see exactly the same distribution of colours, because no two can see it from exactly the same point of view, and any change in the point of view makes some change in the way the light is reflected.

—Bertrand Russell

5. What would be the best title for this passage?
   (1) How the Sun Makes Things Appear Different
   (2) The Desk in My Office
   (3) Looking Carefully at Everyday Objects
   (4) How People See Things Differently
   (5) Observations of the Sun

6. The way people perceive the desk in the author's office is an example of

    (1) cause and effect

    (2) detail

    (3) compare and contrast

    (4) inference

    (5) main idea

7. If the author uses how the table is perceived as an effect, what is the cause?

    (1) the shape of the table

    (2) the reflection of the light on the table

    (3) several people looking at the table

    (4) our immediate experiences

    (5) the color of the table

8. What can the reader infer from this passage?

    (1) The author looks at things differently than other people do.

    (2) The author believes that the sun makes things look different to different people.

    (3) A change in point of view will change how people look at his table.

    (4) The author feels that the table is just an example of how people see everything differently according to their point of view.

    (5) The reflection of sunlight on an object will cause people to see it differently.

Answers

1. **(2)** The main idea of the passage is that the author had wonderful childhood memories. Although the other answers are true statements, they are details that support the main idea.

2. **(3)** The second paragraph of the passage details what the author did at the shore during the summer, so the main idea of the paragraph is to enumerate the author's activities.

3. **(5)** Because the main idea is that the author had wonderful childhood memories, the detail that would support that idea is the overall statement that the children would spend all day at the shore.

4. **(1)** In the second sentence of the passage, the author describes how the shore had more activity then it does now. The final sentence of the first paragraph also states that there are no fishing houses on the shore now.

5. **(4)** Although the author discusses each of the other answer choices, these choices are details that support the main idea. The main idea is to convey the message that people look at things differently because of their individual experiences, so choice (4) would reflect the main idea.

6. **(3)** The way people perceive the desk is an example of comparison and contrast. The author points out that everyone will agree to the feel of the table and the sound of the table being hit. These are the points of comparison. The contrast includes the statements of how the reflection of light would cause different people to see the table differently.

7. **(2)** How people see the table is the effect, and the play of light on the table is the cause, or the reason different people see it differently.

8. **(4)** The example the author uses of the table is only one instance of people seeing things differently. The point the author wants us to learn is that these differences can also be extended to everything we see in our daily lives.

COMMENTARY

Commentary is a type of nonfiction in which the author's main purpose is to evaluate a book, a movie, a play, or a piece of music or art. It is a very subjective form of writing—that is, the author is offering an opinion of his subject. Often, the writer only implies the opinion, and it is up to the reader to infer what the author thinks. One way to identify the author's purpose is to be aware of the tone of writing he or she uses. **Tone** refers to the author's attitude toward the subject being reviewed. The tone will give the reader an indication as to whether the reviewer liked or disliked the subject. Some reviewers are noted for being negative in their reviews, and this can sometimes be seen clearly in the commentary.

Practice

Choose the *one* best answer to each question.
Items 9–14 refer to the following passages.

The wife of Shelley was much more successful, and her inimitable *Frankenstein; or, the Modern Prometheus* (1817) is one of the horror-classics of all time. Composed in competition with her husband, Lord Byron, and Dr. John William Polidori in an effort to prove supremacy in horror-making, Mrs. Shelley's *Frankenstein* was the only one of the rival narratives to be brought to an elaborate completion; and criticism has failed to prove that the best parts are due to Shelley rather than to her. The novel, somewhat tinged but scarcely marred by moral didacticism, tells of the artificial human being moulded from charnel fragments by Victor Frankenstein, a young Swiss medical student. Created by its designer "in the mad pride of the intellectuality," the monster possesses full intelligence but owns a hideously loathsome form. It is rejected by mankind, becomes embittered, and at length begins the successive murder of all whom Frankenstein loves best, friends and family. It demands that Frankenstein create a wife for it and when the student finally refuses in horror lest the world be populated with such monsters, it departs with a hideous threat "to be with him on his wedding night." Upon that night the bride is strangled, and from that time on Frankenstein hunts down the monster, even into the wastes of the Arctic. In the end, whilst seeking shelter on the ship of the man who tells the story, Frankenstein himself is killed by the shocking object of his search and creation of his presumptuous pride. Some of the scenes in Frankenstein are unforgettable, as when the newly animated monster enters its creator's room, parts the curtains of this bed, and gazes at him in the yellow moonlight with watery eyes — "If eyes they may be called." Mrs. Shelly wrote other novels, including the fairly notable *Last Man*; but never duplicated the success of her first effort. It has the true touch of cosmic fear, no matter how much the movement may lag in places. Dr. Poldori developed his competing idea as a long short story, *The Vampyre*; in which we behold a suave villain of the true Gothic or Byronic type, and encounter some excellent passages of stark fright, including a terrible nocturnal experience in a shunned Grecian wood.

—H. P. Lovecraft

9. What distinguished Mrs. Shelley's story from the other stories?

    (1) Her version was scarier.

    (2) In her version, the monster kills more people.

    (3) She created a wife for Frankenstein.

    (4) Some of her scenes are unforgettable.

    (5) Her version has an elaborate conclusion.

10. What is the author's purpose in writing this review?

    (1) to show that a woman can write horror fiction

    (2) to point out how Mrs. Shelley's version is superior to others

    (3) to explain the story of Frankenstein

    (4) to show how all of Mrs. Shelley's stories were popular

    (5) to show how *Frankenstein* is a true Gothic novel

11. What is the author's tone in this review?

    (1) negative

    (2) sarcastic

    (3) positive

    (4) hostile

    (5) unflattering

12. Which of the following is a criticism of *Frankenstein*?

    (1) The story is one of the greatest horror-classics of all time.

    (2) Some of the scenes are unforgettable.

    (3) It has the true touch of cosmic fear.

    (4) The novel is tinged by moral didacticism.

    (5) The novel was brought to an elaborate conclusion.

The songs are, for the most part, tedious mockeries of social convention performed by a lackluster band. Although the group has achieved a great following, this is not one of their best albums. They have compromised their artistic integrity by using hackneyed rhyme and old rhythms in an effort to get the music to the public before their next concert tour. The only saving grace is "Rain," a song that explores the themes of guilt and redemption. There is a glimmer of the old genius here, but not enough to save the album.

13. What is the author's tone in this commentary?

    (1) hostile

    (2) flattering

    (3) sarcastic

    (4) enthusiastic

    (5) bored

14. What is the author's theory for the album being made?

    (1) the band has a large audience

    (2) to get the music to the public before the concert tour

    (3) to explore the themes of guilt and redemption

    (4) to prove their artistic integrity

    (5) to promote the song "Rain"

Answers

9. **(5)** The author feels the main reason Mrs. Shelley's version of the story is the best version is her conclusion to the story. She provided an elaborate conclusion while the others did not.

10. **(2)** The author's purpose in writing the review was to point out how this version is superior to other versions. He does so by explaining how this version is different and how the differences make a better story.

11. **(3)** Although the author does point out some flaws in the story, overall the tone is positive.

12. **(4)** The only real criticism of the book is that Mrs. Shelley was sometimes guilty of writing with a preachy overtone.

13. **(1)** The reviewer did not like the album at all and makes his feelings known in a hostile way.

14. **(2)** The author feels that the main reason the album was made was to have the music released to the public before the group made its next concert tour.

FICTION

People usually read fiction for enjoyment and entertainment. It differs from nonfiction because the story and the characters are imaginary, although some fiction is based on factual events or a real person. Fiction generally takes the form of a novel or a short story. The **plot** in fiction is the story line. It is the series of events in the story that are strung together in a particular **sequence** or order. A work of fiction, however, does not always begin with the first event. The author may choose to begin the story with the final event and then unravel the plot by going back to the first event in order to explain what led up to the event.

The **narrator** of a story is the voice that tells the story. It is the point of view from which the reader sees the events being relayed. Usually a story is told from either a first person or a third person point of view. **First person** point of view is the story being told from the perspective of the narrator. Throughout, the author uses "I" to explain the events. First person point of view is limiting because although the reader is aware of what the narrator is thinking, the reader must interpret the actions and thoughts of the other characters through the eyes of the narrator. The reader responds to the other characters through the influence of the narrator's opinions. **Third person** point of view, on the other hand, allows the reader to observe the thoughts and actions of the characters through an all-knowing, or omniscient, narrator.

Authors often use figures of speech to get a point across to the reader. A **figure of speech** is the use of a common word or phrase in such a way as to give something other than the literal meaning to the phrase. A figure of speech can be used to make an abstract idea concrete or to vitalize an idea. Often a figure of speech will compare two seemingly different things to reveal their similarities. You can find figures of speech in all kinds of writing. Look at the example below.

> The children were on pins and needles waiting for Christmas.

Obviously, the children were not literally on pins and needles. The expression, however, does convey their excitement about Christmas.

Characters in a story are revealed to the reader in several different ways. The author describes how the characters look and gives the reader some information about their personalities. This information usually gives the reader the first insights about the characters. How characters act is a second way they are revealed. A third way the personalities of characters are disclosed is by what they say and how they say it. Often the author has a character use poor grammar, or he might give the character a dialect. Finally, characters are understood by what the others in the story say or think about them.

The **tone** of a story is the attitude of the narrator or the author toward the subject or event. The reader's impression of the subject or event may be colored by how the narrator or author feels about it. The **mood** is an overall atmosphere the author creates by carefully selecting certain words and details.

The **setting** of a story is the author's description of the time and place in which the story occurs. Not only does the setting make the story more real for the reader, it also helps to create the mood of the story. An event that occurs at midnight on a rainy night creates more of a mood of fear than the same event occurring on a sunny day.

Practice

Choose the *one* best answer to each question.
Items 15–23 refer to the following passages.

Now this is the point. You fancy me mad. Madmen know nothing. But you should have seen me. You should have seen how wisely I proceeded—with what caution—with what foresight, with what dissimulation, I went to work! I was never kinder to the old man than during the whole week before I killed him. And every night about midnight I turned the latch of his door and opened it oh, so gently! And then, when I had made an opening sufficient for my head, I put in a dark lantern all closed, closed so that no light shone out, and then I thrust in my head. Oh, you would have laughed to see how cunningly I thrust it in! I moved it slowly, very, very slowly, so that I might not disturb the old man's sleep. It took me an hour to place my whole head within the opening so far that I could see him as he lay upon his bed. Ha! Would a madman have been so wise as this? And then when my head was well in the room I undid the lantern cautiously—oh, so cautiously—cautiously (for the hinges creaked), I undid it just so much that a single thin ray fell upon the vulture eye. And this I did for seven long nights, every night just at midnight, but I found the eye always closed, and so it was impossible to do the work, for it was not the old man who vexed me but his Evil Eye. And every morning, when the day broke, I went boldly into the chamber and spoke courageously to him, calling him by name in a hearty tone, and inquiring how he had passed the night. So you see he would have been a very profound old man, indeed, to suspect that every night, just at twelve, I looked in upon him while he slept.

—E. A. Poe

15. According to the narrator

    (1) He was a madman.

    (2) The old man was wise.

    (3) The old man vexed him.

    (4) He was wise.

    (5) The old man suspected what he was going to do.

16. When did the events take place?

    (1) one night

    (2) over seven nights at midnight

    (3) in the morning

    (4) as soon as the old man fell asleep

    (5) over an hour

17. Which of the following words best describes the narrator?

    (1) deranged

    (2) timid

    (3) inventive

    (4) depressing

    (5) predictable

18. Which word best describes the mood of the story?

    (1) frivolous

    (2) somber

    (3) horrifying

    (4) tranquil

    (5) tense

   The opened half-door was opened a little further, and secured at that angle for the time. A broad ray of light fell into the garret, and showed the workman with an unfinished shoe upon his lap, pausing in his labour. His few common tools and various scraps of leather were at his feet and on his bench. He had a white beard, raggedly cut, but not very long, a hollow face, and exceedingly bright eyes. The hollowness and thinness of his face would have caused them to look large, under his yet dark eyebrows and his confused white hair, though they had been really otherwise; but, they were naturally large, and looked unnaturally so. His yellow rags of shirt lay open at the throat, and showed his body to be withered and worn. He, and his old canvas frock, and his loose stockings, and all his poor tatters of clothes, had, in a long seclusion from direct light and air, faded down to such a dull uniformity of parchment-yellow, that it would have been hard to say which was which.

—Charles Dickens

19. It can be inferred from the context that a "garret" is

    (1) a large apartment

    (2) a place to shop

    (3) a place to eat

    (4) a home

    (5) a workshop

20. Although the narrator does not directly say it, the reader can infer that the man was

    (1) young and alert

    (2) old and shabby

    (3) middle class

    (4) lazy

    (5) well respected

21. The man

    (1) mended clothes

    (2) was a beggar

    (3) repaired shoes

    (4) was a bookkeeper

    (5) was a blacksmith

Dark spruce forest frowned on either side the frozen waterway. The trees had been stripped by a recent wind of their white covering of frost, and they seemed to lean towards each other, black and ominous, in the fading light. A vast silence reigned over the land. The land itself was a desolation, lifeless, without movement, so lone and cold that the spirit of it was not even that of sadness. There was a hint in it of laughter, but of a laughter more terrible than any sadness—a laughter that was mirthless as the smile of the sphinx, a laughter cold as the frost and partaking of the grimness of infallibility. It was the masterful and incommunicable wisdom of eternity laughing at the futility of life and the effort of life. It was the Wild, the savage, frozen-hearted North-land Wild.

—Jack London

22. The figure of speech "a laughter that was mirthless as the smile of the sphinx" implies

    (1) a joyful smile

    (2) warmth and happiness

    (3) a sarcastic smile

    (4) a smile without warmth

    (5) a wise smile

23. The atmosphere of the setting is one of

    (1) desolation

    (2) peacefulness

    (3) sadness

    (4) joyfulness

    (5) tranquility

Answers

15. **(4)** The narrator felt that he was sly in the proceedings that led up to his murdering the old man. His caution in looking in on the old man every night was, to him, a sign that he was wise.

16. **(2)** The narrator spent seven nights looking in on the old man at precisely midnight each night.

17. **(1)** The narrator makes a point of telling the reader that he is not mad, but then he goes on to describe in great detail how and why he decided to kill the old man. His pride in the details of the murder is a mark of his derangement.

18. **(3)** The mood of the story is horrifying both in the elaborate preparations for the murder of the old man and in the reasons for the narrator's killing.

19. **(5)** Because of the description of the room, the reader can assume that a garret is a place where the man lived and worked.

20. **(2)** The words "white beard, raggedly cut," "confused white hair," and "withered and worn" all lead to a picture of the man being old and shabby.

21. **(3)** "The unfinished shoe on his lap," and "various scraps of leather" indicate that the man was a cobbler who repaired and made shoes.

22. **(4)** Both the fact that the sphinx is made of stone and the narrator describes the scene as cold and lonely indicate that the smile of the sphinx is one without warmth.

23. **(1)** The author suggests desolation from such details as the forest frowning, the trees being black and ominous, the fading light, and the land being lifeless.

DRAMA

Generally, a drama is written to be performed by actors. Rather than using quotation marks to indicate dialogue, the name of the character is written, and then the words the character speaks are written. **Stage directions** for the actors are written in parentheses, sometimes interrupting the dialogue. The purpose of the stage directions is to give suggestions to the actors of how the author wants the lines to be delivered or any movements the actors should make while saying the lines. A play or drama is divided into acts and scenes. Usually, the author describes the setting of the act or scene at the beginning of each. The time and place of the action might influence the drama, so it is important that the reader is aware of setting. Reading a play is more difficult than reading a story since the author is not speaking directly to the reader. In order to completely understand a play, the reader must infer a great deal from the setting, the characters, the dialogue, and the stage directions. The writer indicates the mood of a play to the audience through the speeches and actions of the actors rather than setting the scene through a paragraph of descriptive writing.

Practice

Choose the *one* best answer to each question.
Items 24–30 refer to the following passages.

Covent Garden at 11:15 p.m. Torrents of heavy summer rain. Cab whistles blowing frantically in all directions. Pedestrians running for shelter into the market and under the portico of St. Paul's Church, where there are already several people, among them a lady and her daughter in evening dress. They are all peering out gloomily at the rain, except one man with his back turned to the rest, who seems wholly preoccupied with a notebook in which he is writing busily.

The church clock strikes the first quarter.

THE DAUGHTER. (*in the space between the central pillars, close to the one on her left*) I'm getting chilled to the bone. What can Freddy be doing all this time? He's been gone twenty minutes.

THE MOTHER. (*On her daughter's right*) Not so long. But he ought to have got us a cab by this.

A BYSTANDER. (*On the lady's right*) He won't get no cab not until half-past eleven, missus, when they come back after dropping off their theatre fares.

THE MOTHER. But we must have a cab. We can't stand here until half-past eleven. It's too bad.

THE BYSTANDER. Well, it ain't my fault, missus.

THE DAUGHTER. If Freddy had a bit of gumption, he would have got one at the theatre door.

THE MOTHER. What could he have done, poor boy?

THE DAUGHTER. Other people got cabs, Why couldn't he?

Freddy rushes in out of the rain from the Southampton Street side, and comes between them closing a dripping umbrella. He is a young man of twenty, in evening dress, very wet around the ankles.

THE DAUGHTER. Well, haven't you got a cab?

FREDDY. There's not one to be had for love or money.

THE MOTHER. Oh, Freddy, there must be one. You can't have tried.

THE DAUGHTER. It's too tiresome. Do you expect us to go and get one ourselves?

FREDDY. I tell you they're all engaged. The rain was so sudden: nobody was prepared; and everybody had to take a cab. I've been to Charing Cross one way and nearly to Ludgate Circus the other; and they were all engaged.

THE MOTHER. Did you try Trafalgar Square?

FREDDY. There wasn't one at Trafalgar Square.

THE DAUGHTER. Did you try?

FREDDY. I tried as far as Charing Cross Station. Did you expect me to walk to Hammersmith?

THE DAUGHTER. You haven't tried at all.

THE MOTHER. You really are very helpless, Freddy. Go again; and don't come back until you have found a cab.

FREDDY. I shall simply get soaked for nothing.

THE DAUGHTER. And what about us? Are we to stay here all night in this draught, with next to nothing on. You selfish pig.

—G.B. Shaw

24. Why are the characters outside while it is raining?
    (1) They've been out shopping.
    (2) They've just left the theatre.
    (3) They've forgotten their umbrellas.
    (4) They refuse to take a bus.
    (5) They've been visiting friends.

25. Which of the following phrases best describes the daughter?
    (1) a down to earth girl
    (2) a girl in love with Freddy
    (3) a reasonable girl
    (4) a pleasant person
    (5) an unreasonable person

26. Which of the following statements is true about the mother?
    (1) She is trying to look out for the best interests of Freddy.
    (2) She wants what is best for her daughter.
    (3) She doesn't care about other people.
    (4) She is a loving person.
    (5) She is concerned about those around her.

27. What will the daughter most likely think about Freddy in the future?
    (1) He isn't good enough for her.
    (2) He truly loves her.
    (3) He is sensible.
    (4) He has her best interests at heart.
    (5) He is amusing to her.

KROGSTAD. Your father was very ill, I believe?

NORA. He was on his death-bed.

KROGSTAD. Tell me, Mrs. Helmer; do you happen to recollect the day of his death? The day of the month, I mean?

NORA. Father died on the 29th of September.

KROGSTAD. Quite correct. I have made inquiries. And here comes in the remarkable point—(*Produces a paper.*) which I cannot explain.

NORA. What remarkable point? I don't know—

KROGSTAD. The remarkable point, madam, that your father signed this paper three days after his death!

NORA. What! I don't understand—

KROGSTAD. Your father died on the 29th of September. But look here: he has dated his signature October 2nd! Is not that remarkable, Mrs. Helmer? (*NORA is silent*) It is noteworthy, too, that the words "October 2nd" and the year are not in your father's handwriting, but in one which I believe I know. Well, this may be explained; your father may have forgotten to date his signature, and somebody may have added the date at random, before the fact of your father's death was known. There is nothing wrong in that. Everything depends on the signature. Of course it is genuine, Mrs, Helmer? It was really your father himself who wrote his name here?

NORA. (*After a short silence, throws her head back and looks defiantly at him.*) No, it was not. I wrote father's name.

KROGSTAD. Ah!—You are aware, madam, that that is a dangerous admission?

NORA. How so? You will soon get your money.

KROGSTAD. May I ask you one more question? Why did you not send the paper to your father?

NORA. It was impossible. Father was ill. If I had asked him for his signature, I should have had to tell him why I wanted the money; but he was so ill I really could not tell him that my husband's life was in danger. It was impossible.

KROGSTAD. Then it would have been better to have given up your tour.

NORA. No, I couldn't do that; my husband's life depended on that journey. I couldn't give it up.

KROGSTAD. And did it never occur to you that you were playing me false?

NORA. That was nothing to me. I didn't care in the least about you. I couldn't endure you for all the cruel difficulties you made, although you know how ill my husband was.

KROGSTAD. Mrs. Helmer, you evidently do not realize what you have been guilty of. But I can assure you it was nothing more and nothing worse that made me an outcast from society.

NORA. You! You want me to believe that you did a brave thing to save your wife's life?

KROGSTAD. The law takes no account of motives.

—H. Ibsen

28. Of what has Nora been accused?

    (1) putting the wrong date on a document

    (2) lying to Krogstad

    (3) taking a journey when her father was ill

    (4) falsifying her father's signature

    (5) forgetting to have her father sign a document

29. From the dialogue, the reader can infer that

    (1) Krogstad had lent Nora's father some money

    (2) Krogstad and Nora had been friends

    (3) Nora didn't want her husband to know that she had borrowed money from Krogstad

    (4) Nora's husband and Krogstad were business partners

    (5) Nora had intentionally signed the document with the wrong date

30. From the dialogue, the reader can infer that

    (1) In the future, Nora will give Krogstad what he wants

    (2) Krogstad will threaten to tell Nora's husband what has happened

    (3) Nora and her husband will sue Krogstad

    (4) Krogstad will take Nora to court

    (5) Nora's husband will intervene to save Nora

Answers

24. **(2)** The stage directions at the beginning of the passage indicate that the characters are wearing evening dress, and the bystander comments that there will be no more cabs until they come back after dropping off their theatre fares.

25. **(5)** The daughter is unreasonable and refuses to accept Freddy's explanation for why he couldn't get a cab. She insists that Freddy didn't really try.

26. **(3)** The mother's telling Freddy that he is helpless and insisting that he go back out into the rain reveals that she cares little about his welfare.

27. **(1)** Because she is so demanding, the daughter is difficult to please. She feels that Freddy is not really trying his hardest to make her happy.

28. **(4)** Nora has been accused of signing her father's name to a document three days after her father's death.

29. **(3)** Nora implies that she didn't want to tell her husband she borrowed money because his life was in danger.

30. **(2)** Krogstand is upset by Nora's deceit and wants to hurt her. Telling her husband would cause Nora the most harm.

POETRY

A poem is the expression of an author's or narrator's feelings and ideas about certain experiences. A poem is generally much shorter than a story or play, but is often more difficult to read and understand. Although there is obviously less detail in poetry than in other forms of literature, the emphasis is more on form or arrangement of detail. The poet will often use figurative language to make the most powerful points. Two of the most common figures of speech used by the poet are the simile and the metaphor. A **simile** is a comparison that uses the words "like" or "as." The following is an example of a simile.

He was *like* a raging lion.

A **metaphor**, on the other hand, is a comparison that identifies one object with another.

Life *is* a dance.

Personification is another devise used by poets. **Personification** occurs when the poet gives human attributes to an inanimate object or to something not human. Look at the example below.

The mountains *watched* the villagers below.

It is obvious that mountains don't have eyes, but the author chose to give the mountains the human attribute of seeing, giving the impression that the mountain was protecting the villagers.

Reading a poem is sometimes difficult because of the form in which it is written. Often, the poet rearranges typical sentence patterns to produce a particular rhyme or rhythm scheme. People find reading a poem confusing because the lines are frequently broken instead of continuing all the way across the page. When you are reading a poem, try to blend the lines together instead of stopping at the end of one line. Try to pause only at the punctuated words.

The mood of a poem is created not only by the words the poet chooses and the rhythm of the poem, but the poet will also imply a mood by certain sounds. For example, the poet may choose to string together a series of words that all have the same beginning letter as in the example below.

The wind whispered through the willows.

The repetition of the letter "w" creates a particular mood of quiet movement.

Practice

Choose the *one* best answer to each question.
Items 31–38 refer to the following passages.

When reeds are dead and a straw to thatch the marshes,
And feathered pampas-grass rides into the wind
Like aged warriors westward, tragic, thinned
Of half their tribe, and over the flattened rushes,
Stripped of its secret, open, stark and bleak,
Blackens afar the half-forgotten creek, —
Then leans on me the weight of the year, and crushes
My heart. I know that Beauty must ail and die,
And will be born again, —but ah, to see
Beauty stiflened, staring up at the sky!
Oh, Autumn! Autumn! —What is the Spring to me?

—Edna St. Vincent Millay

31. The mood of the poem is one of

    (1) joy

    (2) loneliness

    (3) hostility

    (4) despair

    (5) resentment

32. "Beauty must ail and die" is an example of

    (1) personification

    (2) simile

    (3) metaphor

    (4) rhythm

    (5) rhyme

33. The point of this poem is to convey the author's

    (1) joy of the season

    (2) feelings about growing older

    (3) anxiety for spring to return

    (4) description of the landscape during autumn

    (5) feelings about autumn being a kind of death

Whose woods these are I think I know,
His house is in the village though.
He will not see me stopping here,
To watch his woods fill up with snow.

My little horse must think it queer,
To stop without a farmhouse near,
Between the woods and the frozen lake,
The darkest evening of the year.

He gives his harness bells a shake,
To ask if there is some mistake.
The only other sound's the sweep,
Of easy wind and downy flake.

The woods are lovely, dark and deep,
But I have promises to keep,
And miles to go before I sleep,
And miles to go before I sleep.

—Robert Frost

34. What is the author's purpose in repeating the last two lines of the poem?

    (1) to make the number of lines throughout the poem even

    (2) to make the rhyme consistent throughout the poem

    (3) to enhance the mood of the poem.

    (4) to emphasize his stopping briefly to enjoy the woods before assuming his responsibilities

    (5) to emphasize the loneliness of the woods at night

35. The mood of the poem is one of

    (1) fear of the woods at night

    (2) loneliness

    (3) tranquility

    (4) despair

    (5) isolation

36. What is the theme or main idea of the poem?

    (1) The narrator's detachment from everything around him.

    (2) The narrator's enjoyment at being alone.

    (3) The narrator's pleasure at enjoying nature before going back to his responsibilities.

    (4) The narrator's relationship with his neighbors in the farmhouse.

    (5) The narrator's feelings of isolation and depression.

I asked the professors who teach the meaning of life to tell
    me what is happiness.
And I went to famous executives who boss the work of
    thousands of men.
They all shook their heads and gave me a smile as though
    I was trying to fool with them
And then one Sunday afternoon I wandered out along
    the Desplaines river
And I saw a crowd of Hungarians under the trees with
    their women and children and a keg of beer and an
    accordion.

—Carl Sandburg

37. How did the narrator find the meaning of happiness?

    (1) by asking the professors

    (2) by talking to famous executives

    (3) by seeing how people enjoy the simple things in life

    (4) by trying to fool the professors and executives

    (5) by walking to the river

38. What is the mood of the poem?

    (1) reflective

    (2) angry

    (3) hopeful

    (4) sarcastic

    (5) sad

Answers

31. **(4)** The mood of the poem is one of despair. She refers to the weight of another year passing as crushing her heart. Although she looks forward to another spring, she is depressed about the coming winter.

32. **(1)** The author has attributed the human qualities of sickness and death to the inanimate object, beauty. This is an example of personification.

33. **(5)** The point of the poem is to emphasize how the author feels about another year coming to an end. She sees autumn as a sort of death of the year.

34. **(4)** The narrator is emphasizing that he has responsibilities to return to.

35. **(3)** The mood of the poem is one of tranquility. The "easy wind and downy flake" hold no threat.

36. **(3)** The narrator is relating his enjoyment of nature in the form of the snowy woods before he resumes his journey and the responsibilities of his life.

37. **(3)** The narrator finally finds the meaning of happiness by visiting the river and seeing ordinary people enjoying themselves.

38. **(1)** The mood of the poem is one of reflection. The narrator finds it ironic that the professors and executives don't know the meaning of happiness, but ordinary people do.

TEST YOURSELF

Choose the one best answer to each question.
Items 1–3 refer to the following.

The tendency nowadays to wander in wildernesses is delightful to see. Thousands of tired, nerve-shaken, over-civilized people are beginning to find out that going to the mountains is going home; that wildness is a necessity; and that mountain parks and reservations are useful not only as fountains of timber and irrigating rivers, but as fountains of life. Awakening from the stupefying effects of the vice of over-industry and the deadly apathy of luxury, they are trying as best they can to mix and enrich their own little ongoings with those of Nature, and to get rid of rust and disease. Briskly venturing and roaming, some are washing off sins and cobweb cares of the devil's spinning in all-day storms on mountains; sauntering in rosiny pinewoods or in gentian meadows, brushing through chaparral, bending down a parting sweet, flowery sprays; tracing rivers to their sources, getting in touch with the nerves of Mother Earth; jumping from rock to rock, feeling the life of them, learning the songs of them, panting in whole-souled exercise, and rejoicing in deep, long-drawn breaths of pure wildness. This is fine and natural and full of promise. So also is the growing interest in the care and preservation of forests and wild places in general, and in the half wild parks and gardens of towns. Even the scenery habit in its most artificial forms, mixed with spectacles, silliness, and kodaks; its devotees arrayed more gorgeously than scarlet tanagers, frightening the wild game with red umbrellas,—even this is encouraging, and may well be regarded as a hopeful sign of the times.

—John Muir

1. What is the overall mood of the passage?
   (1) sarcastic
   (2) depressing
   (3) optimistic
   (4) reflective
   (5) tense

2. Why does the author feel that enjoying nature is necessary for humans?
   (1) He feels that nature has the capacity of restoring life.
   (2) He feels that humans will take more care preserving the wild if they enjoy it.
   (3) He feels that "over-industry" is bad for people.
   (4) He feels that people need to wash off their sins.
   (5) He feels that people generally need the exercise of roaming in the woods.

3. How does the narrator feel about people who come to the woods with their cameras and frighten the animals?

    (1) He's angry with them for frightening the animals.

    (2) He would like to ignore them.

    (3) He is encouraged that they are there.

    (4) He feels they are artificial to the surroundings.

    (5) He is hopeful they won't stay.

Choose the *one* best answer to each question.
Items 4–6 refer to the following.

The day is done, and the darkness
Falls from the wing of Night,
As a feather is wafted downward
From an eagle in its flight.

I see the lights of the village
Gleam through the rain and mist,
And a feeling of sadness comes o'er me,
That my soul cannot resist.

A feeling of sadness and longing,
That is not akin to pain,
And resembles sorrow only
As the mist resembles rain.

Come, read to me some poem,
Some simple and heartfelt lay,
That shall soothe this restless feeling
And banish the thoughts of day …

And the night shall be filled with music,
And the cares that infest the day,
Shall fold their tents like the Arabs,
And as silently steal away.

                   —Henry Wadsworth Longfellow

4. "the cares that infest the day, shall fold their tents like Arabs, and as silently steal away" is an example of

    (1) personification

    (2) simile

    (3) rhyme

    (4) rhythm

    (5) metaphor

5. Which choice best tells what the poem is about?

    (1) the lights of the village

    (2) the sadness of the poet's life

    (3) how reading a poem makes the narrator happy

    (4) the end of the day

    (5) filling the night with music

6. To what does the poet compare night falling?

    (1) a feeling of sadness

    (2) the mist

    (3) the mist resembling the rain

    (4) tents

    (5) a feather

Choose the one best answer to each question.
Items 7–9 refer to the following passage.

I heartily accept the motto, "That government is best which governs least"; and I should like to see it acted up to more rapidly and systematically. Carried out, it finally amounts to this, which also I believe—"That government is best which governs not at all"; and when men are prepared for it, that will be the kind of government which they will have. Government is at best but an expedient; but most governments are usually, and all governments are sometimes, inexpedient. The objections which have been brought against a standing army, and they are many and weighty, and deserve to prevail, may also at last be brought against a standing government. The standing army is only an arm of the standing government. The government itself, which is only the mode which the people have chosen to execute their will, is equally liable to be abused and perverted before the people can act through it. Witness the present Mexican war, the work of comparatively a few individuals using the standing government as their tool; for in the outset, the people would not have consented to this measure.

—Henry David Thoreau

7. Which sentence best states the main idea of this passage?

    (1) The less government interferes, the better.

    (2) The army is an important function of government.

    (3) The people choose what government they want.

    (4) The government is abused and perverted.

    (5) The Mexican war was the result of too much government.

8. Which is the supporting detail that shows how inexpedient government is?

    (1) The standing army is an arm of the government.

    (2) The people would not have consented to the Mexican war.

    (3) The best government is one that doesn't interfere with the will of the people.

(4) The same objections against the army could be brought against government.

(5) People are prepared to do away with the government.

9. What conclusion can be drawn from the passage?

    (1) The author hates his government.

    (2) The author wishes government would not interfere with the will of the people.

    (3) The author is against having an army.

    (4) The author is bitter against the government.

    (5) The author does not want any government.

Choose the *one* best answer to each question.
Items 10–12 refer to the following.

He said:
"In the winter dusk
When the pavements were gleaming with rain,
I walked thru a dingy street
Hurried, harassed,
Thinking of all my problems that never are solved.
Suddenly out of the mist, a flaring gas-jet
Shone from a huddled shop.
I saw thru the bleary window
A mass of playthings:
False-faces hung on strings,
Valentines, paper and tinsel,
Tops of scarlet and green,
Candy, marbles, jacks
A confusion of color
Pathetically gaudy and cheap.
All of my boyhood
Rushed back.
Once more these things were treasures
Wildly desired.
With covetous eyes I looked again at the marbles,
The precious agates, the pee-wees, the chinies
Then I passed on.

In the winter dusk,
The pavements were gleaming with rain;
There in the lighted window
I left by boyhood."

—Sara Teasdale

10. What does the man mean when he says he left his boyhood in the lighted window?

    (1) All the things he loved were in the window.

    (2) He wished he was young again.

    (3) He sold all his boyhood toys.

    (4) He briefly remembered his boyhood with joy but then had to return to adulthood.

    (5) He was sorry he was grown up.

11. Using the context for clues, what does "covetous" mean?

    (1) charitable

    (2) unselfish

    (3) greedy

    (4) neutral

    (5) joyful

12. For what purpose does the author repeat the second and third lines at the end of the poem?

    (1) to show it was still raining

    (2) to show that the man wishes to return to his everyday problems

    (3) to contrast the night with the lighted window

    (4) to emphasize the brightness of the toys in the window

    (5) to emphasize the brief moment the man relived his boyhood

Choose the *one* best answer to each question.
Items 13–14 refer to the following passage.

    This book is about a man who suffers from a deep depression that makes his life and the lives around him miserable. The struggles Jack endures are as painful for the reader as they are for him. For all of the author's good intentions, Jack, although he suffers mightily, is still a shallow character. Much better drawn are the characters of his wife and mother. These are two women who have lived through all the perils Jack brings upon himself. The fact that they become disgusted with him halfway through the book only serves to make them more realistic. Although the book moves along at a rapid pace, the author has included so many tragedies for poor Jack, his plight becomes almost humorous instead of tragic.

13. What conclusion can be drawn from the review?

    (1) Although he doesn't like the main character, the reviewer likes the other characters.

    (2) The reviewer thinks the book is good.

(3) The reviewer likes all the tragedies the main character suffers.

(4) The reviewer thinks the book is well written.

(5) The reviewer doesn't like the author of the book.

14. What is the reviewer's attitude toward the book?

(1) sarcastic

(2) indifferent

(3) hostile

(4) objective

(5) approving

Choose the *one* best answer to each question.
Items 15–16 refer to the following passage.

If ever a girl of the working class had led the sheltered life, it was Genevieve. In the midst of roughness and brutality, she had shunned all that was rough and brutal. She saw but what she chose to see, and she chose always to see the best, avoiding coarseness and uncouthness without effort, as a matter of instinct. To begin with, she had been peculiarly unexposed. An only child, with an invalid mother upon whom she attended, she had not joined in the street games and frolics of the children of the neighbourhood. Her father, a mild-tempered, narrow-chested, anaemic little clerk, domestic because of his inherent disability to mix with men, had done his full share toward giving the home an atmosphere of sweetness and tenderness.

—Jack London

15. Which of these statements does NOT account for Genevieve's character?

(1) the fact she was an only child

(2) the other children in the neighborhood

(3) her invalid mother

(4) her mild mannered father

(5) her sheltered life

16. Which of the following best describes Genevieve?

(1) inventive

(2) predictable

(3) timid

(4) rude

(5) confused

Choose the *one* best answer to each question.

Items 17–19 refer to the following passage.

Lady Britomart is a woman of fifty or thereabouts, well dressed and yet careless of her dress, well bred and quite reckless of her breeding, well mannered and yet appallingly outspoken and indifferent to the opinion of her interlocutors, amiable and yet peremptory, arbitrary, and high-tempered to the last bearable degree, and withal a very typical managing matron of the upper class, treated as a naughty child until she grew into a scolding mother, and finally settling down with plenty of practical ability and worldly experience, limited in the oddest way with domestic and class limitations, conceiving the universe exactly as it were a large house in Wilton Crescent, through handling her corner of it very effectively on that assumption, and being quite enlightened and liberal as to the books in the library, the pictures on the walls, the music in the portfolios, and the articles in the papers.

Her son, Stephen, comes in. He is a gravely correct young man under 25, taking himself very seriously, but still in some awe of his mother, from childish habit and bachelor shyness rather than from any weakness of character.

STEPHEN. What's the matter?

LADY BRITOMART. Presently, Stephen. (*Stephen submissively walks to the settee and sits down. He takes up* The Speaker.)

LADY BRITOMART. Don't begin to read, Stephen. I shall require all your attention.

STEPHEN. It was only while I was waiting—

LADY BRITOMART. Don't make excuses, Stephen. (*He puts down* The Speaker.) Now! (*She finishes her writing; rises; and comes to the settee.*) I have not kept you waiting very long, I think.

STEPHEN. Not at all, Mother.

LADY BRITOMART. Bring me my cushion. (*He takes the cushion from the chair at the desk and arranges it for her as she sits down on the settee.*) Sit down. (*He sits down and fingers his tie nervously.*) Don't fiddle with your tie, Stephen: there is nothing the matter with it.

STEPHEN. I beg your pardon. (*He paddles with his watch chain instead.*)

LADY BRITOMART. Now are you attending to me, Stephen?

STEPHEN. Of course, Mother.

LADY BRITOMART. No: it's not of course. I want something much more than your everyday matter-of-course attention. I am going to speak to you very seriously, Stephen. I wish you would let that chain alone.

—George Bernard Shaw

17. Stephen fidgets around his mother because

    (1) he doesn't like her

    (2) he is afraid of her

    (3) he doesn't care much about her

    (4) she makes him uncomfortable

    (5) he just wants to get away from her

18. Based on the stage directions, what kind of life do Lady Britomart and Stephen lead?

    (1) middle class

    (2) a working class life

    (3) lower class

    (4) a life of privilege

    (5) a life dedicated to charity work

19. From the dialogue in the passage, how does Lady Britomart treat her son?

    (1) with respect

    (2) as if he were a child

    (3) as a disciplinarian

    (4) she is in awe of him

    (5) she is mean to him

Answers

1. **(3)** The writer is optimistic that people will use the wilderness to rejuvenate themselves.

2. **(1)** The author feels that nature has the ability to restore life for people and allow them to overcome the adverse effects of society.

3. **(3)** Although he feels that some of the people who go to the wilderness behave inappropriately, he is still encouraged that they are making the attempt to be there.

4. **(2)** "shall fold their tents like Arabs" is an example of a simile because the word *like* is used to make the comparison.

5. **(4)** The poem explains how the end of the day affects the author.

6. **(5)** In line 3 of the poem, the author compares the night to a feather drifting downward.

7. **(1)** The main idea of this passage is the author's discontent with interference by the government.

8. **(2)** The author feels that the people would not have consented to the war had they had the opportunity to voice an opinion.

9. **(2)** The author is not opposed to government. He is, however, opposed to too much government, and he is opposed to a government that does not act according to the wishes of the people.

10. **(4)** The author was happily reminded of his boyhood when he looked through the window. When he moved on, he moved back into the adult world.

11. **(3)** Because he was yearning for his boyhood, the man was greedy for the reminders of this happier time.

12. **(5)** Looking through the window was only a brief escape for the man. Before he looked into the window, he was an adult with all the adult problems, and afterward, he returned to being an adult.

13. **(1)** Although the reviewer did not like the main character, he generally liked the other characters and how they reacted to Jack.

14. **(4)** The reviewer tried to be objective when reviewing this book. He pointed out some flaws, but he also praised what he felt was good about the book.

15. **(2)** All the selections with the exception of (2) are factors that influenced Genevieve's character. The children in the neighborhood did not influence her because she had little contact with them.

16. **(3)** Genevieve tended to keep to herself. She made her decisions about people through her father's eyes.

17. **(4)** Stephen's mother is overbearing, and she tends to make Stephen uncomfortable. This is evidenced by his trying to say and do what she wants.

18. **(4)** Lady Britomart and Stephen lead a life of privilege. She is well bred and a matron of the upper class.

19. **(2)** Lady Britomart treats Stephen as if he were a child. She is constantly watching over him and telling him how to act.

CHAPTER 3

Language Arts, Writing

TEST-TAKING TIPS

The GED Language Arts, Writing test is a two-part test. On the first part, you will be tested on your knowledge of basic English grammar. You already know many of the conventions of the English language, but sometimes, writing is more difficult than speaking. This review covers structure, usage, and mechanics.

For many, the most difficult part of the Language Arts, Writing test is actually writing an essay. When you take the GED, you will be given the opportunity to express yourself on a topic in an essay of about 200 words. This part of the test is not examining your knowledge of a topic, but it is assessing your ability to express yourself in a clear, precise manner. The actual writing of the essay will occupy only part of your allotted time. You will also have to spend time planning your essay and proofreading and editing, so the essay you turn in is an effective one.

The essay part of the test is scored in a different fashion from the rest of the GED. As you know, the majority of the GED is multiple-choice questions with only one right answer. Because the essay is the one part of the test in which you can express your own opinions, it has no answer key. The essay is scored holistically—that is, your essay will be given a score of 0 to 6, and this reflects the essay as a whole. The highest score you can get is 6, and a 6 indicates an essay that is clear and well organized. The writer offers good ideas that are well supported by detail. An occasional flaw will not mar a score of 6.

Scores of 4 and 5 do not mean that the essay is poorly written. These scores indicate the author generally observes the conventions of accepted English, but there might be some errors in usage. The supporting detail might not be as sufficient as an essay marked with a 6, but the writer's general organizational plan is apparent.

Scores of 3 and 2 show a lack of planning or development of ideas. These essays often indicate a struggle on the part of the author to think of enough to say about the topic to meet the required length. In these cases, the writer simply includes lists of generalizations that only somewhat support the topic. A score of 2 or 3 is also a sign of numerous or repeated errors in usage.

A score of 1 indicates that the writer has not accomplished the goal of writing a clear, well-organized essay. There is neither an apparent plan nor is there control over the English language.

The score of 0 indicates that a blank or illegible document was turned in, or the writer chose not to write about the assigned topic.

THE LANGUAGE ARTS, WRITING TEST PART I—WRITING A COMPLETE SENTENCE

A sentence is a group of words that expresses a complete thought. We speak in sentences every day, but when we are speaking to another person, our sentences do not necessarily have to reflect a complete thought because in a conversation, both people know what the subject of conversation is. In writing, however, the author does not have immediate feedback from someone else, so it is the writer's job to write complete thoughts for the reader. The following is part of a conversation:

> Bill said, "I went to a movie last night."
>
> "Really?"

The word "really" does not express a complete thought; but in a conversation, both parties know what the subject of the conversation is, so the reply is simply one word.

The **subject** of a sentence is the word or phrase that explains what the sentence is about. In the conversation above, the complete subject is *I*. A **complete subject** is the noun or pronoun plus any of the words directly related to the noun or pronoun.

The **predicate**, or **verb**, is the part of the sentence that says something about the subject. The **complete verb** is the words that, together, say something about the subject. In our example above, *went* is the complete verb.

A **compound subject** is a case where there is more than one subject in a sentence. Compound subjects are joined by *and*, *or*, or *nor*. Compound subjects share the same verb. In the following sentence, the compound subjects are in italics.

> *The batter* and *the umpire* confronted each other.

In this sentence, both the batter and the umpire were involved in the action of confrontation, so they are both the subjects.

A **compound verb** is a case where two or more verbs are joined by *and*, *or*, or *nor*. Compound verbs share the same subject or subjects. Look at the following sentence.

The batter and the umpire *screamed* and *shouted* at each other.

In this sentence, both the batter and the umpire, the two subjects, did two separate things: They screamed and they shouted.

Practice

Identify the complete subjects and complete verbs in the following sentences.

1. The werewolf and his girlfriend prowled the countryside at night.
2. He proposed to her at dawn.
3. The caterer baked and frosted six cakes and prepared some very rare roast beef for the reception.
4. He and she were married at dusk and left for their honeymoon shortly after.
5. They went to Las Vegas and lost a great deal of money.
6. The newlyweds returned home to the castle and vowed not to travel far away again.
7. In spite of being poor, never before had the werewolf been so happy. **HINT:** This one is tricky

Answers

1. Subject—werewolf, girlfriend
    Verb—prowled
2. Subject—he
    Verb—proposed
3. Subject—caterer
    Verb—baked, frosted, prepared
4. Subject—he, she
    Verb—were married, left
5. Subject—they
    Verb—went, lost
6. Subject—newlyweds
    Verb—returned, vowed
7. Subject—werewolf
    Verb—had been

SUBJECT-VERB AGREEMENT

Subject-verb agreement means that the number of the subjects must agree with the number indicated in the verb. Look at the following sentences.

> Thelma and Louise know many routes to the mountain.
>
> Grandma only knows one route to the mountain.

In the first sentence, *Thelma and Louise* is a compound subject. The verb *know* is a plural verb indicating that it goes with a plural subject. In the second sentence, the subject is singular—there is only one grandma. The verb *knows* is singular to match the subject. HINT: Very often, a singular verb ends in the letter "s."

Frequently, the subject of the sentence is separated from the verb by other words. Be alert to these conditions, and don't be fooled by them. Look at the following sentences.

> The *boys* in the senior class *work* harder than the girls do.
>
> The *boy* with multiple tattoos *works* hard at being different.

In the first sentence, the subject is plural. It is separated from the verb by a group of words containing a singular noun—*class*. In the second sentence, the subject is only one boy, so the verb *works* is also singular even though the noun *tattoos* is plural and is the word that directly precedes the verb.

There are a number of special circumstances that will arise occasionally. These exceptions are listed below.

- When the word *each* or *every* appears before a compound subject, treat the subject as if it were a singular subject. Example: Each tulip and rose has its own special beauty. (This does not hold true when the word *each* comes after the compound subject. Example: Joseph and Allen each have different ideas about going away for college.)

- When a compound subject is connected by *or* or *nor* (or by *either...or* or *neither...nor*), the verb will agree with the part of the subject that is closest to it. Example: Neither the dog nor the cat wants to come in the house.

- Most indefinite pronouns are treated as singular. An **indefinite pronoun** is one that does not refer to a specific person or thing. The following is a list of the most common indefinite pronouns.

any	each	everybody	none
anyone	either	everything	no one
anybody	everyone	neither	someone
			something

Example: Anyone going to the party needs to bring something to eat for everyone to share.

- A collective noun is usually treated as singular. A **collective noun** generally names a group as a whole. Some common collective nouns are family, audience, crowd, and class. Example: The whole family was late for the reunion.

Practice

Choose the correct verb form to match the subject in the following sentences.

1. Remember that your safety and health (is, are) under your own control.
2. A good set of dishes (cost, costs) a great deal of money.
3. Both Joan and Jackie (is, are) competing in the Science Fair.
4. High levels of cholesterol (cause, causes) heart disease.
5. Neither Jason nor Zachary (is, are) old enough to drive.
6. Christmas Eve and New Year's Eve (is, are) usually holidays from work.
7. None of these books (is, are) very interesting.
8. Everyone on the team (yell, yells) when someone makes a goal.
9. The shirts in the closet (need, needs) to be ironed.
10. Neither my sister nor her friend (was, were) able to attend graduation.

Answers

1. are	4. cause	7. is	10. was
2. costs	5. is	8. yells	
3. are	6. are	9. need	

SENTENCE FRAGMENTS

A **clause** is a group of words that contains a subject and a verb. If this definition seems to you to be suspiciously like the definition for a sentence, you are right. An **independent clause** can stand alone as a sentence. An independent clause, however, is this same group of words as part of a longer sentence. A **dependent clause** cannot stand alone as a sentence, in spite of the fact that it also contains a subject and a verb. The difference between the two is that a dependent clause is introduced by a word or group of words known as a **subordinate conjunction**. If an author writes a dependent clause standing alone as a sentence, he will be guilty of writing a sentence fragment. Look at the following sentence.

When Jane watches television, she sits too close to the set.

The first part of the sentence contains the subject *Jane* and the verb *watches*. The second part of the sentence contains the subject *she* and the verb *sits*. The first part of the sentence, *When Jane watches television*, cannot stand alone as a sentence because of the word *when*. This word is responsible for making the first part of the sentence dependent on the second part in order to make sense. The following is a list of words that commonly introduce dependent clauses.

after	how	that	which
although	if	though	while
as	in order that	unless	who
as if	rather than	until	whom
because	since	when	whose
before	so that	where	why
even though	than	whether	

A dependent clause can appear anywhere in a sentence. Writing a dependent clause as a sentence is among the most common grammatical errors in writing. A dependent clause written as a sentence is one form of a sentence fragment, but other errors lead to sentence fragments, as well.

Other groups of words that are commonly fragmented include parts of compound verbs and examples introduced by *also*, *and*, *but*, *for example*, *or*, *such as*, or similar expressions. Most sentence fragments can be corrected in one of two ways: You can either include the fragment in a nearby sentence, making sure you punctuate properly, or you can create an entirely new sentence out of the fragment. If a dependent clause cannot logically be pulled into a nearby sentence, it should be rewritten to stand alone as a sentence.

Practice

Identify the dependent clauses in the following sentences.

1. If the price is too high, I won't buy a new car this year.
2. This test seemed to go on forever, although the clock said it was only one hour.
3. I would prefer to take a trip to New York, although it's also beautiful in Arizona.
4. Because you came home too late to eat dinner, I'll fix you a snack.
5. While you were gone, your cousin left for college.
6. Because the weather is terrible, we won't be able to have the reception outside.
7. When the girls complained too much, their father said they couldn't go to the dance.
8. He wrote a note to his mother before he left home for good.

Answers

1. If the price is too high
2. although the clock said it was only one hour
3. although it's also beautiful in Arizona
4. Because you came home too late to eat dinner
5. While you were gone
6. Because the weather is terrible
7. When the girls complained too much
8. before he left home for good

Practice

If the following contain sentence fragments, correct them by either including the fragment with a nearby sentence or by creating a new sentence.

1. Michael went for a ride on his motorcycle. But forgot his helmet.
2. Angela was confined to her room. After she stayed out too late the night before.
3. Because he was restless. He wanted to keep moving from place to place.
4. Jennifer eats too many sweets. Such as candy, cake, and pies.
5. Jose was exhausted. Having worked for 12 hours straight.
6. While she was at the mall, Maria did some window shopping at a new store. One that specializes in furniture.
7. He hid the Christmas presents he bought for his family under his bed. Hoping no one would find them.
8. When she thought she was finally ready for the party, she discovered that she had forgotten to buy enough paper plates. Also the party favors she wanted to give to her guests.

Answers

These are suggested corrections. Answers may vary.

1. Michael went for a ride on his motorcycle, but he forgot his helmet.
2. After she stayed out too late the night before, Angela was confined to her room.
3. Because he was restless, he wanted to keep moving from place to place.
4. Jennifer eats too many sweets such as candy, cake, and pies.
5. Having worked for 12 hours straight, Jose was exhausted.
6. While she was at the mall, Maria did some window shopping at a new store that specializes in furniture.
7. Hoping no one would find them, he hid the Christmas presents he bought for his family under his bed.
8. When she thought she was finally ready for the party, she discovered that she had forgotten to buy enough paper plates and the party favors she wanted to give to her guests.

RUN-ON SENTENCES

When two independent clauses have been joined together incorrectly, the result is either a run-on sentence or a comma splice. A run-on sentence occurs when there is no punctuation joining two independent clauses. A comma splice occurs when the writer has joined two independent clauses incorrectly with a comma.

If two independent clauses have been written together, forming a run-on sentence, the easiest way to make the correction is to place a period after the first independent clause and create a new sentence from the second independent clause.

There are three ways to correct a comma splice.

- Separate the two independent clauses by a comma <u>and</u> a coordinating conjunction (such as *and*, *but*, *or*, *nor*, *for*, *so*, *yet*).
- Separate the two independent clauses by a semicolon.
- Separate the two independent clauses by a semicolon <u>and</u> a conjunctive adverb or phrase (such as *also*, *besides*, *finally*, *then*, *for example*, *however*, *of course*, *on the other hand*, *still*, *therefore*) followed by a comma.

Look at the following sentence.

One way to cook a chicken is to fry it, another way is to roast it.

This is an example of a comma splice. It can be corrected in any of the ways listed above. The following sentences are examples of how it would look when fixed each way.

- One way to cook a chicken is to fry it, and another way is to roast it.
- One way to cook a chicken is to fry it; another way is to roast it.
- One way to cook a chicken is to fry it; of course, another way is to roast it.

The point to remember here is that you have a choice. How you join two independent clauses will depend on the sentence you want to create.

Practice

Correct the following examples of comma splices or run-on sentences.

1. She did her grocery shopping for the week; however, she forgot to buy the ingredients she needed for dinner that night, consequently they ended up going to a restaurant.
2. The best way to find a lost pet is to put an ad in the paper, another way is to ask the neighbors if they saw it.
3. Tragedy strikes every family sometime, how they deal with it differs from case to case.
4. Why shouldn't people receive a pension, they worked for it all their lives?

5. Alexander didn't want to pay to have the car repaired, after all he wasn't the one who had the accident.

6. For the first time in his life, Dad had time to relax, he took up fishing as a hobby.

7. Maria gave half the cookies she baked to her nieces and nephews then she saved the rest for her own family.

8. I raked all the leaves in the front yard when I turned around, I discovered they had all blown back.

9. It was too late to go to the movie we wanted to see, therefore, we decided to go to Rachel's party.

10. He left the house only to go to the post office, otherwise he stayed home and studied all day.

Answers

These are suggested corrections. Answers may vary.

1. She did her grocery shopping for the week; however she forgot to buy the ingredients she needed for dinner that night. Consequently, they ended up going to a restaurant.

2. The best way to find a lost pet is to put an ad in the paper; another way is to ask the neighbors if they saw it.

3. Tragedy strikes every family sometime; how they deal with it differs from case to case.

4. Why shouldn't people receive a pension? They worked for it all their lives.

5. Alexander didn't want to pay to have the car repaired; after all, he wasn't the one who had the accident.

6. For the first time in his life, Dad had time to relax. He took up fishing as a hobby.

7. Maria gave half the cookies she baked to her nieces and nephews; then she saved the rest for her own family.

8. I raked all the leaves in the front yard. When I turned around, I discovered they had all blown back.

9. It was too late to go to the movie we wanted to see; therefore, we decided to go to Rachel's party.

10. He left the house only to go to the post office; otherwise, he stayed home and studied all day.

WORD CHOICE

We all know thousands of words. Generally, we don't think of words as we go through our everyday lives. When we speak, as long as the meaning of what we say is clear, we don't spend much time trying to think of one word that would be more precise than another. When we write, however, the correct wording is important for getting a meaning conveyed to the reader.

We are not there with the reader to clarify anything, so the words we choose to use in written communication are vitally important.

The dictionary definition of a word is its denotation. Many words also have a connotation. A connotation of a word is the emotional impact a word can have on a reader. A connotation can be positive or negative. For example, the word *skinny* has a negative connotation. Being skinny is not something we strive for. The word *slender*, on the other hand, has a positive connotation. In our culture, slender connotes an attribute of fashion models. It implies good health and grace.

When you write your essay for the GED, you will be writing a formal paper. This means that the appropriate writing style will be one that emphasizes the importance of the subject. For this reason, slang is inappropriate. Slang is very informal, and not everyone understands it. In a formal paper, you would not write, "The food grossed me out." Instead, you would perhaps write, "The food was unappetizing."

Instead of using general words, try to be specific in your language. A general word refers to a whole group or class of things, and a specific word names a narrower class. For example, instead of using the term *football team*, you might choose to write *Pittsburgh Steelers,* which names the exact team to which you are referring.

In an effort to write the required number of words for the GED essay, many people repeat themselves unnecessarily or use inflated phrases. Look at the following sentence.

> The CD that is the most valuable in his collection is a jazz CD that features Miles Davis.

This sentence would be more effective if it were rewritten as below.

> The most valuable in his collection is a jazz CD that features Miles Davis.

Practice

Edit the sentences below to eliminate words with inappropriate connotations, slang, general rather than specific words, and unnecessary repetition.

1. I have talked to you about your behavior countless numbers of times.

2. The third person standing in line is not a very nice person.

3. I worked twenty-four seven on that project, and now it's down the tubes.

4. You will be the contact person for making all the arrangements for the wedding reception.

5. In order that you may graduate next year, you must complete all the forms that need to be filled out.

6. He sweated up a storm working outside all day.

7. He pitched for a baseball team for a lot of numbers of years.

8. Joseph became rich by penny-pinching.

9. You must stay here until such time as I deem it appropriate that you leave.

10. At the present time, we have to work much harder in order to finish on time.

Answers

These are suggested corrections. Answers may vary.

1. I have talked to you about your behavior countless times.
2. The third person standing in line is not very nice.
3. I worked all week on that project, and now it's a wasted effort.
4. You will make all the arrangements for the wedding reception.
5. In order to graduate next year, you must complete all the forms.
6. He was drenched in perspiration from working outside all day.
7. He pitched for the Red Sox for many years.
8. Joseph became rich by saving his money.
9. You must stay here until I decide that you can leave.
10. We have to work much harder to finish on time.

SENTENCE STRUCTURE

Sentences can be classified by their structures as well as by their purposes. Depending on the number and types of clauses they contain, sentences are classified as simple, compound, complex, or compound-complex. A simple sentence is one independent clause with no subordinate clauses.

> Isabel experienced a life threatening disease.

A simple sentence may have two or more subjects or verbs, but as long as it does not contain more than one independent clause, it remains a simple sentence.

A compound sentence contains two or more independent clauses with no subordinate clauses. The independent clauses are generally connected with a comma and a coordinating conjunction (*and*, *but*, *or*, *nor*, *for*, *so*, *yet*) or with a semicolon.

> Isabel experienced a life threatening disease, but she remained cheerful and optimistic.

A complex sentence contains one independent clause with one or more subordinate clauses.

> When she was a young girl, Isabel experienced a life threatening disease.

A compound-complex sentence is composed of at least two independent clauses and at least one subordinate clause.

> Isabel experienced a life threatening disease when she was a young girl, but she made a complete recovery because she followed her doctor's orders.

In the above sentence, *Isabel experienced a life threatening disease when she was a young girl* is an independent clause containing a dependent clause. The second part of the sentence, *she made a complete recovery because she followed her doctor's orders* is the second independent clause, also containing a dependent clause.

The purpose of a sentence is the second way a sentence can be classified. There are four types of sentences.

- **declarative**—Makes a statement. *Autumn is the most beautiful time of the year.*
- **imperative**—Issues an order or a request. *Stop at the post office on your way home.*
- **interrogative**—Asks a question. *Why don't you want to go to Europe on your vacation?*
- **exclamatory**—Makes an emphatic statement. *Close the door before we all freeze!*

Practice

Identify the following sentences as simple, compound, complex, or compound-complex.

1. The winner of the contest is the person who has the ugliest tie.
2. If you don't wear your seatbelt, you could be seriously hurt in an accident.
3. The princess attended the ball alone, but she had more dance partners than she ever imagined.
4. The dangers of living too well are bad; the dangers of not living well enough are even worse.
5. She was a vivacious flirt who broke men's hearts, but one day her own heart would be broken.
6. When Jack spoke to the police, he was evasive about his whereabouts on the night of the crime.
7. Wendy spent many years in the classroom, but her heart was somewhere else.
8. Leaving everything familiar behind, Janine ran away from home; however, she only got as far as her grandmother's house.

Answers

1. complex	4. compound	6. complex	8. compound-complex
2. complex	5. compound-complex	7. compound	
3. compound			

TEST YOURSELF

For each item, choose the answer that would result in the most effective writing. Some sentences may be correct as written.

Paragraph 1

(1) When we were small Mother would pack us all into the car and take us on picnics. (2) Sometimes we would go to the beach and sometimes we would go to the park. (3) If it was raining, we had indoor picnics. (4) An indoor picnic was when we would pack a lunch; and then we would spread a blanket on the living room floor and just pretend we were outdoors. (5) One time she even brought in some sand from the sandbox and spread it on the blanket. (6) We listened to music on the old record player and we pretended we were at the beach. (7) We even put on sunglasses and beach hats.

1. Sentence 1: **When we were small Mother would pack us all into the car and take us on picnics.**

   What correction should be made to this sentence?
   (1) Add a comma after car
   (2) Add a comma after small
   (3) Add a comma after and
   (4) Add a period after car
   (5) No correction is necessary

2. Sentence 2: **Sometimes we would go to the beach and sometimes we would go to the park.**

   What correction should be made to this sentence?
   (1) Add a comma after beach
   (2) Add a comma after and
   (3) Add a semicolon after beach
   (4) Add a comma after the first use of sometimes
   (5) No correction is necessary

3. Sentence 3: **If it was raining, we had indoor picnics.**

   What correction should be made to this sentence?
   (1) Remove the comma after raining
   (2) Replace the comma after raining with a semicolon
   (3) Add a comma after if
   (4) Replace the comma after raining with a period
   (5) No correction is necessary

4. Sentence 4: **An indoor picnic was when we would pack a lunch; and then we would spread a blanket on the living room floor and just pretend we were outdoors.**

    What correction should be made to this sentence?
    (1) Add a comma after was
    (2) Add a comma after floor
    (3) Replace the semicolon with a comma
    (4) Replace the semicolon with a period
    (5) No correction is necessary

5. Sentence 5: **One time she even brought in some sand from the sandbox and spread it on the blanket.**

    What correction should be made to this sentence?
    (1) Add a comma after time
    (2) Add a comma after sandbox
    (3) Add a semicolon after sandbox
    (4) Add a comma after sandbox
    (5) No correction is necessary

6. Sentence 6: **We listened to music on the old record player and we pretended we were at the beach.**

    What correction should be made to this sentence?
    (1) Add a period after player
    (2) Add a semicolon after player
    (3) Add a comma after pretended
    (4) Add a comma after player
    (5) No correction is necessary

7. Sentence 7: **We even put on sunglasses and beach hats.**

    What correction should be made to this sentence?
    (1) Add a comma after sunglasses
    (2) Add a semicolon after sunglasses
    (3) Add a period after sunglasses
    (4) Add a comma after we
    (5) No correction is necessary

Paragraph 2

(1) Painting a room can be a time consuming task that can take a long time. (2) First, all the pictures must be removed from the walls then the nail holes must be patched and sanded. (3) After all this is done the furniture must be covered so paint doesn't splash on it and ruin it. (4) The trim takes a long time, it has to be done carefully. (5) Finally, the walls can be painted. (6) When the job looks done it really isn't. (7) Cleaning up, and re-hanging the pictures can take a long time.

8. Sentence 1: **Painting a room can be a time consuming <u>task that can take a long time.</u>**

    Which is the best way to write the underlined portion of this sentence? If you think the original is the best way, choose option (1).

    (1) task that can take a long time

    (2) task, that can take a long time

    (3) task.

    (4) task; that can take a long time

    (5) task that can, take a long time

9. Sentence 2: **First, all the pictures must be removed from the <u>walls then</u> the nail holes must be patched and sanded.**

    Which of the following is the best way to write the underlined portion of this sentence? If you think the original is the best way, choose option (1).

    (1) walls then

    (2) walls, then

    (3) walls; then

    (4) walls. Then

    (5) walls then,

10. Sentence 3: **After all this is done the furniture must be covered so paint doesn't splash on it and ruin it.**

    What correction should be made to this sentence?

    (1) Add a comma after done

    (2) Add a comma after covered

    (3) Add a comma after it

    (4) Add a semicolon after covered

    (5) No correction is necessary

11. Sentence 4: **The trim takes a long <u>time, it</u> has to be done carefully.**

    Which of the following is the best way to write the underlined portion of this sentence? If you think the original is the best way, choose option (1).
    (1) time, it
    (2) time; it
    (3) time. It
    (4) time, and
    (5) time, because

12. Sentence 6: **When the job looks done it really isn't.**

    What correction should be made to this sentence?
    (1) add a semicolon after done
    (2) add a comma after when
    (3) add a comma after looks
    (4) add a comma after done
    (5) No correction is necessary

13. Sentence 7: **Cleaning up, and re-hanging the pictures can take a long time.**

    What correction should be made to this sentence?
    (1) remove the comma
    (2) replace the comma with a semicolon
    (3) add a comma after pictures
    (4) add a comma after re-hanging
    (5) no correction is necessary

Answers

1. **(2)** *When we were small* is a dependent clause used to introduce the independent clause. An introductory dependent clause requires a comma after it.
2. **(1)** Two independent clauses joined by *and* require a comma to link them.
3. **(5)** No correction is necessary.
4. **(3)** Two independent clauses joined by *and* require a comma to link them.
5. **(5)** No correction is necessary.
6. **(4)** Two independent clauses joined by *and* require a comma to link them.
7. **(5)** No correction is necessary.
8. **(3)** *time consuming task* and *can take a long time* mean the same thing. Including both is redundant.
9. **(3)** Although it would be possible to place a period after *walls* and begin a new sentence, the sentences would be short and choppy. A semicolon separates the independent clauses but keeps the ideas together in one sentence.
10. **(1)** *After all this is done* is a dependent clause, which must be separated from the independent clause by a comma.
11. **(2)** A semicolon after *time* is appropriate for joining the two short independent clauses.

12. **(4)** *When the job looks done* is a dependent clause introducing the dependent clause.

13. **(1)** No comma is necessary in this sentence.

GRAMMAR REVIEW
Misplaced and Dangling Modifiers

Look at the following sentence.

At the age of eight, her mother took Janice to her first concert.

Was the mother eight years old at the time, or was Janice eight years old? This is a case of a misplaced modifier. Look at the corrected sentence.

When Janice was eight years old, her mother took her to her first concert.

Now it is clear that Janice was eight years old at the time. The group of words that is used to describe Janice has been placed near her name.

A misplaced modifier is a group of descriptive words that has been written in an incorrect location in the sentence. When you are writing your essay, one of your jobs is to make sure that each sentence is clear in meaning.

A dangling modifier is a group of words that does not logically refer to any other word in the sentence. Most likely, a dangling modifier will appear at the beginning of a sentence. Look at the sentence below.

While watching the movie, the popcorn spilled on the floor.

The introductory phrase *while watching the movie* appears to be referring to the popcorn. Now look at the corrected sentence below.

While we were watching the movie, the popcorn spilled on the floor.

Now it is clear that people (not popcorn) were watching the movie.

Practice

Rewrite the following sentences to correct any misplaced or dangling modifiers.

1. Marshmallows were roasted by the Boy Scouts on sharply pointed sticks.
2. I took a picture of the giraffe with my camera.
3. Soon after graduating from high school, my father bought me the car I had been dreaming about.
4. While still just a baby, Bob's father began to save for his college education.
5. The man with a criminal record was falsely accused of committing the burglary by the witness.
6. When reaching up to adjust the visor, the car swerved off the road.

Answers

These are suggested corrections. Answers may vary.

1. The Boy Scouts roasted marshmallows on sharply pointed sticks.
2. I took a picture with my camera of the giraffe.
3. Soon after I graduated from high school, my father bought me the car I had been dreaming about.
4. While Bob was still just a baby, his father began to save for Bob's college education.
5. The witness falsely accused the man with a criminal record of committing the burglary.
6. When I was reaching up to adjust the visor, the car swerved off the road.

Pronoun Agreement

A pronoun is a word that takes the place of a noun (a person, place, or thing). The noun for which it is substituting is called the antecedent. A noun and a pronoun agree when they are both singular or both plural. Do not use plural pronouns to refer to singular antecedents.

One of the most frequent pronoun errors is not treating an indefinite pronoun as singular. The following indefinite pronouns are singular.

any	each	everything	no one
anybody	either	neither	someone
anyone	everyone	none	something

Everyone in class works at *his* or *her* own ability.

If you have mistakenly referred a plural pronoun to a singular pronoun, you can correct your mistake in one of three ways:

- Replace the plural pronoun with *he* or *she* (or *his* or *her*).
- Make the antecedent plural.
- Rewrite the sentence so that no problem of agreement exists.

Treat a collective noun such as team or family as singular unless the members function as individuals.

The *committee* worked all night on *its* proposal.

The *audience* stamped *their* feet and shouted.

If the antecedents are compound and connected by *or*, *nor*, *either...or*, or *neither...nor*, make the pronoun agree with the nearer antecedent.

> *Neither Bill nor James* won a prize for *his* entry.
>
> Either Jennifer or her teammates should carry their equipment.

When you are proofreading your essay, make sure you read each sentence as an individual unit. By doing this, you will avoid the common mistake of assuming that pronouns agree with their antecedents. Every time you spot a pronoun, look back in the sentence and double check that the antecedent agrees with the pronoun. Look in each sentence for instances where you have written key words such as *or* or *nor*.

Practice

Correct the following sentences that have problems with pronoun-antecedent agreement. Not all sentences contain errors.

1. No one admitted they had taken the last piece of pie.
2. If any student loses their book, they will have to pay for it.
3. Everyone should do his or her own work.
4. Neither you nor Joseph are responsible for locking that door.
5. Fortunately, none of the boys was involved in their accident.
6. The group has announced that their next meeting will be in July.
7. If a person plans to work, they should get their resume in order.
8. Either Susan or Deborah has agreed to take their car.
9. Either the mayor or his representatives will attend their meetings.

Answers

These are suggested corrections. Answers may vary.

1. No one admitted he or she had taken the last piece of pie.
2. If any student loses his or her book, they will have to pay for it.
3. Correct
4. Neither you nor Joseph is responsible for locking that door.
5. Fortunately, none of the boys was involved in the accident.
6. The group has announced that its next meeting will be in July.
7. If people plan to work, their resumes should be in order.
8. Either Susan or Deborah has agreed to take her car.
9. Correct

Punctuation Review

There are several general rules for capitalizing words. Of course, you will capitalize the first word in each new sentence, but there are instances where you will capitalize a word that falls somewhere within the sentence, also.

Capitalize all proper nouns and words derived from them. Do not capitalize common nouns. A proper noun is the name of a specific person, place, or thing. All other nouns are common nouns. This can sometimes be confusing with words such as *father*. Look at the examples below.

> A good father will spend time with his children.
>
> After we went shopping, Father took us for ice cream.

In the first sentence, fathers are referred to as a general group of people. In the second sentence, only the writer's father is being discussed. In this case, the word *father* is used to mean the name of the person. The above rule also applies with titles of people.

> When I was in college, Professor Johnson taught that course.
>
> All the local professors attended the seminar.

The first, last, and all major words in titles of books, magazines, movies, songs, and similar works are capitalized.

> The first book I read in high school was *Catcher in the Rye*.

Capitalize north, south, east, and west when they refer to specific geographical sections of the country or world. Do not capitalize them when they are used to name directions.

> The North and South fought the Civil War for several years.
>
> When you get to the light, turn north.

Using commas correctly is often a problem for writers. There are several general rules that apply to the use of commas. Learning these rules will help you to avoid major errors in writing your essay.

Use a comma to separate all items in a series. Do not, however, use a comma before the first item in the series.

> The children brought their new pencils, pens, lunch boxes, and notebooks on their first day of school.
>
> NOT
>
> The children brought their new, pencils, pens, lunch boxes, and notebooks on their first day of school.

Use a comma to set off nonrestrictive elements. Do not use a comma to set off restrictive elements in a sentence. A nonrestrictive element is a group of words that describes a noun or a pronoun. A restrictive element defines or limits the meaning of the word it modifies, so it is essential to the meaning.

Nonrestrictive

Her new car, which is equipped with airbags, is the first major purchase she made in years.

Restrictive

Cars that are equipped with airbags have been proven to be safer than other cars.

Use a comma before a coordinating conjunction joining independent clauses. Do not use a comma after the coordinating conjunction. The seven coordinating conjunctions are *and*, *but*, *or*, *nor*, *for*, *so*, and *yet*.

The car suddenly swerved to the right, but the driver was able to pull it back to the center of the road.

NOT

The car suddenly swerved to the right but, the driver was able to pull it back to the center of the road.

Use a comma after an introductory phrase or clause. An introductory phrase or clause usually tells when, where, how, why, or under what conditions the main action of the sentence occurred.

After Alexander had spent the night studying, he felt sleepy when he finally sat down to take the test.

Use a comma between coordinate adjectives not joined by *and*. Do not use a comma between cumulative adjectives. Coordinate adjectives are words that describe a noun separately. Cumulative adjectives are words that do not describe the noun separately. Cumulative adjectives cannot be joined by *and*. Their order in the sentence cannot be changed.

Coordinate Adjectives

He grew to be a strong, independent, intelligent man.

Cumulative Adjectives

There were four large dark shadows looming in the hallway.

Practice

Correct all errors in capitalization and comma usage in the following sentences.

1. When we traveled to europe we especially enjoyed the french countryside.

2. We had no problems on our vacation until we got to the city of north braddock where we had a flat tire.

3. The plane with its engines roaring landed in the field behind the mall.

4. Gerald is a warm affectionate gentle father to his sons.

5. Various religious groups including the catholics and protestants joined together to ask for peace.

6. We bought a home in chicago where I worked as a chemist.

7. Her children are impossible spoiled demanding brats.

8. As time passed and we got used to the new routine we settled in happily to our new lives.

9. Our lawyer explained the will but we weren't sure we really understood it.

10. Jennifer mother's favorite sister is going to visit us soon.

Answers

These are suggested corrections. Answers may vary.

1. When we traveled to Europe, we especially enjoyed the French countryside.

2. We had no problems on our vacation until we got to the city of North Braddock where we had a flat tire.

3. The plane, with its engines roaring, landed in the field behind the mall.

4. Gerald is a warm, affectionate, gentle father to his sons.

5. Various religious groups, including the Catholics and Protestants, joined together to ask for peace.

6. We bought a home in Chicago where I worked as a chemist.

7. Her children are impossible, spoiled, demanding brats.

8. As time passed and we got used to the new routine, we settled in happily to our new lives.

9. Our lawyer explained the will, but we weren't sure we really understood it.

10. Jennifer, Mother's favorite sister, is going to visit us soon.

Apostrophes

Apostrophes are used in three ways. An apostrophe is used to form a possessive of a noun or pronoun. To form the possessive of a singular noun or pronoun, add an apostrophe and *s* (*'s*).

The boy's skates need to be sharpened.

When the noun is plural and ends in *s*, add only an apostrophe.

The boys' skates need to be sharpened.

(In this sentence, more than one boy needs to have his skates sharpened.)

To form the possessive of a plural noun not ending in *s*, add *'s* just as with a singular possessive.

Those men's coats all look the same.

To show joint possession use *'s* or *s'* with the last noun only. To show individual possession, make all the nouns possessive.

Maria and Manuel's new car is the latest model.

Rita's and Mary's choices of boyfriends couldn't have been more different.

A common misuse of the apostrophe is using it with the possessive pronouns *us*, *whose*, *his*, *hers*, *ours*, *yours*, and *theirs*.

Those books in the back of the room are hers.

NOT

Those books in the back of the room are her's.

An apostrophe is used to indicate the omission of letters in contractions. In a contraction, the apostrophe takes the place of the missing letters.

We can't go to the graduation.

(*Can't* takes the place of *cannot*)

It's too cold to go outside without a coat.

(*It's* takes the place of *it is*)

Use an apostrophe to form the plural of numbers and letters.

They are asking to see ID's at the door.

A semicolon is used between sentence elements that are of equal rank or between items in a series that contain internal punctuation. A colon is mainly used to call attention to the words that follow it. Look at the examples below.

They did not go to Spain; they went to Germany.

That new bookstore has books about travel in Charleston, West Virginia; American antiques; and museums in Paris, France.

The perfect husband should have these qualities: intelligence, stability, kindness, and a sense of humor.

In the first sentence, the two independent clauses are equal in value. A period between the independent clauses, although grammatically correct, would have created two short choppy sentences that did not show any relationship to each other.

The second sentence uses a semicolon to avoid confusion between separate parts of items in a series and the items themselves.

The colon is used in the third sentence as an introduction to the series of qualities of a perfect husband.

Quotation marks are generally used to set off a person's exact words. The exact words make up a direct quote. An indirect quote, on the other hand, reports someone's ideas without using that person's exact words. An indirect quote is not set off by quotation marks. Look at the examples below.

Direct Quote

She said, "These shoes aren't the right size for me."

Indirect Quote

She said that the shoes didn't fit her properly.

Always place periods and commas inside the quotation marks. Question marks and exclamation marks are placed inside quotation marks unless they refer to the whole sentence.

"This is not right," said the senator. "My constituents deserve better than this!"

Did you hear him say, "Everyone is entitled to one vote"?

Notice in the first sentence that the direct quote is followed by words that explain who is making the statement. When this occurs, the period is placed at the end of the explanatory words, and a comma is placed before the ending quotation mark. If the direct quote is broken up by explanatory words, commas are used on both sides of the explanatory words.

"After you get back from the store," said Scott, "please stop in to see me."

In the second sentence, the direct quote is not a question, but the sentence as a whole is a question, so the question mark appears at the end of the whole sentence and not inside the quotation mark.

Practice

Correct the errors in the use of apostrophes, colons, semicolons, and quotation marks in the sentences below. Not all sentences have errors.

1. The point of our vacation was to see the three largest rivers in the world. The Nile, the Amazon, and the Mississippi.
2. Im sure its time for the car to have its oil changed.
3. One of Jackies friends moved out of the state and took the gloves that were hers.
4. Werent you angry to hear Ms. Leopold say "youll all stay after school for this?"
5. "Its getting dark: lets head for home soon." Said the scout leader.
6. The teacher said that we all needed to take care of our own research papers.
7. "The point of the test isnt to scare us." Maxine explained. "its just to get us used to taking a test."
8. Shes here now, but she didn't bring the twins books with her.
9. You've lost John and Marys car keys, havent you?
10. My mother asked what I had in my pockets.

Answers

1. The point of our vacation was to see the three largest rivers in the world: the Nile, the Amazon, and the Mississippi.
2. I'm sure it's time for the car to have its oil changed.
3. One of Jackie's friends moved out of the state and took the gloves that were hers.
4. Weren't you angry to hear Ms. Leopold say, "You'll all stay after school for this"?

5. "It's getting dark; let's head for home soon," said the scout leader.

6. Correct

7. "The point of the test isn't to scare us," Maxine explained. "It's just to get us used to taking a test."

8. She's here now, but she didn't bring the twins' books with her.

9. You've lost John and Mary's car keys, haven't you?

10. Correct

TEST YOURSELF

For each item, choose the answer that would result in the most effective writing. Some sentences may be correct as written.

Paragraph 1

(1) Parenthood has a way of making people grow up fast. (2) One day people can have no cares the next day they are responsible for another life. (3) Its sometimes overwhelming. (4) Parents are responsible for the care of another person. (5) If a parent is careless the results could be disastrous. (6) Parents must feed, clothe, and shelter their children as well as provide medical attention when necessary. (7) If a parent doesn't take care of their child, who will?

1. Sentence 2: **One day people can have no <u>cares the</u> next day they are responsible for another life.**

   Which is the best way to write the underlined portion of this sentence? If you think the original is the best way, choose option (1).

   (1) cares the

   (2) cares, the

   (3) cares; the

   (4) cares. The

   (5) cares: the

2. Sentence 3: **Its sometimes overwhelming.**

   What correction should be made to this sentence?

   (1) Add a comma after *sometimes*

   (2) Add a comma after *its*

   (3) It's

   (4) Replace the period with a question mark

   (5) No correction is necessary

3. Sentence 4: **Parents are responsible for the care of another person.**

What correction should be made to this sentence?

(1) Parent's

(2) Parents'

(3) Add a comma after *responsible*

(4) Add a comma after *parents*

(5) No correction is necessary

4. Sentence 5: **If a parent is <u>careless the</u> results could be disastrous.**

Which is the best way to write the underlined portion of this sentence? If you think the original is the best way, choose option (1).

(1) careless the

(2) careless: the

(3) careless; the

(4) careless, the

(5) careless. The

5. Sentence 6: **Parents must feed, clothe, and shelter their children as well as provide medical attention when necessary.**

What correction should be made to this sentence?

(1) Add a comma after *children*

(2) Add a period after *children*

(3) Change *their* to *his or her*

(4) Add a comma after *attention*

(5) No correction is necessary

6. Sentence 7: **If a parent doesn't take care of their child, who will?**

What correction should be made to this sentence?

(1) Remove the comma after *child*

(2) Change *their* to *his or her*

(3) Add a comma after *if*

(4) Remove the apostrophe in *doesn't*

(5) No correction is necessary

Paragraph 2

(1) Someone once said "Once you have children, your life changes for ever." (2) Imagine my surprise when I went to the Doctor, and she told me I was going to have twins. (3) She said, "Are you ready for a shock"? (4) I thought I was ready, but your never ready for something like that. (5) That was years ago, now my children are grown. (6) Now I look back on those times and can't believe how much work it was.

7. Sentence 1: **Someone once said "Once you have children, your life changes for ever."**

   What correction should be made to this sentence?
   (1) Add a comma after *said*
   (2) Remove the comma after *children*
   (3) Change *your* to *you're*
   (4) Change *Once* to *once*
   (5) No correction is necessary

8. Sentence 2: **Imagine my surprise when I went to the Doctor, and she told me I was going to have twins.**

   What correction should be made to this sentence?
   (1) Remove the comma after *Doctor*
   (2) Add a comma after *surprise*
   (3) Change *Doctor* to *doctor*
   (4) Add a comma after *me*
   (5) No correction is necessary

9. Sentence 3: **She said, "Are you ready for a shock"?**

   What correction should be made to this sentence?
   (1) Change *Are* to *are*
   (2) Remove the comma after *said*
   (3) Add a comma after *ready*
   (4) Move the question mark to the inside of the quotation mark
   (5) No correction is necessary

10. Sentence 4: **I thought I was ready, but your never ready for something like that.**

    What correction should be made to this sentence?
    (1) Remove the comma after *ready*
    (2) Change *your* to *you're*
    (3) Add a comma after *thought*
    (4) Add a comma after *ready*
    (5) No correction is necessary

11. Sentence 5: **That was years <u>ago, now</u> my children are grown.**

    Which is the best way to write the underlined portion of this sentence? If you think the original is the best way, choose option (1).

    (1) ago, now

    (2) ago: now

    (3) ago. Now

    (4) ago; now

    (5) ago now

12. Sentence 6: **Now I look back on those times and can't believe how much work it was.**

    What correction should be made to this sentence?

    (1) Add a comma after *Now*

    (2) Add a comma after *times*

    (3) Add a comma after *and*

    (4) Add a semicolon after *times*

    (5) No correction is necessary

Answers

1. **(3)** A semicolon is most appropriate here because both the independent clauses have equal value in the sentence, and they are showing a relationship.

2. **(3)** *It's* is a contraction of the words *it is*. *Its* is a possessive pronoun.

3. **(5)** No correction is necessary in this sentence.

4. **(4)** *If a parent is careless* is a dependent introductory clause that needs a comma to separate it from the independent clause.

5. **(5)** No correction is necessary in this sentence.

6. **(2)** *A parent* is a singular antecedent for the pronoun. The pronoun *their* is plural.

7. **(1)** The explanatory introduction to the quote is separated from the direct quote by a comma.

8. **(3)** The word *doctor* is not referring to a particular doctor by name, so the word is not capitalized.

9. **(4)** The whole sentence is not a question. Only the direct quote is a question, so the question mark goes inside the quotation mark.

10. **(2)** *You're* is a contraction of the words *you are*. *Your* is a possessive pronoun.

11. **(4)** This is a case of two independent clauses that are directly related. Making them two separate sentences would result in short choppy sentences.

12. **(5)** No correction is necessary in this sentence.

THE LANGUAGE ARTS, WRITING TEST
PART II—WRITING AN ESSAY

When you take your GED, you will be given a topic to write about, and you will have only 45 minutes in which to complete your essay. This means that it is extremely important to know how to plan, organize, and edit efficiently.

When you are given your topic, the first step is to use a piece of scratch paper to narrow the topic sufficiently so that you have no more than four main points. Each of these main points will become a separate paragraph in your completed essay. For example, if you are to discuss the advantages and disadvantages of television, you might want to list only two advantages and two disadvantages. Think through what you wish to say about the topic. What is your purpose in writing the essay?

After you have decided on the purpose of the essay, state the purpose in sentence form. This will then be revised to become your thesis statement. Looking at our example above, your purpose might be to discuss the advantages and disadvantages of television, but this is not your thesis. You will use your attitude about the topic to develop your thesis statement. Maybe you feel that television should be censored because of the violent shows. Your thesis statement might be: "Although there are some advantages to television, the violence portrayed on many shows leads to juvenile delinquency." You have now stated your feelings about television, and you have given the reader an idea of what you will be saying in your essay. This statement will be written in the first paragraph of your essay, and the rest of the essay will be directly related to it. By crafting a good thesis statement, you will be giving yourself direction for the rest of the essay.

Practice

Rewrite the following thesis statements to reflect a more exact attitude toward the subject.

1. I like all kinds of books.
2. Winter sports are the best.
3. Everyone has strange relatives.
4. Dreams are interesting.
5. I have a lot of friends.

Answers

Answers may vary.

1. Although I enjoy reading all kinds of books, my favorites are those that are based on fact because they are educational.
2. Participating in winter sports is a good way to stay in shape since most winter sports require a great deal of stamina and strength.
3. I have three aunts who are all eccentric in different ways.
4. There is a theory that dreams are a person's unexpressed desires and hopes that lurk in the subconscious.
5. I take pride in the fact that my friends come from all walks of life.

DEVELOPING PARAGRAPHS

After you have written your thesis statement and have decided on the points you will discuss, you are ready to begin to write your first draft. Interesting writing is more than a series of general statements. Ideally, you will have only a few general statements, and the majority of your writing will be dedicated to creating purposeful, specific details. This means that you will include facts, comparisons, definitions, reasons, and examples to illustrate the point you are trying to make.

Each paragraph in your essay will reflect back to the thesis statement; but within each paragraph, you will need to write a topic sentence. The topic sentence of each paragraph will be one of the points you choose to discuss. The paragraph will be the development of these points through a series of supporting sentences. Each supporting sentence in a paragraph should give more information about the idea or thought expressed in the topic sentence.

The sentences that make up a paragraph should be presented in a logical order and should be varied in style and length. An entire paragraph written in short choppy sentences is distracting and not very interesting to read. Look at the following paragraph.

> Some television shows have too much violence. This is not good for young children. They may learn to be violent themselves. They see too much fighting and shooting on television.

Now look at the revised paragraph.

> The television shows that have too much violence may not be good for young children. The fighting and shooting on these shows may teach children to be violent themselves.

Practice

Combine or restructure the sentences in the following paragraphs.

1. Many books are interesting. I especially enjoy science fiction. I like it because it deals with the future sometimes. One of my favorite authors is Jules Verne. He wrote about some things that came true.

2. During the fall and winter, I like to hunt. My father and uncle taught me how. We always stayed at my father's camp when we went. It was a tradition for us to go during Thanksgiving vacation.

3. Smoking is bad for people. It can cause lung cancer. Other people who breathe smoke can get sick too. This is from secondhand smoke. Smoking is a habit, though, so a lot of people have trouble stopping.

4. I've always liked to travel. One of my favorite places to travel is Texas. I really enjoy the warm weather. There are a lot of interesting places to visit when I go to Texas.

Answers

Answers will vary.

1. Although I enjoy a variety of books, my favorite type is science fiction. One of my favorite authors is Jules Verne. Verne wrote many of his stories about the future, and much of what he wrote about has actually come true.

2. My father and uncle taught me how to hunt, and I still enjoy it. It was a tradition for us to go hunting during Thanksgiving vacation, and each time we went, we stayed at my father's camp.

3. Cigarettes are not only bad for the person smoking them, but they can also be bad for those around the smoker. Secondhand smoke may cause lung cancer just as inhaling can. Those who smoke are victims of their own habit.

4. I've always enjoyed traveling, and Texas is one of my favorite places to visit because of the warm weather and the interesting sites.

PARALLEL STRUCTURE

If two or more ideas are parallel, they should be expressed in parallel form. This means that statements that are similar should be written in the same way. Look at the example below.

You are responsible for organizing, writing, and to edit your essay.

In this sentence the three responsibilities are expressed in two different ways. *Organizing* and *writing* are parallel because they are written in the same form. The words *to edit* do not fit the pattern. The corrected sentence is below.

You are responsible for organizing, writing, and editing your essay.

Now the sentence is written in parallel form and the sentence is balanced. Any time you are writing a series of items, check that you have written them in parallel form. Single words should be balanced with single words, and phrases or clauses should be balanced with other phrases or clauses.

Practice

Edit the following sentences to correct faulty parallelism.

1. We began the project by looking in the library for information and called an expert in the field.
2. The game had gone well in the first quarter, but the team found itself losing at the end.
3. The boys were expected to clean their rooms, rake the leaves and were going to the store before lunch.
4. He was told either to change his attitude or change his job.
5. Reckless driving can result in losing your license or even some jail time.
6. The three sports she participated in were skiing, swimming and she liked to bowl.
7. Even though Sarah liked to read, she preferred to spend her free time sewing.

Answers

1. We began the project by looking in the library for information and calling an expert in the field.
2. The game had gone well in the first quarter, but the team was losing at the end.
3. The boys were expected to clean their rooms, rake the leaves, and go to the store before lunch.
4. He was told either to change his attitude or change his job.
5. Reckless driving can result in losing your license or even spending some time in jail.
6. The three sports she participated in were skiing, swimming, and bowling.
7. Even though Sarah liked reading, she preferred to spend her free time sewing.

TRANSITIONS

An essay that flows well from one paragraph to another is said to be coherent. Creating a coherent essay means that you will use transitions to link paragraphs throughout the essay. Just as the reader expects the sentences in a paragraph to support and flow from the topic sentence, the reader also expects the paragraphs to be directly related to the thesis statement. The paragraphs should be arranged in a clear, logical order. There are several ways of achieving coherence in an essay.

Repetition of key words or variations of them will help to make an essay coherent. As new ideas are introduced, keep your reader grounded by repeating words or phrases that have already been explained in previous paragraphs.

Parallel structure throughout the essay will also help in achieving coherence. Consistency in point of view and in style will eliminate confusion for the reader.

As the reader moves from one paragraph to the next, the transitions that link the paragraphs should be logical. The final paragraph should sum up all the ideas presented in the body of the essay just as the introductory paragraph presented the ideas.

Leaving time to proofread and edit your essay is an important step that shouldn't be left out. This is the step that will make the difference between a good essay and a great essay. There are several specific steps to proofreading your essay.

- **Strengthen the content**—Review the content of your essay with your original purpose in mind. Do you need to add something to make the purpose clear? Have your ideas been clearly outlined in the body of the essay?

- **Sharpen the focus**—Is there one central focus in your essay? Have you gone into too much detail and strayed from the original purpose? Can the reader tell from your introductory paragraph where you are going with your ideas? Does the introduction clearly reflect the ideas in the body of the essay?

- **Improve the organization**—Do you have to add to or revise the topic sentences in the paragraphs? Do you have to reorganize the order of the paragraphs so they are in a logical order? A good way to review the order of the paragraphs is to just read the topic sentences. They should make sense in both sequence and subject matter.

- **Proofread for grammar**—After you have read your essay for content, you will have to reread for grammar and punctuation. Each sentence should be read as a separate unit. This reading is often difficult because you have just finished writing the essay, and you do not have the time to go back at a later time to review it. Often, you will read what you *think* you wrote instead of what you actually wrote. Because your mind works faster than your pen, you might have left out words or punctuation in your haste to record your ideas. One way to help solve this problem is to read your essay backward. This means that, instead of reading from the beginning to the end, you will read the last sentence first and work your way up to the start of the essay. This way, you are forcing your mind to see each sentence separately instead of reading a sentence as it relates to the one before.

TEST YOURSELF

Choose one of the following topics. You have 45 minutes to draft, write, and edit an essay of about 200 words. Your essay should reflect your point of view, and you should give reasons and examples to support your position.

1. For many, capital punishment is viewed as a deterrent to crime. Others feel that the death sentence does nothing to stop others from committing crimes and that it is cruel and unusual punishment. Those who are opposed to capital punishment feel that rehabilitation is possible for even the most hardened criminal.

2. Many feel that rigid gun control laws will help stop senseless shootings. Others feel that stiffer laws will not stop criminals from obtaining guns, but will only make it more difficult for law abiding citizens to protect themselves.

3. Many states operate a lottery to earn money that is used for senior citizen programs or to build playgrounds for children. Some people think that the lottery promotes gambling and that the people who can least afford it are spending their valuable dollars buying lottery tickets.

4. The Internet is a valuable tool for everyone to use, but some people have created Web sites that are questionable for children to view. There are groups of people who feel that the Internet should be monitored so these questionable sites can be censored. Others feel that it would be unconstitutional to do so. Those who oppose censorship feel that all people have a right to put whatever they want on the Web and that it is up to the parents to decide what their children can and cannot view.

CHAPTER 4

Social Studies

TEST-TAKING TIPS

The first step to succeeding in the Social Studies test is to read the passages for the main idea. Very often, the main idea will be located in the beginning of the first paragraph. It is the sentence that gives the reader an idea of what the paragraph is about. It is usually followed by a variety of details that support the main idea. The details are usually in the form of specific examples or reasons that support the main idea.

The subject area of social studies will also require that you sometimes make inferences and draw your own conclusions using the passages as the base for this. When you make an inference, you will take a statement of fact and try to decide what else is being said, even if it is not written explicitly. This means that when you read, you will be reading critically so you can distinguish between fact and opinion. Remember, a fact can be proven, and an opinion expresses the author's feelings or thoughts. Opinions cannot be proven.

When working on social studies, you will often have to determine cause and effect. A cause is the reason why something happened, and the effect is the event that happened. In history, many of the questions will involve your deciding either a cause or an effect. For example, if the question asks you to choose a reason why the Civil War began, and you are given a choice of possibilities, you are searching for the reason an event took place. The event itself, in this case the Civil War, is the effect. Events do not happen as isolated incidents. For an event to happen, there must be a reason why.

The ability to understand how to compare and contrast ideas and events will be helpful to you as you work in social studies. A question could, for example, require that you read the passage to find out how two political parties are the same or how they differ. When comparing two items, you will be looking for ways they are similar. When you are contrasting two items, you will have to understand how they are different from each other.

Finally, your ability to read maps and charts will be important for the Social Studies test. Many questions, particularly those dealing with geography will ask that you interpret information that is found on a map. Remember to examine the map carefully, looking at the key as well as the map itself to understand it completely. The math section of this book will assist you in interpreting and analyzing charts and graphs.

GEOGRAPHY

Items 1–2 refer to the following passage.

Geography is the science that studies the relationship between man and the earth. It includes the size and distribution of the land masses, seas and resources, climatic zones, and the plant and animal life that exist on Earth. It is different from other sciences, such as geology, because it tries to find the relationships between the features of the earth and man's existence on Earth. For example, many of the people who came to America were farmers in the countries from which they emigrated. When they arrived in this country, they sought an area in which to live where they could continue their livelihood. The natural resources of a particular geographical area would help them to determine where they would settle.

1. You can infer from this passage that
    (1) immigrants all wanted to settle in the same area
    (2) settlers who came to this country looked for a geographical area that was similar to the area from which they came
    (3) people have a difficult time finding enough farm land
    (4) early settlers did not want to come to America because it was hard to find a place to live
    (5) immigrants had a hard time finding a place to settle

2. Which of the following is NOT part of the study of geography?
    (1) weather
    (2) the forms of wildlife in a given area
    (3) the amount of available farm land of an area
    (4) the availability of fresh water for farming
    (5) the amount of natural resources available in a given area

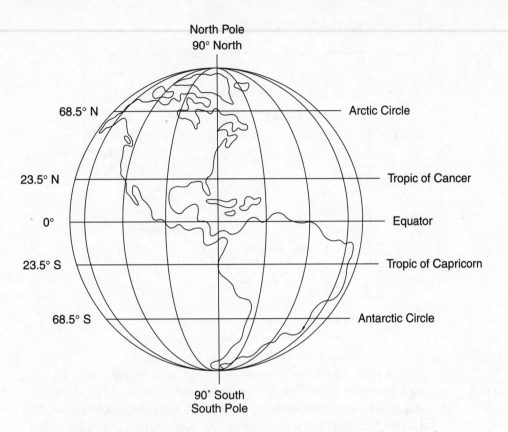

North Pole
90° North

68.5° N — Arctic Circle

23.5° N — Tropic of Cancer

0° — Equator

23.5° S — Tropic of Capricorn

68.5° S — Antarctic Circle

90° South
South Pole

3. Latitude and longitude on a map are measured in degrees, minutes, and seconds east or west of a prime meridian or line of longitude, and north or south of the equator. The North and South Poles are the points at which the Earth's axis meets the Earth's surface. Halfway between the poles is an east-west line which divides the Earth into two hemispheres. According to the map, this line is known as the

(1) Tropic of Cancer

(2) Equator

(3) Tropic of Capricorn

(4) North Pole

(5) Antarctic Circle

4. The East-West lines of latitude are numbered from 0 at the equator to 90° near the poles. The lines that are drawn from pole to pole to complete the grid are the lines indicating longitude. North-South lines are numbered from 0 at the North-South base line both east and west to the 180th North-South line. The zero line and the 180th line together form a complete circle that cuts the Earth into the Eastern and Western Hemispheres. The latitude and longitude lines intersect at the Tropic of Cancer at what measurement?

(1) 90°N

(2) 68.5°S

(3) 68.5°N

(4) 23.5°N

(5) 23.5°S

Items 5–6 refer to the map below.

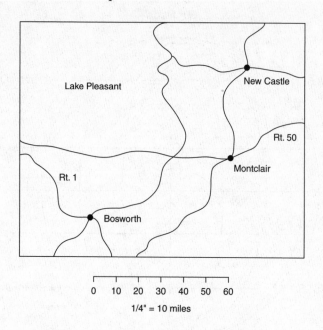

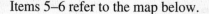

Maps are generally drawn to scale—that is, the mathematical relationship, or ratio, between the size of the features of the map and the size of the features in real size. The ruled line indicating the scale is usually marked off in miles. To find the distance between two points on the map, a strip of paper can be used if there is no ruler handy. Place the paper between the two points and place marks on the paper indicating the points. Then, place the paper along the scale with one mark at zero, and the other mark will indicate the distance.

5. The distance between Montclair and New Castle is approximately

   (1) 25 miles

   (2) 50 miles

   (3) 35 miles

   (4) 40 miles

   (5) 60 miles

6. The distance between New Castle and Bosworth is approximately

   (1) 110 miles

   (2) 80 miles

   (3) 200 miles

   (4) 75 miles

   (5) 150 miles

Items 7–9 refer to the following map.

Deposits of Fertilizer Minerals

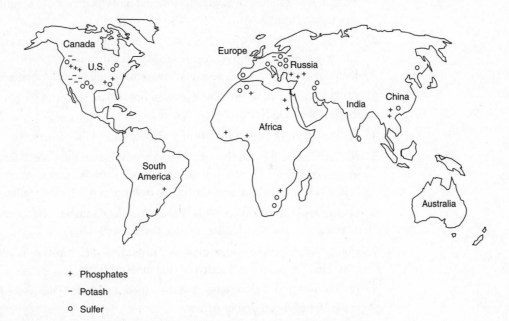

+ Phosphates

− Potash

o Sulfer

The purpose of some maps is to indicate geographical information in a pictorial manner. The title and the legend of the map will give the reader essential clues to the information contained in the map. The legend explains the symbols on the map, and the title gives an overall explaination of the content.

7. The map above explains

    (1) what the world looks like

    (2) where phosphates are located

    (3) all minerals in the world

    (4) what countries have natural resources

    (5) where deposits of fertilizer minerals are found in the world

8. The major phosphate producers are

    (1) Canada

    (2) Africa

    (3) the United States and Africa

    (4) the United States and South America

    (5) Africa and Russia

9. The continent producing the least amount of fertilizer minerals overall is

    (1) South America

    (2) Australia

    (3) Africa

    (4) Russia

    (5) China

Answers

1. **(2)** Settlers who came to this country would logically seek an area that was similar to the area they left so they could continue their livihood. For example, if a man was a farmer in England, he would most likely choose to settle in an area inland from the Atlantic Coast so he could farm.

2. **(1)** Although climate is part of the study of geography, since it has a great deal to do with the relationship between man and the earth, weather refers to short term conditions rather than long term conditions that could affect how people live.

3. **(2)** The Equator is the invisible east-west line, which separates the planet into the Southern and Northern Hemispheres.

4. **(4)** The Tropic of Cancer is north of the Equator, so its lines intersect at 23.5°N.

5. **(4)** Each line on the scale is $\frac{1}{4}$ inch from the next line on the scale. Each $\frac{1}{4}$ inch section represents 10 miles on the map. Since there is approximately 1 inch between Montclair and New Castle, the distance is $4 \times 10 = 40$ miles.

6. **(1)** Because the measurement is slightly less than 3 inches, the approximate distance between New Castle and Bosworth is 110 miles.

7. **(5)** The purpose of the map, as explained in its title, is to indicate where deposits of fertilizer minerals are located around the world.

8. **(3)** The + indicates phosphates, and the majority of these symbols are located in the United States and in Africa.

9. **(2)** Australia has none of the symbols indicating any deposits of fertilizer minerals.

BEHAVIORAL SCIENCE

Items 10–13 refer to the following passage

Psychology is the study of how people think and behave. Among the many branches of psychology are physiological psychology, abnormal psychology, cognitive psychology, social psychology, and developmental psychology.

Physiological psychology deals with the neurological and physiological aspects of a people's lives that influence how they think and act. To do this, many physiological psychologists attempt to map the functions of the brain or study the effects of drugs on human behavior.

An abnormal psychologist studies behaviors that lie outside the norm. These behaviors can be simple habit disorders or may be linked to the most severe mental disturbances. Abnormal psychology examines the causes of these behaviors and tests various treatments for the behaviors.

Cognitive psychology applies to the study of thinking, concept formation, and problem solving. Cognitive psychologists are concerned with how people learn to decode symbols and think logically.

Social psychology examines humans as social creatures who constantly interact with others. Social psychologists study the development of human relationships.

Developmental psychology deals with the process of growth and development of individuals from childhood through adulthood. The mental, social, and emotional changes a person goes through in life are the subject matter of a developmental psychologist.

10. A person who had a severe addiction to gambling would seek the help of

    (1) a physiological psychologist

    (2) a congnitive psychologist

    (3) a social psychologist

    (4) a developmental psychologist

    (5) an abnormal psychologist

11. A new drug is coming out on the market. The person who would most likely be asked to help test the drug would be

    (1) a cognitive psychologist

    (2) a developmental psychologist

    (3) an abnormal psychologist

    (4) a physiological psychologist

    (5) a social psychologist

12. The person who would most likely study the effects of cooperation and competition among athletes would be

    (1) a physiological psychologist

    (2) a developmental psychologist

    (3) an abnormal psychologist

    (4) a social psychologist

    (5) a cognitive psychologist

13. The person who studies how children learn both inside and outside school is

    (1) a social psychologist

    (2) a cognitive psychologist

    (3) a developmental psychologist

    (4) an abnormal psychologist

    (5) a physiological psychologist

14. Conditioning and learning examine how people's experiences influence their thoughts and behaviors. Conditioning is the learned process by which an act or emotion is triggered by a certain stimulus. The emotion will repeat itself each time the stimulus is introduced. This is sometimes refered to as "maladaptive learning." Real learning, on the other hand, deals with the level of proficiency of performance a person acquires in mastering a task. Which of the following is NOT an example of conditioning?

    (1) learning to recite the alphabet

    (2) learning to be afraid of snakes

    (3) learning to fear tests

    (4) learning to buckle your seat belt

    (5) learning to watch for cars before crossing the street

Items 15–16 refer to the following passage.

Sociology is the study of human behavior in groups. It examines everything about a group of people that gives the group its distinctive characteristics. It includes the group's customs, traditions, patterns of historical development, and the institutions that have emerged, such as its government. Society shapes and controls individuals by expecting acceptance of its social rules (norms) and occupancy of certain social postions (roles). Socialization, or the process of becoming a social being, occurs as people learn the norms of their society and the groups within the society in which they live.

15. You can infer from this passage that
    (1) people have no choice as to how they fit into society
    (2) norms and roles are bad things
    (3) people are forced to observe traditions and customs according to the group they are in
    (4) people act the way society wants them to act
    (5) people often accept social rules as their own standard of behavior

16. An example of a norm would be
    (1) a person who was born to be a king
    (2) laws against theft
    (3) thinking of women only as wives and mothers
    (4) how a society develops
    (5) government

Item 17 refers to the following passage.

Anthropology is divided into two distinct studies. Physical anthropology deals with the biological aspects of humans. A physical anthropologist may study fossil remains to determine how a society lived long ago and may be able to theorize why an ancient society no longer exists. Cultural anthropology is mainly concerned with the growth of human societies and the behavior of the groups in terms of the group's religion, social customs, technical developments, and family relationships.

17. A cultural anthropologist would study
    (1) how the ancient Greeks lived
    (2) why societies have unique marriage ceremonies
    (3) how fossils are formed
    (4) how today's people are biologically different from their ancestors
    (5) the physiological makeup of different groups of people

Item 18 refers to the following passage.

Charles Darwin first formally presented the idea of evolution in 1859 in *On the Origin of Species*. In it, he argued that successful species have adapted to changes in their environment, and that only the most adaptable creatures or groups have survived through time. This process of natural selection is known as "survival of the fittest."

18. Darwin's theory could be supported by

    (1) the fact that dinosaurs as well as other species no longer exist because they could not adapt to their surroundings

    (2) the idea that humans are superior to animals

    (3) the way humans have become civilized

    (4) watching groups of animals in the wild

    (5) the fact that we live in a complex society

Answers

10. **(5)** Gambling is considered a disorder that lies outside the norm similar to alcoholism or drug addiction, so it would most likely be treated by an abnormal psychologist.

11. **(4)** Because a physiological psychologist is concerned with the neurological and physiological aspects of what influences a person's thoughts and actions, he would be most likely to test a new drug for changes in behavior that stem from physiological influences.

12. **(4)** A social psychologist studies human interaction with other humans. Competition and cooperation both involve humans interacting in different ways.

13. **(3)** Children both in and out of school are involved in mental, social, and emotional changes as they grow and develop, so a developmental psychologist would most likely study children as they grow.

14. **(1)** Learning to recite the alphabet is not an example of conditioning because it deals with learning a task that has no emotional stimuli connected with it. The other choices are all conditioned responses that are triggered by some sort of stimulus.

15. **(5)** As people become social and learn the norms of their society, in order to be accepted in that society, they generally adopt the social rules as standards of behavior. People do have a choice in how they fit into a society, or they may choose not to fit in at all. People are not generally forced to observe traditions in their society and, again, they have a choice whether to accept certain traditions or not.

16. **(2)** Because a norm is a social rule, laws against theft would be considered norms. They are rules explicitly outlining what is acceptable and what is not in that society.

17. **(2)** Because a cultural anthropologist is concerned with human society and behavior of groups, a unique marriage ceremony would be something he would study as a custom that influences a particular cultural group.

18. **(1)** Natural selection is one theory as to why the dinosaur no longer exists. As the world changed, dinosaurs could not adapt to the changes, so they became extinct as opposed to other animals who learned how to adapt to changing surroundings.

ECONOMICS

Items 19–21 refer to the following passage.

The purpose of an economic system is to decide what should be produced, how it should be produced, and for whom it should be produced. The main distinguishing features between systems are those that have private ownership of producer goods and market control over the system and those that are characterized by some authoritarian structure where economic decisions are made by planning agencies.

Capitalism, communism, and socialism have been the most predominent economic systems in the modern world. Capitalism is dependent on the motive of profit to survive. The theory of capitalism is that as the search for higher profits continues, each owner of a commodity is forced to sell the resource in a way consumers want. If he fails to do so, his competition will take over. There is very little government interference, and consumers are free to make whatever choices they want. The United States operates under a capitalistic system.

Communism is both a political and an economic system in which the major means of production and distribution of goods and products are held in common amongst all the people. In its purest form, communism would mean even the sharing of all property. The term is generally used to describe the economic systems in Russia and China.

Socialism is an economic system which relies on the majority of productive resources, both man-made and natural, to be owned and controlled by the state or its agency. Because production is divided among the population, it is assumed that it is more equitable and efficient than in capitalism.

19. Communism and Socialism have in common

    (1) the theory of private ownership of resources

    (2) the theory that competition is good

    (3) the fact that both are political as well as economic systems

    (4) the division of production amongst all the people

    (5) the idea that consumers are free to choose different products

20. What is NOT a purpose of an economic system?

    (1) to decide what should be produced

    (2) to decide for whom a product should be produced

    (3) to decide what consumers want

    (4) to decide how a product should be produced

    (5) to decide what agencies will regulate the system

21. The main difference between Capitalism and Communism is

    (1) Capitalism encourages competition

    (2) Capitalism allows for everyone to share equally in profits

    (3) Communism is both a polital and an economic system

    (4) Communism is only practiced in China

    (5) In Communism, the government doesn't interfere with production of goods

22. The central bank of the United States is the Federal Reserve Bank. Most commercial banks belong to the Federal Reserve system's banking network. Consumers do business with commercial banks, and these are supported by the Federal Reserve Bank. In return, the central bank may from time to time require the commercial banks to increase the proportion of their liquid funds deposited with the central bank that, in turn, forces the commercial banks to call in some loans so their liquid assets are adequate to cover any normal claims on them.

   The central bank can also change its minimum lending rate to commercial banks. When the rate of interest for borrowing from the central bank rises, all other interest rates will also soon be raised. In this way, the Federal Reserve Bank can influence the money supply. You can infer from this that

   (1) consumers can do their banking with the Federal Reserve Bank

   (2) if the Federal Reserve Bank lowered its interest rates, commercial banks would also lower their rates.

   (3) the commercial banks control the central bank

   (4) the Federal Reserve Bank is not fair to the commercial banks

   (5) the interest rates do not affect consumers

23. Every January, the president of the United States sends a budget message to Congress. The purpose of the message is to ask Congress to set aside funds he feels are necessary to keep the government running for another year. The government runs on a fiscal year that begins on October 1 and runs until the end of the following September. Congress is responsible for making the final decisions on the federal budget. When Congress receives the budget message, it is handed over to committees whose job it is to decide specific expenditures as a spending guide in the form of a resolution. After the resolution is approved, a spending bill cannot be passed that would cause the government to exceed the goal nor collect revenues that would be less than the total collection outlined in the resolution until the new fiscal year begins. Ultimate control over the spending policies in this country comes

   (1) from the president

   (2) the committees who write the resolution

   (3) from Congress

   (4) the American people

   (5) in the form of a budget message

24. A lobbyist is a person who represents a group of people and whose job it is to work for the special interests of that group. A lobbyist will contact members of Congress in order to make sure that money is allocated for the group's work. Not every group will get all that it asks for, but the lobbyist will try to persuade members of Congress that the interests he or she represents are more worthy than others to receive a share of available financial resources. One can infer from this passage that

   (1) some groups are not worthwhile to give money to

   (2) every group will get an equal share of available financial resources

   (3) lobbyists work for Congress

   (4) the most influencial lobbyist will receive the greatest share of financial resources

   (5) lobbyists have everyone's interests in mind

Items 25–27 refer to the following passage.

Inflation is an economic condition where prices in general increase, and the value of the dollar decreases since each dollar has less purchasing power. During a time of inflation, those who borrow money may actually profit by paying back their debts in dollars that have less buying power, while banks who loan money may suffer. In general, inflation raises the demand for goods and services past the ability of the economy to satisfy the demand. A major cause of inflation is the government's capability to print money. When the government pays its bills by printing money rather than raising taxes, inflation is created by having more money in circulation. During a time of prolonged inflation, the government may choose to limit the rate at which the supply of money is put into circulation. When this occurs, it becomes more difficult for people to obtain loans and causes interest rates to rise. Unemployment is often a result of an attempt to curb inflation, causing an economic slump or recession.

25. You can infer from this passage that an inflation would generally
    (1) encourage people to save more money
    (2) be good for the country in the long run
    (3) make the government stronger
    (4) help the banking system
    (5) encourage people to borrow more money

26. During a recession
    (1) the government may choose to print less money
    (2) banks will lower the interest rate
    (3) people will spend more money
    (4) people will have more purchasing power
    (5) more people will be employed

27. An inflation could be damaging to
    (1) businesses
    (2) people who live on a fixed income
    (3) people who want to borrow money
    (4) people who want to pay back their debts
    (5) the Federal Reserve

28. The term "industry" refers to all goods and services produced in a country. A nation's wealth is, to a large degree, determined by its industry. A nation with a productive industry is considered a wealthy nation whose standard of living is usually high compared to other nations. The total value of goods and services produced each year in a country is the Gross National Product (GNP) of the country. If the GNP were divided by the number of consumers in the country, the measure is called the "per capita," or per person, amount. The dollar value of this amount is an average indicator of the standard of living for the people of the county. GNP refers to
    (1) the standard of living
    (2) the per capita
    (3) the total value of all goods and services produced by a nation
    (4) the number of consumers in a nation
    (5) the dollar value of the per capita

Items 29–30 refer to the following passage.

Three major causes of unemployment are: changes in industry and the economy, changes in wages, and changes in government policies. Industrial changes have had a profound effect on the economy. Manufacturing, or blue-collar jobs have been declining because, with the advent of automation, many jobs have been lost. Before blue-collar workers can be employable again, they must be retrained for new jobs. Largely because of organized labor, wages in Europe, North America, and Japan are quite high when compared with wages of other countries. The problem this creates is that many companies have moved manufacturing jobs to countries, such as Mexico, where wages are much lower. Although this has helped many companies, some workers have lost their jobs in this country due to the shift in manufacturing sites. Often, the federal government will institute new policies aimed at helping the economy adust to change, but some economists argue that policies such as unemployment compensation and welfare only serve to promote or prolong unemployment.

29. Many blue-collar jobs have been lost due to

    (1) high wages in Japan and Europe

    (2) government policies

    (3) unemployment

    (4) automation

    (5) unemployment compensation

30. Many economists feel that government policies

    (1) help out the unemployed

    (2) help to keep wages high

    (3) increase production

    (4) help out other countries

    (5) prolong unemployment

Item 31 refers to the following passage.

International trade is based on manufacturers in one country producing goods to be sent to other countries (exporting), and buying goods to be brought into their own country (importing). Often, governments can raise money by imposing taxes (tariffs) on imports. Although these tariffs are paid for by the manufacturers, the cost of the tax is built into the product itself, and this, in turn, is passed along to the consumer. A manufacturer is often able to realize a profit by producing an excess of goods and then exporting the surplus. When the manufacturer can do this, often the cost of production is lowered on each unit produced, so the final selling price is reduced for the products sold in the country of production.

31. Lowest prices on goods are often realized when a manufacturer can

    (1) impose a tariff

    (2) export a surplus of goods

    (3) import goods

    (4) pass along a tariff to consumers

    (5) only sell products in the country of production

Answers

19. **(4)** Neither Communism nor Socialism promotes private ownership of resources, nor does either promote competition in business. Only Communism is considered both a political as well as an economical system. Both systems, however, believe in the division of production amongst all the people. How the division is made may differ, but both support the theory that division is good.

20. **(3)** An economic system can decide what should be produced and for whom a product should be produced as well as how a product should be produced. It can also choose which agencies will regulate the system, but their system itself will not decide what consumers want.

21. **(1)** The main difference between Capitalism and Communism is that Capitalism encourages competition. Through competition, everyone has an equal opportunity to share in profits.

22. **(2)** Since commercial banks raise their interest rates in accordance with the Federal Reserve Bank, it can be inferred that they would also lower their rates if the Federal Reserve Bank chose to lower its rates.

23. **(3)** Although the president sends a proposed budget to Congress on a yearly basis, the budget is not automatically approved. Congress has the responsibility for ultimately approving the proposed budget.

24. **(4)** If a lobbyist is successful in convincing members of Congress that his group's special interests are more important than another group's, he will stand a good chance of receiving more financial resources than another. Not all special interest groups receive the same amount of financial support.

25. **(5)** During an inflation, commercial banks are being paid back with money that has less buying power, and consumers have more money in general, so they would be encouraged to borrow more money. Traditionally, during an inflation, the interest rates banks charge are lowered.

26. **(1)** During an inflation, the government often prints more money. The opposite of an inflation is a recession, and during this period, the federal government would print less money so there isn't so much in circulation.

27. **(2)** Because during an inflationary period, goods generally cost more, those people who are on a fixed income such as people who rely on Social Security would suffer since their income does not change to keep up with prices rising.

28. **(3)** The GNP, or Gross National Product, refers to all goods and services produced by a nation.

29. **(4)** Automation in manufacturing jobs causes a need for fewer workers since machines often do many of the menial tasks that were formerly done by workers. If workers do not have the skills to move into a new job, they will be laid off, creating more unemployment.

30. **(5)** Many economists feel that government policies, such as welfare and unemployment compensation, prolong unemployment because many people are not encouraged to seek new employment while they are receiving monetary benefits through the government.

31. **(2)** If a manufacturer can produce more goods, the cost of production per item is often reduced. The surplus of manufactured goods can be exported, and the manufacturer can pass the production savings on to customers in the country where the product was produced.

POLITICAL SCIENCE

Items 32–33 refer to the following definitions.

Democracy—A system in which the people are involved in some way in the ruling of society.

Dictatorship—A system in which only a few or, in some cases, only one person has absolute power over everyone.

Autocracy—One person or a small group rules society and enforces only what would be in the interest of the ruler without consulting any other group.

Totalitarian—A system in which only one political party rules everyone without regard for any other political party.

Monarchy—A system in which a king or queen holds absolute power.

32. A system of government in which people vote on candidates and policy is a(n)

   (1) dictatorship

   (2) monarchy

   (3) democracy

   (4) totalitarian system

   (5) autocracy

33. A system of government in which the head of government is born into his/her position is a(n)

   (1) dictatorship

   (2) monarchy

   (3) democracy

   (4) totalitarian system

   (5) autocracy

34. The men who framed the Constitution of the United States divided the authority of the federal government into three branches: the legislative, the executive, and the judicial. The intention of having three branches of government was so that they would serve as a system of checks and balances—no one branch has sole authority over the entire system. Congress makes up the legislative branch, and they are the ones who make laws. The president, who is head of the executive branch, is empowered to enforce the laws created by the legislative branch. The Supreme Court is the highest judicial authority in the country. It is the court of highest appeal, and its rulings are law for all citizens, including the president. The system of checks and balances was created to

   (1) give sole authority to the president

   (2) keep the president from enforcing the laws

   (3) give more authority to the Supreme Court

   (4) ensure that no one branch had authority over the others

   (5) give Congress authority over court rulings

Items 35–36 refer to the following passage.

The Congress was created by Article I, section 1, of the Constitution. The powers of Congress are outlined in section 8 of Article I. One of the most important powers is that of assessing and collecting taxes. Congress also exerts legal control over all government employees, and it can initiate amendments to the Constitution if it sees fit to do so. Congress is made up of the members of both the Senate and the House of Representatives. Generally, most of the work of Congress is done through the 16 standing committees in the Senate and the 22 standing committees in the House. Congressional terms last from each odd-numbered year to the next odd-numbered year.

35. The powers of Congress are carried out
    (1) by the group as a whole
    (2) by committees from both the House and the Senate
    (3) only in odd-numbered years
    (4) through collecting taxes
    (5) through the Senate

36. A Congressman's term lasts
    (1) one year
    (2) three years
    (3) as long as he or she wants to be there
    (4) as long as the president's term
    (5) two years

Items 37–38 refer to the following passage.

Members to the House of Representatives are elected by the people. Although the number of representatives varies according to the population of a state, no state has less than one representative. After each census, representation is reconfigured. The House has two special powers: the right to originate revenue bills, and the right to begin impeachment proceedings. The Speaker of the House presides over its meetings and is a member of the majority party controlling the House. The Speaker of the House is elected by his fellow party members. Each party has a House leader who is called the "whip." The job of the whip is to keep his party members in line.

37. The Speaker of the House is elected by
    (1) the majority party
    (2) everyone in the House
    (3) the whip
    (4) a vote from the people
    (5) the president

38. Each state is represented in the House by
    (1) less than one member
    (2) as many members as a state chooses
    (3) a number in proportion to the state's population
    (4) the pary whip
    (5) one member

Items 39–40 refer to the following passage.

The Senate is made up of 100 members, two from each state, and its powers and rules are outlined in Article I, section 3, of the Constitution. Its special powers include approving presidential appointments, aproving treaties, and it serves as the court for impeachment trials. The presiding head of the Senate is the vice president of the United States. Interestingly, this is the only power accorded to the vice president under the Constitution. The full term of a senator is six years. Every two years, the terms of one third of the members of the senate expire so at any given time, two-thirds of the senators are not new to the job.

39. Senators may NOT

    (1) try impeachments

    (2) approve presidential appointments

    (3) disapprove presidential appointments

    (4) begin impeachment proceedings

    (5) approve treaties

40. A senator's term

    (1) lasts for two years

    (2) is renewed every two years

    (3) lasts for six years

    (4) is voted on by two-thirds of the senators

    (5) is renewed every six years

41. The president holds office for four years and, according to the 22nd Amendment that was ratified in 1951, can be reelected for no more than a second term. Among the president's jobs is the task of enforcing all federal laws and supervising all federal administrative agencies. The president also has the power to grant reprieves and pardons to those who have been convicted of committing crimes against the United States. The president negotiates treaties with other countries and is the commander in chief of all the armed forces. In order to maintain a good relationship with Congress, the president must keep Congress informed of the need for new legislation and must submit his yearly budget to Congress. The president does NOT have the authority to

    (1) enforce all federal laws

    (2) enact laws

    (3) grant pardons to those convicted of crimes against a particular state

    (4) supervise all federal administrative agencies

    (5) grant pardons to those conviced of crimes against the United States

42. The Supreme Court is the highest court in the country. The nine associate justices and one chief justice are appointed by the president and are able to sit on the court for life. The Supreme Court hears two types of cases: those that are tried directly before it without involving any of the lower courts, and those that are under appeal from a lower court. Original cases are those that arise because of controversy between states, between a state and the federal government, between a state and citizens of another state, and cases involving ambassadors or other public ministers. Cases that come before the Court as appeals are those that challenge a state or federal law as being unconstitutional. These cases have already been tried in a lower court and, after a preliminary hearing, the Court will decide whether to grant a trial. The Supreme Court will hear

    (1) original cases involving two citizens from the same state
    (2) any case under appeal from a lower court
    (3) original cases involving two different states
    (4) some original traffic cases
    (5) original cases involving personal injury

Answers

32. **(3)** Of the political systems listed, a democracy is the only one in which ordinary citizens have a voice in their government through elections of officials.

33. **(2)** A monarchy is a system that is headed by royalty. Kings and queens are born into the system through a line of other monarchs.

34. **(4)** The system of checks and balances is designed to assure that no one branch of the government has total authority over the country. The division of power is set up so that one branch of the government is incapable of making all the decisions for the country.

35. **(2)** Congress is a large group of people who have been directly or indirectly elected by citizens. The elected officials are either state representatives or senators. When these groups meet together, they form the body known as Congress. Members of both groups work on committees together to carry out the work of Congress.

36. **(5)** Because a congressman's term runs from one odd-numbered year to the next odd-numbered year, the term is two years total. For example, if a congressman were to begin his term in 1997, he would end his term in 1999.

37. **(1)** The Speaker of the House is elected by his peers. At any given time, one political party has more members in the House than another, and this majority party is responsible for electing the Speaker.

38. **(3)** In the House of Representatives, membership is dependent upon the number of people who reside in any state. The states with a higher population have more representatives than those with a smaller population. Each time the government does a census that counts the poplulation of a state, the numbers of alloted representatives are altered to reflect any population shifts in the country.

39. (4) Impeachment is an example of the system of checks and balances in place in the government. The Senate has the authority to try an impeachment proceding, but it is the House that initiates an impeachment.

40. (3) A senator serves for six years. Elections are held in various districts at different times. Only one-third of senators are new to the job at any given time, with the other two-thirds completing their terms.

41. (2) The president, who represents the executive branch of the government, is charged with enforcing all federal laws, but it is the legislative branch of the government that enacts the laws for the federal government. This is an example of the system of checks and balances of the system.

42. (2) The Supreme Court will not hear original cases. Individual states have their own court systems that handle such cases. Traffic laws are under the jurisdiction of individual states. The only way the Supreme Court would consider such a case would be if it somehow involved a Constitutional issue, and then the case would come before the Supreme Court on an appeal. Disputes betweeen states are handled in the Supreme Court.

HISTORY

Items 43–44 refer to the map below.

The First 13 Colonies

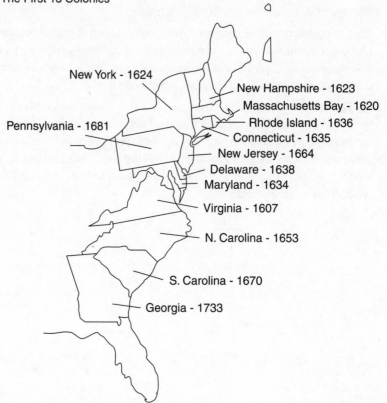

New York - 1624

New Hampshire - 1623

Massachusetts Bay - 1620

Rhode Island - 1636

Pennsylvania - 1681

Connecticut - 1635

New Jersey - 1664

Delaware - 1638

Maryland - 1634

Virginia - 1607

N. Carolina - 1653

S. Carolina - 1670

Georgia - 1733

43. According to the map, which was the first colony established in North America?

    (1) New York

    (2) Virginia

    (3) New Hampshire

    (4) Deleware

    (5) Connecticut

44. According to the map, the last colony established was

    (1) Rhode Island

    (2) Pennsylvania

    (3) North Carolina

    (4) Massachusetts Bay

    (5) Georgia

Items 45–46 refer to the following passage

In 1763, when the French and Indian War was settled, Great Britain and the American Colonies enjoyed friendly relations; but soon after, Britain began to enforce restrictions on American trade, and taxes were levied on the colonists. After Americans protested, most taxes—with the exception of a few, including the tax on tea—were lifted. Tension continued, however, and in 1770, British troops fired on a crowd in Boston, killing five people. This act became known as the Boston Massacre. Finally, on December 16, 1773, the Boston Tea Party occurred. It was then that patriots dressed as Indians boarded British ships and dumped chests of tea into the sea as an open protest to Britain's tyranny. This was followed by the first battle of the American Revolution, which started in April of 1775. During the war, in 1776, the Congress voted for independence from Britain. Finally, in 1781, Britain surrendered to the colonists, and this marked the beginning of freedom for the United States.

45. The Boston Tea Party symbolized

    (1) anger at the Boston Massacre

    (2) the beginning of the American Revolution

    (3) anger at all of Britain's injustices

    (4) American's distaste for tea

    (5) anger at taxes in general

46. The American Revolution lasted

    (1) six years

    (2) three years

    (3) four years

    (4) eight years

    (5) five years

Items 47–49 refer to the following map.

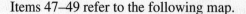
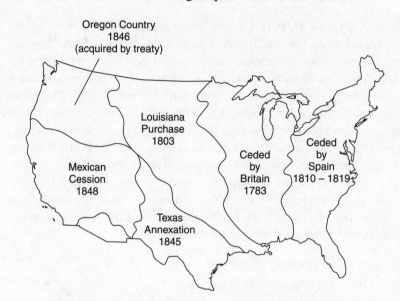

47. After the east coast of America was colonized, the second frontier, which was the region lying between the Appalachians and the Mississippi River, began to be explored and settled. The third frontier was the West, which stretched from the Mississippi River all the way to the Pacific Ocean. The United States acquired the largest section of land through the

    (1) Annexation of Texas

    (2) Louisiana Purchase

    (3) Mexican Cession

    (4) British Cession

    (5) Spanish Cession

48. Which of the following on the map reflects the boundaries of a current state?

    (1) Florida

    (2) Mexico

    (3) Louisiana

    (4) Oregon

    (5) Ohio

49. By the middle of the nineteenth century, the United States had become a country that spread from the Atlantic Ocean to the Pacific Ocean with a huge variation of people and ways of life. The North was becoming industrialized with large pockets of population, while the South remained mainly agricultural with large plantations growing cotton and tobacco and a comparitively sparse poplulation. People in the North were becoming critical of the plantation owners in the South who used slaves to work the plantations, and they began to talk about doing away with the institution of slavery. These people were called abolitionists. The issues of slavery and individual states' rights became points of contention on both sides. When Abraham Lincoln was elected president in 1860, South Carolina seceded (withdrew) from the Union. This action was followed in 1861 by six other Southern states seceding from the Union. These states organized a new government called the Confederate States of America, and they elected Jefferson Davis as their president.

You can infer from this passage that an abolitionist opposed

    (1) the growing of tobacco and cotton

    (2) states who seceded from the Union

    (3) the use of slaves on plantations

    (4) states' rights

    (5) Abraham Lincoln as president

Items 50–52 refer to the following passage.

The Civil War started in 1861 and continued until 1865. The period after the Civil War is known as Reconstruction. During this time, Americans tried to recover from the devestating losses of the war, but there was still a great deal of animosity between the North and the South. Some Northerners migrated south with the intention of taking over and controlling sections of the South. These people were called carpetbaggers, and they created new tensions. In the immediate aftermath of the war, Northern troops continued to patrol some Southern states, which served to increase hostilities. The 13th and 14th Amendments were added to the Constitution in 1865 and 1868. These amendments abolished slavery and established civil rights for all and helped to put an end to the bitter feelings still dividing the country.

The industrial development in the rest of the country, however, was rapid. Coal, iron ore, copper, lead, and other minerals were being mined all over the country, and oil wells were being built. Electric lighting and the telephone were invented, and agriculture began to flourish with the inventions of farm machinery that enabled farmers to expand. It was during this time that the cross-country railroad was completed.

50. Reconstruction was hampered by

    (1) industrial development

    (2) the cross-country railroad

    (3) oil wells being built

    (4) continued hostility between the North and the South

    (5) carpetbaggers

51. The cross-country railroad would help to

    (1) ease the tension between the North and the South

    (2) help mining of minerals

    (3) link industry and agriculture with their markets

    (4) make it easier for carpetbaggers to move south

    (5) patrol the southern states

52. The 14th Amendment

    (1) made the North more bitter

    (2) established civil rights for all

    (3) abolished slavery

    (4) helped the carpetbaggers

    (5) allowed Northern troops to continue patrolling

Items 53–54 refer to the following passage.

In the early years of the 1900s, the United States continued to enjoy a great business boom, but war had begun in Europe in 1914. (America, under the leadership of President Wilson, tried to stay neutral during the conflict, but in 1917, Germany started unrestricted submarine warfare and struck U.S. ships causing America to be drawn into World War I on the side of the 23 Allied nations led by France and Britain against the Central Powers (Germany, Austria-Hungary, Turkey, and Bulgaria)).

The war persisted until 1918 when an armistace was signed on November 11. In January, 1919, the Paris Peace Conference convened and was dominated by the major victors of the war—America, France, the British Empire, Italy, and Japan. After a series of delays, the treaty at Versailles was signed. President Wilson had put forth his "Fourteen Points" as a basis for the peace agreement, but was forced to compromise many points. When the Senate refused to join the League of Nations, the United States retreated into isolation, a policy advocating noninvolvement in European wars and alliances.

53. The Allied nations included

    (1) France

    (2) Germany

    (3) Turkey

    (4) Bulgaria

    (5) Austria-Hungary

54. The United States became isolationist because

    (1) President Wilson refused to join the League of Nations

    (2) the signing of the treaty was delayed

    (3) they had to compromise away many of the "Fourteen Points"

    (4) they were bitter about losing the war

    (5) they didn't agree with the peace agreement

Item 55 refers to the following chart.

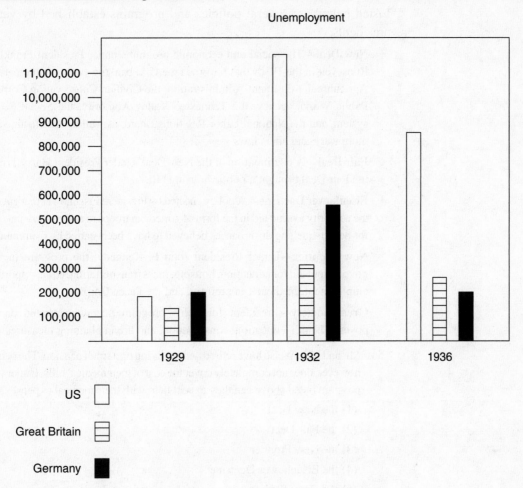

55. With the stock market crash of 1929, most countries suffered from unemployment. Which country or countries were most affected?

(1) the United States and Great Britain

(2) Great Britain and Germany

(3) the United States and Germany

(4) Germany

(5) Great Britain

Items 56–58 refer to the following.

Listed below are several policies and programs established by various presidents.

New Deal—The social and economic programs under President Franklin D. Roosevelt in the 1930s that reformed the U.S. banking system and created the Agricultrual Adustment Administration, the Civilian Conservation Corps, the Public Works agency, the Tennessee Valley Authority, the Social Security system, and the National Labor Relations Board, as well as establishing minimum wage and hours laws.

Fair Deal—A continuation of the New Deal. Under President Harry Truman, the Fair Deal brought a public housing bill.

Eisenhower Doctrine—A policy enacted by President Eisenhower that gave him the authority to send aid in the form of American troops to any country that asked for help in quelling disturbances believed to have been started by Communists.

New Frontier—Under President John F. Kennedy, the program included government aid for education, housing, mass transportation, equal opportunity employment, medicare, tax reform, and the Peace Corps.

Great Society—President Johnson's program that concentrated on anti-poverty, health, education, conservation, and urban planning measures.

56. Mr. and Mrs. Welsh have retired and are living on a small pension. The pension, however, does not completely cover the cost of their medical bills. Under which program listed above can they expect help with their medical expenses?

(1) the New Deal

(2) the Fair Deal

(3) the New Frontier

(4) the Eisenhower Doctrine

(5) the Great Society

57. Frank is 15 years old and wishes to secure employment after school. When he applies for a job, he is told that he may only work a certain number of hours each week because of his age. Which program is responsible for protecting him from working too many hours for his age?

(1) the New Deal

(2) the Fair Deal

(3) the New Frontier

(4) the Eisenhower Doctrine

(5) the Great Society

58. A special interest group is lobbying to receive money to save a particular piece of land from strip mining. The group wants to keep the land from being destroyed by the mining. Under which program could they seek help?

(1) the New Deal

(2) the Fair Deal

(3) the New Frontier

(4) the Eisenhower Doctrine

(5) the Great Society

59. In 1972, Republican President Nixon's Committee for the Re-Election of the President hired people to break into the Democratic National Committee headquarters, and the infamous Watergate Scandal began. The hired agents installed listening devices and penetrated the files. The President denied all wrongdoing on the part of the White House, but several of his advisers resigned. The implication of this act on the part of the advisers would suggest that

   (1) they were embarrassed to be associated with the President

   (2) the president was guilty of wrongdoing

   (3) the advisors did not want to stand up for the President

   (4) the advisors were guilty of wrongdoing

   (5) the advisors were afraid

Answers

43. (2) The first colony, Virginia, was established in 1607.

44. (5) The last colony, Georgia, was established in 1733.

45. (3) There were a number of injustices Americans felt were restricting them. Besides the tax on tea, American trade was also restricted, and when British troops fired on Americans, the patriots rebelled by staging the Boston Tea Party.

46. (1) The American Revolution began in 1775, two years after the Boston Tea Party, and lasted until 1781.

47. (2) The Louisiana Purchase of 1803 was responsible for accumulating the largest single mass of land.

48. (4) Oregon is the territory that reflects most closely a current state.

49. (3) The use of slaves on the plantations was the main concern of the abolitionists. The dispute over states' rights to choose was secondary to the humanitarian issues.

50. (4) The continued hostilities between the North and the South were responsible for slowing down the process of reconstruction, particularly for the South.

51. (3) The cross country railroad made it possible for farmers and manufacturers to take their products to other cities to sell. This, in turn, helped to complete the process of reconstruction more quickly.

52. (2) The 14th Amendment established civil rights for all. It came quickly afer the 13th Amendment, which abolished slavery, and was a natural outgrowth of the 13th Amendment since the newly freed slaves needed the protection of the Constitution to keep from having their rights violated.

53. (1) France was one of the Allied nations who fought against the Central Powers of Germany, Austria-Hungary, Turkey, and Bulgaria.

54. (5) The United States drew back from its involvement in Europe when the peace agreement was signed without President Wilson's recommendations added to it, and the Senate refused to join the League of Nations.

55. (3) The United States and Germany both suffered from unemployment although, overall, the United States fared the worst.

56. (3) President Kennedy's New Frontier was responsible for the advent of medicare, a program designed to financially help the elderly with medical care costs.

57. (1) The New Deal, a program under President Roosevelt, established laws that prohibited people from working long hours and also made sure they received a minimum wage that could be classified as a living wage.

58. (5) President Johnson's Great Society was concerned with conservation, and it provided resources for groups to make efforts to preserve land and animals that were threatened by progress.

59. (2) The fact that several advisers resigned would imply that they felt President Nixon was guilty of being involved with the Watergate break-in.

TEST YOURSELF

Items 1–3 refer to the following.

Listed below are several amendments to the Constitution.

Amendment IV—The right of the people to be secure in their persons, houses, papers, and effects, against unreasonable searches and seizures, shall not be violated.

Amendment VI—In all criminal prosecutions, the accused shall enjoy the right to a speedy and public trial, by an impartial jury of the State and district wherein the crime shall have been committed.

Amendment XVI—The right of citizens of the United States who are eighteen years of age or older, to vote shall not be denied

Amendment XIX—The right of citizens of the United States to vote shall not be denied or abridged by the United States or by any State on account of sex.

Amendment XXIV—The right of citizens of the United States to vote in any primary or other election…shall not be denied or abridged by reason of failure to pay any poll tax or other tax.

1. Sarah is a 17-year-old black woman. Under which amendment can she be denied the right to vote?

   (1) Amendment IV

   (2) Amendment VI

   (3) Amendment XIX

   (4) Amendment XXIV

   (5) Amendment XVI

2. Joseph is a 32-year-old male who has never paid his taxes. Which amendment protects his right to vote?

   (1) Amendment IV

   (2) Amendment VI

   (3) Amendment XIX

   (4) Amendment XXIV

   (5) Amendment XVI

3. Bill has been accused of commiting a serious crime in Chicago, Illinois, where he lives and is well liked by his neighbors. The prosecution does not want to try the case in Chicago. Which amendment can the defense attorney evoke to keep the case in Chicago?

   (1) Amendment IV

   (2) Amendment VI

   (3) Amendment XIX

   (4) Amendment XXIV

   (5) Amendment XVI

Items 4–5 refer to the following chart.

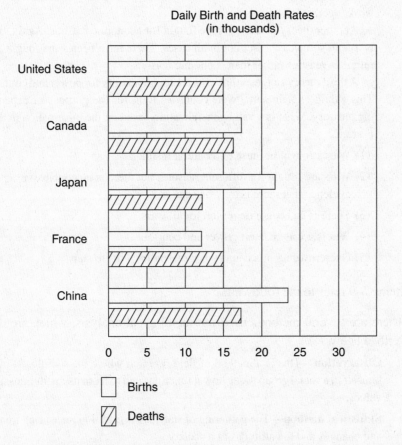

Daily Birth and Death Rates
(in thousands)

4. According to the chart, the countries with the highest daily birth rate are

   (1) the United States and Japan

   (2) China and the United States

   (3) Japan and China

   (4) Canada and Japan

   (5) China and Canada

5. According to the chart, the countries with the lowest ratio of births to deaths are

   (1) France and Canada

   (2) Canada and Japan

   (3) the United States and France

   (4) China and France

   (5) Canada and the United States

6. There have been a number of theories explaining the causes of war. One theory is that man is, like all animals, an aggressive creature whose natural tendencies to fight cannot be denied. On the other hand, man, as well as certain other species, also seems to have a natural tendency to cooperate and work together.

   Another theory is that wars are fought for economic reasons. Again, this is true in some cases, but not in all cases. There have been wars fought for religious reasons rather than economic reasons.

   A third theory suggests that wars are fought mainly for power and control. This would explain some wars countries fight for the purpose of expanding territory. What is a valid generalization based on the information in this passage?

   (1) War is fought because of a natural instinct.

   (2) Wars are fought for different reasons, but there is no conclusive evidence that there is only one cause.

   (3) There is an economic reason for all wars.

   (4) War is a way to exert power and control.

   (5) Overcrowding in a country is a reason for wars to start.

Items 7–9 refer to the following.

There are several methods used for sociological analysis, which are described below.

Observation—This is a method of field research where the sociologist puts himself in a social group to see how it functions and to learn its institutions and values.

Statistical method—The gathering of statistics is useful in measuring trends and changes and the attitudes of a society.

Data collection—The interview and the questionnaire are common to data collection.

Experiments—These are procedures conducted in artificial conditions, usually laboratories or classrooms.

Ecological methods—Sociological research is often done in the field with researchers mapping distribution of population, often in urban areas.

7. A sociologist who wanted to study crime and delinquency in a city would most likely use which method of data collection?

    (1) observation

    (2) statistical method

    (3) data collection

    (4) experiments

    (5) ecological

8. A sociologist would most likely use which method of data collection to examine the effects of a disease on a community?

    (1) observation

    (2) statistical method

    (3) data collection

    (4) experiments

    (5) ecological

9. In order to accomplish small group research, a sociologist would use which method of analysis?

    (1) observation

    (2) statistical method

    (3) data collection

    (4) experiments

    (5) ecological

Items 10–12 refer to the following passage.

The purpose of a map or a globe is to find the location of a place. A map is a graphic representation of various geographical, geologic, political, ecological, physiographic, or meteorological variables on the earth's surface. Below are brief definitions of several types of maps most commonly used.

Political map—Emphasizes man-made or cultural features such as states or counties.

Physical map—Emphasizes natural features such as lakes and rivers.

Physical thematic map—Emphasizes a particular theme such as the distribution of minerals in a geographic location.

Globe—A map drawn on a sphere usually showing the earth's grid system.

Spherical map—A cutaway disk or globe section.

10. A person who was interested in taking a driving trip across the country would have to plot places to stay overnight during the trip. Which type of map would this person use?

    (1) political

    (2) physical

    (3) physical thematic

    (4) globe

    (5) spherical

11. One of the advantages of using a globe instead of a map would be

    (1) a globe is easier to carry around

    (2) a globe is much more interesting than a map

    (3) a globe could show more detail than a map

    (4) a globe would show distances, and shapes and sizes of areas more accurately

    (5) a globe permits a person to see the whole earth at one time

12. A person who was interested in moving to an area that is not densely populated would refer to which map in planning the move?

    (1) political

    (2) physical

    (3) physical thematic

    (4) globe

    (5) spherical

13. In order for a bill or a resolution to become a law in the United States, it must be passed in identical form by both the House of Representatives and the Senate and signed by the president. The only exception is an amendment to the Constitution, which does not have to be signed by the president. A bill that is not signed by the president can still be passed if two-thirds of both houses vote to do so. If the president does not sign the bill, or if it is returned by the president unsigned, it will automatically be passed after ten working days. A pocket veto occurs if the president does not return the bill and Congress has been adjourned. One can infer from this paragraph that

    (1) a bill that has been returned will not pass if two-thirds of both houses do not vote to pass it

    (2) an amendment to the Constitution is not as important as a bill

    (3) bills are usually automatically passed

    (4) most bills are signed by the president

    (5) the president usually does not sign a bill

14. In the Supreme Court's landmark case *Brown v. The Board of Education of Topeka* (1954), an earlier decision was overturned. In the earlier case, *Plessy v. Ferguson* (1896), the doctrine of "separate but equal" was established with regards to education. In the landmark case, the Court decided that public school segregation, which was a state prescribed issue, was a violation of the equal protection clause of the 14th Amendment to the Constitution. This decision was of great importance because it

    (1) stopped segregation in schools

    (2) protected the equal rights of children

    (3) paved the way for stopping social injustice in the country

    (4) was the first case to overturn a previous decision

    (5) tested the Constitution

15. IQ, or intelligence quotient, is often used as a way to measure the rate of a person's intellectual development. This is done by comparing a person's mental age score with his actual age. Measuring this rate of learning is done by dividing a person's mental age by his actual, or chronological, age. In order to avoid decimal fractions, the answer is multiplied by 100. For example, to measure the IQ of a 6 year old who has a mental age of 8, the formula would be:

$$\frac{8 \text{ yrs. } 0 \text{ mo.}}{6 \text{ yrs. } 0 \text{ mo.}} \times 100 = \frac{96 \text{ mo.}}{72 \text{ mo.}} \times 100 = 133.33, \text{ or (rounded off) } 133$$

The IQ of a child who is 5 years old with a mental age of 6 would be

(1) 100

(2) 120

(3) 130

(4) 125

(5) 115

Items 16–17 refer to the following table.

Life expectancies (in round figures)

Continent	Life Expectancy Male	Life Expectancy Female
Africa	53	56
Asia	63	66
Europe	69	77
North America	69	75
Australia	70	75
South America	64	70

16. According to the table, which continent has the highest disparity between life expectancy in males and females?

(1) Africa

(2) Asia

(3) Europe

(4) North America

(5) South America

17. According to the table, which continent has the longest average life expectancy for males and females combined?

(1) Africa

(2) Asia

(3) Europe

(4) North America

(5) Australia

18. The economic world is made up of industrialized countries such as North America, Western Europe, Australia, and Japan and areas labeled as Third World such as regions in Asia, South America, and Africa. In order for the Third World regions to be successful and raise the standard of living, they will have to be able to sustain economic growth through industrialization. The Organization of Petroleum Exporting Countries (OPEC) has made major inroads in helping the Third World countries become more self sustaining. Because these countries virtually have a monopoly on the export of oil, they have been able to raise prices substantially. Some nations oppose OPEC because

    (1) they don't want the competition
    (2) higher oil prices will raise the cost of some manufactured goods
    (3) some countries don't have oil reserves
    (4) OPEC can become too powerful
    (5) they are afraid the Third World countries will become wealthier than they are

Items 19–21 refer to the following passage.

Crime can be defined in different ways, but generally, a crime is an action against a law. In wartime, many people are killed, but these killings are usually not thought of as criminal actions because they are not against the law; but when one person kills another in day-to-day life, it is considered a criminal action. Not all crimes are considered equally serious by law. In America, a felony is the most serious crime; a misdemeanor is a lesser offense. A misdemeanor is an offense punishable by fines or imprisonment in a local jail. A felony, on the other hand, is punishable by serving terms in state or federal prisons.

A private wrong, or tort, is a civil action that is not considered criminal because it is against the interests of an individual rather than a dangerous action against society as a whole. A tort is generally resolved by payment for damages suffered.

Crimes against people and property are those that violate certain rights of people. Homicide is considered a crime against a person, but there are different degrees of homicide ranging from murder to carelessness. Crimes against property generally involve stealing in some form, but, again, there are distinctions made to indicate the seriousness of the offense. Robbery, for example, involves violence, while theft does not.

A victimless crime is one that generally does not involve a direct attack on a person or a person's property.

White-collar crime is relatively new and involves people who engage in illegal activities through their jobs. Embezzlement and fraud are common white-collar crimes.

19. A person who has rented an apartment for several years is now moving. His landlord has refused to return the security deposit the renter paid when he moved in. The renter intends on suing the landlord to recover the security deposit. The case will be heard as

    (1) a victimless crime
    (2) a white-collar crime
    (3) a misdemeanor
    (4) a felony
    (5) a tort

20. Zachary has been accused of setting fire to an empty building he owned in order to receive insurance money from the destruction of the building. He is accused of commiting

    (1) a tort

    (2) a victimless crime

    (3) a crime against a person

    (4) a crime against property

    (5) a misdemeanor

21. White-collar crime is commited against

    (1) a company or business

    (2) the country or state

    (3) a specific individual

    (4) someone's property

    (5) an officer of the law

22. The United States is comprised of various geographical regions, each with specific climates. The Pacific Northwest, which extends from northwestern California to Alaska, for example, is generally considered wet, and the Southwest is sunny and dry. The Midwest has a more temperate climate that would make it suitable for

    (1) industry

    (2) fishing

    (3) agriculture

    (4) mining

    (5) logging

23. In American history, the series of conflicts between Native Americans and European settlers and their decendents is known as the Indian wars. The majority of conflicts developed as a result of the U.S. government attempting to move Native Americans to reservations. Wounded Knee (1890) in South Dakota is often referred to as the last battle of the era. During this conflict, almost 200 Sioux were killed. In 1973, 200 members of the American Indian Movement (AIM) occupied Wounded Knee for 69 days. It can be assumed from this passage that the occupation

    (1) was mostly done by decendents of the Sioux

    (2) was to reenact the final battle of the Indian wars

    (3) was staged to make the government angry

    (4) was staged to commemorate the end of the Indian wars

    (5) was staged as a protest to the conditions under which Native Americans live

24. In classical economics, the law of supply and demand determines the price of goods and services. Supply refers to the amount of goods or services available to consumers, and demand refers to the quantity of goods and services consumers want at any given price. Market price is ideally at the intersection of the supply curve and the demand curve. It can be inferred that

(1) demand will increase as price increases

(2) demand will decrease as price increases

(3) price will be determined regardless of demand

(4) supply and demand is never equal

(5) price should be set by the government so everyone will have an opportunity to buy goods and services

25. The North Atlantic Treaty Organization (NATO) was formed in 1949 by Belgium, Canada, Denmark, France, Great Britain, Iceland, Italy, Luxembourg, the Netherlands, Norway, Portugal, and the United States. Its goal was to protect its member countries from aggression by the Soviets. NATO is now considered a peacekeeping force throughout the world. It can be assumed that NATO

(1) was sent to Bosnia during its crisis in 1995

(2) will not help Turkey since it did not originally join

(3) will disband since the Soviets are having difficulties of their own right now

(4) is only open to countries with interests in the North Atlantic

(5) will not accept new members

Items 26–27 refer to the following passage.

Modern personality theory began with Sigmund Freud, who felt that the development of personality is the result of childhood impulses and the expressions of those impulses. His three components of personality include: the id, which is a combinbation of all a person's instincts; the ego, which interacts with the reality in the fulfillment of instinctual desires; and the superego, which is responsible for internalizing ideals of behavior. Freud theorized that these three are in constant conflict and this conflict influences how people behave.

A second theory suggests that there are personality traits common to all people, and there are also traits that grow out of individual experience and are unique to each person. This theory implies that personality is the sum of all the separate traits.

In the theory of situationism, human behavior is determined by how a person reacts to a situation rather than to traits within the individual. When a situation changes, a person's behavior or personality will change in accordance.

Interactionism recognizes both situationalism and traits to determine personality. In this theory, a person has a predisposition to a type of response and any variables of a situation.

26. According to Freud, the id

    (1) is solely responsible for how a person acts

    (2) fulfills instinctual desires

    (3) identifies ideals of behavior

    (4) works with the ego and superego to form personality

    (5) helps a child learn how to behave

27. A person who will not steal if he thinks someone is watching but will steal if he is sure he can do so undetected is proving the theory of

    (1) interactionism

    (2) the superego

    (3) situationism

    (4) personality

    (5) traits

28. In the landmark Supreme Court case of *Marbury v. Madison* (1803), the Court held that an act of Congress in conflict with the Constitution was void and that it is the function of the Court to determine whether such a conflict exists. The implication of this landmark case was

    (1) the Supreme Court can overrule Congress if its actions are in conflict with the Constitution

    (2) Congress has no real power

    (3) the Constitution had to be rewritten

    (4) the Constitution was no longer valid

    (5) the Supreme Court can overrule the Constitution

29. In the United States, election of the president and the vice-president is done indirectly through the electoral college. Voters in each state select a group of electors that represents the candidate of their choice. This group then votes for the president and the vice-president. The candidate with the majority of votes from each state receives all that state's electoral votes. Each state is entitled to a number of electors equal to the total number representing it in Congress. Critics of this system feel that a candidate receiving a majority of the popular vote in a state carries all the electoral votes, and that this means that the minority is neglected prior to the final election. Through the electoral college

    (1) only the best candidate will win the election

    (2) the candidate with the most popular votes will win

    (3) the president and vice-president win with a majority of popular votes

    (4) it is possible for a candidate to win with a minority of the popular vote

    (5) each state has the same number of people voting through the electoral college

30. During the late 19th and early 20th centuries, the international monetary system was based on the gold standard. This means that gold was the only true standard of value for all nations. This standard, however, lost its impact because it had an inherent lack of liquidity. Under the new gold-exchange standard, nations fix the value of their currencies to a foreign currency. The foreign currency is then fixed to and redeemable in gold. A two-tier system was then instituted to make up for a drain on U.S. gold reserves. Under this system, in the official tier, the value of gold was set at $35 an ounce. In the free-market tier, the price is free to fluctuate according to supply and demand. Under the two-tier system, in the free market

    (1) gold is always valued the same across the board

    (2) the value of gold will vary

    (3) gold does not have much value

    (4) countries can set their own official value of gold

    (5) foreign currency has no value

Answers

1. **(5)** Sarah is protected under Amendment XIX to vote if she is a female, but she can be denied her right to vote under Amendment XVI, which states that she can vote if she is 18 years of age or older. Because she is only 17, she may not vote.

2. **(4)** Amendment XXIV protects the right of a citizen to vote, even if that citizen has not paid any taxes.

3. **(2)** Amendment VI states that a trial in a criminal prosecution case must be held in the state and district in which the crime was committed.

4. **(3)** Japan and China both exceed all other listed countries in the number of daily births.

5. **(1)** France and Canada both have lower ratios of births to deaths than any of the other countries listed with less than 5,000.

6. **(2)** Because the causes of war are listed as theories, it can be determined that there is no conclusive evidence that one reason for wars is any more valid than any other reason.

7. **(5)** An ecological analysis would be done for a sociologist who wanted to study crime and delinquency in a city. The researcher would look at the population and living conditions in order to draw a conclusion about crime.

8. **(3)** For a sociologist to examine the effects of a disease, he would need to interview or send out questionnaires to those who suffered from the disease in order to glean the information needed to draw a conclusion about the effects of the disease.

9. **(4)** Small group research is usually conducted in an artificial environment with the researcher conducting experiments, logging the results of the experiments, and then comparing the results between the groups of subjects he used for the experiments.

10. **(1)** Maps used for driving are political in nature. The political map would show states, cities, and roads.

11. **(4)** A globe has the advantage because of its shape to show distances, shapes, and sizes of areas. The spherical nature of a globe shows the earth in miniature, so it is not difficult to see relationships of areas.

12. **(3)** A physical thematic map could be found, which uses as its theme the distribution of population across the country.

13. **(1)** If a bill is returned to congress, it will only pass if two-thirds of the members vote on it to pass. If the bill does not have two-thirds voting for it, it will not pass.

14. **(3)** Although *Brown v. The Board of Education of Topeka* dealt specifically with the issue of segregation in schools, it opened the door for later legislation designed to end social injustice in all areas.

15. **(2)** Using the formula for measuring IQ, the answer would be set up as follows:
$$\frac{6 \text{ yrs. } 0 \text{ mo.}}{5 \text{ yrs. } 0 \text{ mo.}} \times 100 = \frac{72 \text{ mo.}}{60 \text{ mo.}} \times 100 = 120$$

16. **(3)** Europe has the highest disparity between life expectancy in males and females with 8 years, followed by North America and South America at 6 years each, Australia with 5 years, and Africa and Asia with 3 years each.

17. **(3)** Europe has the longest average life expectancy for males and females combined at 73 years, followed by Australia at 72.5 years, North America at 72 years, South America at 67, Asia at 64.5 years, and Africa at 54.5 years.

18. **(2)** Because oil is a valuable commodity used in manufacturing, the cost of manufacturing certain goods would rise proportionately to the cost of the raw material.

19. **(5)** A tort is a civil action that is commited against the interest of an individual. A landlord who is refusing to refund a security deposit has not taken a dangerous action against society.

20. **(4)** Even though Zachary has burned his own building and has not damaged anyone else's property, arson is still considered a crime against property.

21. **(1)** Any illegal activity commited through employment is considered white-collar crime. Even relatively petty crime such as taking office supplies adds up and can be punished in court.

22. **(3)** A temperate climate would be most suitable for agriculture because the temperate climate would bring a change of seasons for growing crops.

23. **(5)** Choosing the site of Wounded Knee was a deliberate gesture to emphasize the Native American's outrage at continued poor conditions imposed by the government.

24. **(2)** A delicate balance is maintained with the law of supply and demand. Consumers will demand a product as long as they can afford it. If the price increases too much, consumers will often do without a product they consider to be a luxury rather than a necessity.

25. **(1)** NATO has sent peacekeeping troops to a number of countries, including Bosnia in recent years.

26. **(4)** According to Freud, the id, the ego, and the superego all work together to form an individual's personality. The conflict between how the three interact can often cause behavioral problems.

27. **(3)** According to the theory of situationism, because human behavior is determined by how a person reacts to a situation rather than to personality traits, it is quite possible for a person to commit theft if that situation was one in which he felt he would not be caught. A situation in which he felt he was being observed might prevent him from stealing.

28. **(1)** *Marbury v. Madison* was a landmark case as an important decision that helped to validate the system of checks and balances. Because the Supreme Court can overrule an act of Congress if the act goes against the intent of the Constitution, Congress must ensure that legislation is in keeping with the laws established by the Constitution.

29. **(4)** The fact that it is possible for a condidate to win with a minority of the popular vote is a major concern with critics of the electoral college. The votes of the electors go with the majority even though the number of popular votes could overall be more than the number of electoral votes.

30. **(2)** In the free-market tier of the international monetary system, the value of gold will vary due to supply and demand.

CHAPTER 5

Science

TEST-TAKING TIPS

The majority of the Science test will require you to analyze and apply information from paragraphs of text. You will also need to know how to read charts, diagrams, and illustrations. Reading graphs and charts is covered in the math section of this book, and you might wish to examine that section before proceding with this chapter. A diagram or illustration will point out relationships among items. The labels in a diagram are important because they will frequently supply the information needed to answer the question.

Evaluating and analyzing a question for the science test requires that you be objective. It also requires more complex thinking skills than merely comprehending the material. The information you will read will appear to be factual, but you will need to apply the rules of scientific analysis to determine whether statements are facts or hypotheses. A hypothesis is basically a guess. It might be based on scientific evidence, but it is not a proven conclusion. A proven conclusion is one that has been tested and verified. Your ability to comprehend and analyze information will be tested in the science section of the GED.

Reading carefully is the best way to tackle the science component of the GED. Make sure you read each paragraph as well as any accompanying figures. A thorough understanding of the question will assist you in choosing the correct answer. Be aware that sometimes the question will be in the form of a negative—that is, the question may ask, "Which is NOT…" This kind of question is often confusing because our natural inclination is to be looking for an answer that falls into the pattern of the question.

Answering a question on the Science test will require that you read each answer carefully. The answers might be similar in wording, so it is important that you understand all the choices before you make your selection.

There might be instances where one reading selection will generate several questions. You might find that you have to reread the selection several times in order to answer all the questions. Although the science test is a long one, it will be worthwhile to take your time to read the selections carefully. You might choose to scan each selection for the general idea before you take the time to read it carefully. This will give you a feel for the sequence or the relationships of the subject of the selection. On a more careful reading, you will be able to pick out the details needed to answer the questions.

LIFE SCIENCE

Choose the *one* best answer to each question.

Items 1–10 refer to the following passages.

Neurons are the nerve cells that transmit information throughout the body. Each microscopic neuron has its own job, and together, they allow our bodies to be aware of everything we see, hear, taste, and feel. This is accomplished by the neuron sending and receiving electrical signals through a process of chemical exchange or a mechanical stimulus. These signals or messages are channeled through the brain. **Sensory neurons** are responsible for transmitting messages to the brain and the spinal cord. **Motor neurons** carry commands from the brain and spinal cord to the muscles and glands. **Interneurons** send signals back and forth between the brain and spinal cord to other parts of the body. The process of sending messages takes only a fraction of a second.

1. A pin prick to the finger would be classified as

    (1) a mechanical stimulus

    (2) a chemical exchange

    (3) a neuron sending a message

    (4) an electrical signal

    (5) a sensory neuron

2. The ability to smell a flower is a result of

    (1) motor neurons stimulated by a mechanical stimulus

    (2) motor neurons stimulated by the flower

    (3) interneurons sending signals to the spinal cord

    (4) electrical stimuli

    (5) chemical reaction stimulating sensory neurons

The human eye contains cells in the retina, called **rods**, which register black and white. Other retinal cells, called the cones, are affected by color. Electrical signals from the rods and the cones are sent to the front of the retina. Signals are eventually sent to the brain where they are interpreted and perceived as visual images. Many mammals see the world only in black-and-white images.

3. It can be assumed that

    (1) electrical signals in many mammals are blocked so they can only see in black and white

    (2) many mammals do not have cones in their retinas

    (3) many mammals do not have retinas

    (4) many mammals have more rods than cones in their retinas

    (5) humans are not mammals

In order to successfully transfuse blood from one person to another, blood types have to be matched. There are four blood types: A, B, AB, and O. Type A blood contains an antibody, which works against the antibody found in type B blood, and the antibody in type B blood works against the antibody found in type A. Type AB blood does not contain either antibody, but the red blood cells contain substances found in both A and B blood. Type O blood can be donated to almost anyone because it contains neither substance. Those who have type AB blood have no antibodies at all. A person with type AB blood can receive blood from any of the four blood types.

4. A person with type A blood can receive a blood donation from a persons with the following blood type:

   (1) type B

   (2) type AB

   (3) type O

   (4) types O and A

   (5) types AB and B

Items 5–6 refer to the following passage.

Humans have 23 pairs of chromosomes. Twenty-two of the pairs are the same in males and females. The remaining pair is made up of the sex chromosomes. These determine the sex of a baby. Females have two X chromosomes; males have one X chromosome and one Y chromosome. One of the X chromosomes is always inherited from the mother, and either one X or one Y chromosome is inherited from the father.

5. A male baby has

   (1) 22 pairs of chromosomes

   (2) one X and one Y chromosome

   (3) two X chromosomes

   (4) two Y chromosomes

   (5) three X chromosomes

6. The sex of a baby is determined by

   (1) the number of pairs of chromosomes

   (2) X chromosomes

   (3) Y chromosomes

   (4) the combination of X and Y chromosomes

   (5) the mother's chromosomes

7. Within the chromosomes are smaller units called genes. Genes determine various hereditary traits. Some genes are dominant; others are recessive. The genes for each trait are in pairs, and traits are determined by the combination of the dominant and recessive genes. One or two dominant genes will result in the dominant trait being the hereditary factor. If the gene for brown eyes in humans is dominant over the gene for blue eyes, and an individual inherited two recessive genes for blue eyes from her parents, what color eyes will she have?

   (1) brown

   (2) blue

   (3) one brown and one blue

   (4) green

   (5) hazel

Items 8–9 refer to the following passage.

A food web is made up of linking food chains. The two basic types of food webs are the grazing web and the detrital web. In the grazing web, the chain begins with plants that are passed to **herbivores** (plant eaters) and then to **carnivores** (flesh eaters) or **omnivores** (those that eat both plants and animals). For example, cows, which are herbivores, eat grass, and humans are omnivores who, in turn, might eat beef products.

The detrital web begins with plant and animal matter that become decomposers (bacteria and fungi). The decomposers then pass to **detritivores** (organisms that feed on decomposed matter) and then to carnivores. In this web, the decomposed matter is fed upon by earthworms for example, and some species of birds will eat the worms. The predators that feed upon birds are carnivores.

The two webs can overlap because animals could eat the plants that grow in the decomposed matter, and some animals are both plant and flesh eaters.

8. A carnivore eats

   (1) only plants

   (2) only animals

   (3) both plants and animals

   (4) plants, animals, and decomposers

   (5) plants and decomposers

9. The main idea of this selection is

   (1) food webs are separate and distinct

   (2) animals only fit into the grazing web

   (3) the detrial web overlaps into the grazing web

   (4) decomposed matter is eaten by omnivores

   (5) vegetarians don't eat meat

Item 10 refers to the following passage.

All earth's energy is produced through **photosynthesis**. Photosynthesis is the process by which green plants, algae, and some bacteria take light from the sun and convert it to chemical energy. Only organisms that contain chlorophyll can undergo photosynthesis. **Chlorophyll** is the pigment that makes plants green. The process of photosynthesis usually occurs in the leaves of plants.

10. From reading the selection, it can be assumed that

    (1) if a plant is not green, it cannot produce energy

    (2) on cloudy days, photosynthesis does not occur

    (3) if a plant does not have leaves, it cannot produce energy

    (4) photosynthesis does not occur in the winter

    (5) all living things undergo photosynthesis

Choose the *one* best answer to each question.

Items 11–13 refer to the following diagram

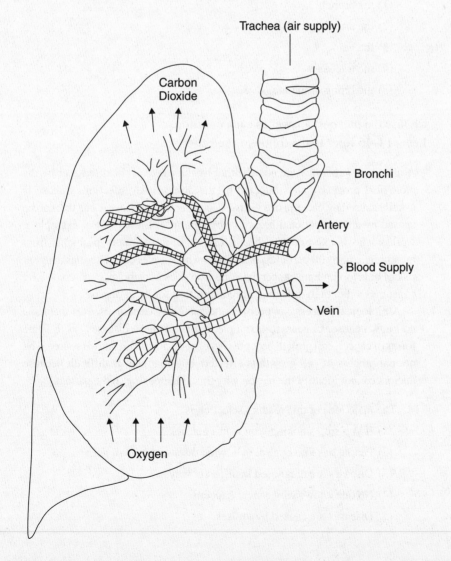

11. Blood enters the lung through

    (1) the trachea

    (2) the bronchi

    (3) the artery

    (4) the vein

    (5) none of the above

12. During the process of breathing

    (1) carbon dioxide is taken in

    (2) air enters the artery

    (3) veins are not operational

    (4) the blood supply is shut off

    (5) oxygen is taken in

13. The air supply enters the lungs through

    (1) the bronchi

    (2) the artery

    (3) the vein

    (4) the trachea

    (5) the lining of the lungs

Choose the *one* best answer to each question.

Items 14–15 refer to the following selection.

A disease is generally diagnosed either by the cause of the disease or by the biological process that is affected by the disease. An infectious disease is usually caused by bacteria or a virus. A noninfectious disease is one that can be caused by an occupational hazard or by a harmful life style. For example, a worker who is exposed to asbestos can develop resiratory problems from breathing in harmful particles, or a person who smokes cigarettes has a higher risk of developing lung cancer than one who does not smoke, or a person who consumes a diet high in fat has a predisposition for heart disease.

A biological process can become interrupted by certain diseases that have no known cause. Cancer, for example, is one of these diseases. With some forms of cancer, cell growth becomes out of control with no known source. The normal process of cell growth is affected, but treatment is difficult because doctors cannot identify the reason why this is happening in the patient.

14. The main idea of this reading selection is:

    (1) If you stop smoking, you won't get sick.

    (2) People have no control over what disease they will get.

    (3) Diseases are diagnosed in different ways.

    (4) No one knows why cancer happens.

    (5) Diseases are caused by viruses.

15. Cancer is a disease that

    (1) has no known cause

    (2) has a known cause

    (3) can be prevented

    (4) is marked by abnormal cell growth

    (5) is caused by working conditions or life style

Answers

1. **(1)** A pin prick is a mechanical stimulus that affects neurons in the finger. These neurons send a message to the brain telling it to feel the pain inflicted by the pin prick.

2. **(5)** Scent triggers a chemical reaction that stimulates the sensory neurons in the nose. These neurons transmit a message to the brain, which allows you to identify the odor.

3. **(2)** The many mammals that can only see in black and white are lacking cones. Cones are the cells that enable the eye to distinguish color.

4. **(4)** A person with any type blood can receive blood from any other person with the same type. A person with type O blood is considered a universal donor and anyone can receive type O blood.

5. **(2)** There is one pair of sex chromosomes. Females have two X chromosomes, and males have one X and one Y chromosome.

6. **(4)** The specific combination of chromosomes determines the sex of a baby. Females will have two X chromosomes, and males will have one X and one Y chromosome, so a combination of X and Y chromosomes will be the determining factor.

7. **(2)** Because the child has only inherited recessive genes, her eyes would be blue.

8. **(2)** A carnivore only consumes meat.

9. **(3)** Food chains link to form webs; decomposed matter, which is made up of plant and animal matter, is consumed by herbivores, and they in turn can be consumed by carnivores resulting in an overlapping of food webs.

10. **(1)** Photosynthesis can only occur in green plants. Because chlorophyll is the pigment that makes plants green, the process cannot occur in anything other than a green plant.

11. **(3)** The arrow on the diagram points out that the blood supply is entering the lung through the artery.

12. **(5)** The arrows in the diagram point upward to indicate that oxygen is taken into the lung.

13. **(4)** The arrow indicates that the air supply goes through the trachea and into the lung through the bronchi.

14. **(3)** A disease can be catagorized as being diagnosed by the cause of the disease or by the biological process that is affected by the disease. The passage also points out that, for some diseases, there is no known cause. The main idea of the passage is to explain that there are a variety of ways to diagnose a disease.

15. **(4)** Although a cause is sometimes known for cancer, all cancers are identified by abnormal cell growth.

EARTH AND SPACE SCIENCE

Choose the *one* best answer to each question.
Items 16–17 refer to the following chart

	Mercury	Venus	Earth	Mars	Jupiter	Saturn	Uranus	Neptune	Pluto
Years to revolve around sun	.24	.62	1	1.88	11.86	29.46	84	164.79	247.7
Radius (Earth = 1)	.38	.45	1	.53	11.2	9.42	4.01	3.88	(.06)

16. Which planet is farthest from the Sun?

    (1) Pluto

    (2) Jupiter

    (3) Neptune

    (4) Mercury

    (5) Saturn

17. Which planet has a radius closest in size to the Earth's radius?

    (1) Venus

    (2) Mars

    (3) Jupiter

    (4) Mercury

    (5) Uranus

Choose the *one* best answer to each question.
Items 18–19 refer to the following diagram.

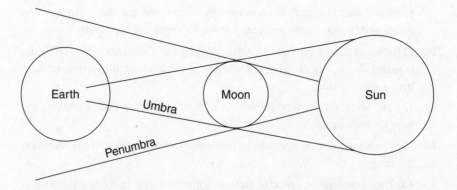

The Earth can experience a solar or a lunar eclipse. When the Earth is between the Sun and the Moon and its shadow darkens the Moon, the episode is called a lunar eclipse. In a solar eclipse, the Moon is between the Sun and the Earth, and its shadow darkens the Earth. The cone-shaped darkening is called the unbra. The lighter shadow cast around the rest of the area is the penumbra.

18. The diagram shows
    (1) a lunar eclipse
    (2) a partial eclipse
    (3) a total eclipse
    (4) either a solar or a lunar eclipse
    (5) a solar eclipse

19. An eclipse occurs because of
    (1) the placement of the Sun
    (2) the speed of the Earth's movement
    (3) the alignment of the Sun, the Earth, and the Moon
    (4) the alignment of the Sun and the Earth
    (5) the alignment of the Earth and the Moon

Choose the *one* best answer to each question.
Items 20–21 refer to the following selection

Erosion is the process by which rock and soil is moved on the surface of the earth, generally by a natural process. There are five basic ways that erosion can take place. Weathering takes place when the climate of an area affects the land. Hot or cold weather can expand or contract rocks and minerals, causing erosion. Rainy weather can have the effect of leeching the soil of minerals, causing erosion. Wind erosion, especially in arid climates causes particles of soil and sand to be moved. Sand dunes are caused by the wind blowing. Glacial erosion occurs over a long period of time and removes rock as the glacier melts. Coastal erosion occurs because of the action of the waves of the oceans and is particulary severe during storms. Water erosion occurs when the ground is saturated with moisture. Excess water runs off carrying with it loose soil.

20. One can infer from the passage that erosion in the Sahara desert is most likely the result of
    (1) weathering
    (2) coastal erosion
    (3) wind erosion
    (4) water erosion
    (5) glacial erosion

21. Hurricanes in Florida can, over a period of time, change the shape of its beaches. This is the result of
    (1) coastal erosion
    (2) wind erosion
    (3) glacial erosion
    (4) weathering
    (5) water erosion

Choose the *one* best answer to each question.
Items 22–24 refer to the following diagram

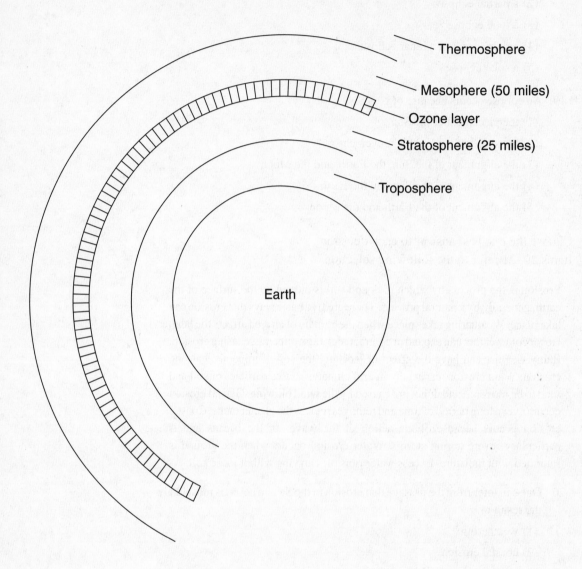

The ozone layer of the stratosphere is responsible for absorbing potentially dangerous ultraviolet rays from the sun. Unchecked, the ultraviolet rays can cause dangerous global warming.

22. By looking at the diagram, which layer of the atmosphere is the one most likely to contain the air we breathe?

    (1) stratosphere
    (2) troposphere
    (3) ozone layer
    (4) mesophere
    (5) thermosphere

23. Which of the following would NOT be a potential effect of global warming?

    (1) The temperature of the oceans would rise.

    (2) Plants will grow better because of more sun.

    (3) The risk of skin cancer would increase.

    (4) Some organisms would die.

    (5) Glaciers would melt faster.

24. Temperature levels fall from ground level to the top of the troposphere, but they rise in the stratosphere. Which of the following would best account for the rise in temperature?

    (1) more gasses in the air at higher altitudes

    (2) thinner air at higher altitudes

    (3) the ozone layer absorbing heat

    (4) the troposhpere blocking the rays of the sun

    (5) global warming

25. The theory of continental drift suggests that at one time the continents were one large land mass. Slowly, sections of this huge plate drifted apart and formed the continents as we know them. In support of this theory are measurements taken on the ocean floor that show the oceans are spreading on both sides from the middle. Assuming this theory is true, one can infer that continental drift is also responsible for

    (1) fossils

    (2) earthquakes

    (3) new forms of plant life

    (4) the formation of new minerals

    (5) some gasses in the air

Answers

16. **(1)** Because Pluto takes the most time to revolve around the Sun, it is the farthest planet from the Sun.

17. **(2)** If the Earth's radius is represented by 1, the planet closest in size to the Earth has a radius closest to 1. Mars, with a radius of .53, has a radius closest to 1.

18. **(5)** The diagram shows a solar eclipse since the Moon is between the Sun and the Earth and its shadow darkening the Earth.

19. **(3)** For an eclipse to take place, the Sun, the Earth, and the Moon must all be aligned in a particular way.

20. **(3)** Although the weather is a factor in erosion on the Sahara desert, the wind plays a greater role, blowing the sand and creating the dunes associated with a desert.

21. **(1)** Florida has most of its land mass on coastal areas, and because hurricanes are storms of great magnitude, they are responsible for the coastal erosion that can change the shape of Florida's beaches.

22. (2) The troposphere is the layer of atmosphere closest to the earth, so it is the layer that contains the air we breath.

23. (2) The ultraviolet rays that would be exposed by a general global warming would be dangerous for plants, as well as for animals, because the rays could potentially burn plants.

24. (3) The stratosophere is closer to the ozone layer than the troposphere, so the effect of the ozone layer would be to raise the temperatures closer to the top of the layer.

25. (2) The measurements taken on the ocean floor support the belief that the continents are still shifting, and this shift could be responsible for earthquakes.

CHEMISTRY

Choose the *one* best answer to each question.
Items 26–30 refer to the following selections.

The smallest unit of an element is the atom. Each atom is made up of a positively charged nucleus that is surrounded by a network of electrons. Atoms combine to form molecules, and every chemical substance is made up of molecules. The distinct way atoms combine in the molecules determines the element. A molecule of water, for example, is made up of two atoms of hydrogen and one atom of oxygen. The symbol for water is H_2O.

In the Periodic Table, all known elements are arranged according to their chemical properties. Elements with similar properties appear together in the table. Besides the symbol for the element, each element has an atomic number associated with it. The weight of the element is indicated by this number. The higher the number, the heavier the element. For example, iron is symbolized by Fe and has the atomic number 26. Mercury is symbolized by Hg and has been assigned the atomic number 80, which means that it is heavier than iron.

26. An element is determined by

    (1) the combination of atoms in the element

    (2) the atomic weight of an element

    (3) the symbol of the element

    (4) how much water is in the element

    (5) the arrangement of the element in the Periodic Table

27. The atomic number of an element indicates

    (1) the number of molecules in the element

    (2) the number of atoms combined with molecules in the element

    (3) the weight of the element

    (4) the chemical properties of the element

    (5) where the element is placed on the Periodic Table

28. The formula for what is commonly known as rust is Fe_2O_3. This means that rust is made up of

    (1) molecules containing iron

    (2) iron and oxygen

    (3) two atoms of iron and three molecules of water

    (4) two atoms of iron and three atoms of oxygen

    (5) a combination of water and iron

There are three forms in which matter occurs: solid, liquid, and gas. Solid matter generally does not change its shape, liquid matter generally does not resist a force to change its shape, and gas that is not contained will diffuse into the air indefinitely and become weaker as it is diffused. Temperature of a substance, however, can change its form.

29. Ice placed into a pot and boiled is an example of

    (1) a liquid state of matter

    (2) a solid changing to a liquid

    (3) a liquid changing to a solid

    (4) a liquid changing to a gas

    (5) a solid changing to a gas

30. When a plastic bag is recycled to make a soda container, it goes from

    (1) a solid to liquid to solid state

    (2) a solid to gas to liquid state

    (3) a solid to liquid to gas state

    (4) a liquid to solid state

    (5) a gas to solid state

Choose the *one* best answer to each question.
Items 31–32 refer to the following table.

Substance	pH	
Gastric juice	1.0	ACID
Tomato juice	4.1	
Milk	6.6	
Pure water	7.0	NEUTRAL
Toothpaste	9.9	
Milk of magnesia	10.5	ALKALINE

The pH of a substance is the measurement of the hydrogen ion concentration in a water based solution. Acids are distinguished by a sour taste, while bases taste bitter. When there is a combination of acids and a base, the substance is neutralized.

31. If a person were suffering from acid indigestion, he or she would help to alleviate the problem by
    (1) doing nothing
    (2) mixing milk of magnesia with tomato juice
    (3) mixing milk of magnesia with pure water
    (4) drinking pure water
    (5) mixing pure water with milk

32. A solution with a pH level of 2.9 would most likely
    (1) taste bitter
    (2) taste sour
    (3) have a neutral taste
    (4) have no taste at all
    (5) none of the above

33. Three types of processes are used for separating a metal from the waste rock in which it is embedded. Mechanical separation employs gravity to remove waste materials, flotation mixes ground ore with a liquid and the waste that is heavier than the ore is dispensed, and electrostatic separation relies on the attraction of unlike charges and the repulsion of like charges for the separation process. Which process explains how one pans for gold?
    (1) flotation
    (2) a combination of flotation and electrostatic
    (3) a combination of mechanical and flotation
    (4) mechanical
    (5) electrostatic

Answers

26. **(1)** Atoms make up molecules, so it is the unique combination of atoms that determines an element.

27. **(3)** In the Periodic Table, each element is assigned a number to indicate the weight of the element

28. **(4)** Since Fe is the symbol for iron, and O is the symbol for oxygen, the formula for rust would include both symbols. The numbers in subscript indicate the number of atoms of each.

29. **(5)** Ice melting and heated to the boiling point goes through three stages. It begins as a solid, and as it heats, it changes to a liquid. Finally, as it begins to boil, it changes to a steam, which is a gas released into the air.

30. **(1)** The plasic bag begins as a solid, and as it is heated, it melts and changes to a liquid. Finally, when it is formed into a soda container, it becomes a solid again.

31. **(3)** A mixture of the milk of magnesia and water would neutralize the acid creating a more balanced pH.

32. **(2)** A solution with a pH level of 2.9 would taste sour because of its acid content.

33. **(4)** Panning for gold is a mechanical process since gravity is used in a sieve to remove waste materials from gold nuggets.

PHYSICS

Choose the *one* best answer to each question.
Items 34–43 refer to the following passages.

The three basic principles of mechanics were formulated by Isaac Newton and are known as Newton's Laws. The first law states that an object will remain in motion or in a state of rest unless something influences it and changes its course. This property is refered to as **inertia.** If you were sitting in an airplane, the force of the airplane taking off would push you against your seat, overcoming your inertia. The second law states that the change of motion is proportional to the force of change. The greater the applied force, the greater the acceleration. If the same force were applied to two objects, a car and a truck, for example, the truck would show a smaller acceleration. The third law states that for every action (or applied force) there is an equal and opposite reaction. The forward thrust of a rocket, for example, takes place from the force of the expanding gases in the rocket's combustion chamber acting equally in all directions. The thrust is produced by the reaction to the force of expansion on the closed front end of the combustion chamber.

34. An example of Newton's second law would be

    (1) two shopping carts colliding in a grocery store
    (2) the whiplash you would experience in a car by suddenly applying the brake
    (3) a mother pushing a baby carriage
    (4) allowing air to escape from a balloon
    (5) a child falling off a bike

35. An example of Newton's first law would be

    (1) two shopping carts colliding in a grocery store
    (2) the whiplash you would experience in a car by suddenly applying the brake
    (3) a mother pushing a baby carriage
    (4) allowing air to escape from a balloon
    (5) a child falling off a bike

36. An example of Newton's third law would be

    (1) two shopping carts colliding in a grocery store
    (2) the whiplash you would experience in a car by suddenly applying the brake
    (3) a mother pushing a baby carriage
    (4) allowing air to escape from a balloon
    (5) a child falling off a bike

37. A fluid can exert a buoyant force as well as an internal force because of the weight of the fluid above it. The suit of a deep sea diver must contain a jacket of compressed air whose pressure counteracts the external water pressure. The reason for the jacket of compressed air is

    (1) to allow the diver to breath without his muscles having to expand his chest against the pressure

    (2) to make the diver more buoyant in the water

    (3) to allow the diver to go to a greater depth

    (4) to keep the diver from drowning in case there is a leak in his suit

    (5) to give the diver an extra source of air

38. Much of the energy we use comes either directly or indirectly from the sun. Coal is the product of forest growth from millions of years ago that was submerged in swamps then buried beneath huge thicknesses of sandstones and shales. The pressure, heat, and breakdown by microorganisms resulted in a combustible solid. Oil, including natural gas, is the product of the decay of single celled plants and animals that lived millions of years ago. Based on this paragraph, conservation of coal and oil is wise because

    (1) it is expensive to get

    (2) coal and oil are not practical to use because both are messy to burn

    (3) there are fewer forests now than millions of years ago

    (4) it's hard to transport coal and oil

    (5) it takes so long to form, we could be using them up faster than new coal and oil is produced

39. Solar collectors provide energy for buildings by pumping water through panels mounted on the roof. The water picks up heat from the sun, and the pump is controlled by a sensor so it operates when the collector is several degrees hotter than the water in the storage tank. This type of energy would work best in

    (1) the Southwest

    (2) the Northeast

    (3) the Great Lakes area

    (4) anywhere in the country

    (5) the Northwest

40. The controlled release of the energy from the atomic nucleus produces electricity in the form of nuclear power. The slow release of energy in a nuclear reactor creates electricity, while a sudden and uncontrolled release produces an atomic bomb. The process of the nucleus dividing into two is called **fission**. Energy can also be produced by the process known as **fusion**. Fusion occurs when light atoms are heated to extreme temperatures so that the atoms are blended together to build heavier atoms. This process, however, is much more difficult to achieve. You can infer from this passage that those who oppose the use of nuclear energy do so because

(1) it would be an expensive form of electric power

(2) it has the potential of being dangerous

(3) it would take too long to produce enough energy to be useful

(4) only trained scientists would know how to produce nuclear energy

(5) most people prefer to use other energy sources

Sound is a form of energy that is produced when an object vibrates and a medium, such as air, vibrates in response. As an object vibrates, it sets the air molecules around it vibrating. A region of higher pressure, or compression, of molecules forms around the vibration. An area of lower presssure, or rarefaction, occurs where the molecules move apart. A sound wave is formed as the compressions and rarefactions move through the air. The farther apart the rarefactions and compressions, the lower the sound. Although sound waves generally travel in straight lines, a sound wave can be reflected when it strikes a surface or diffracted as it passes through an opening. Sound is measured in decibels. The frequency of the vibration of a sound wave is measured in hertz. The range of frequencies for hearing of human beings usually lies between 20 and 20,000 hertz. Sound above this range for man is called ultrasound.

41. If you are sitting in a room with the doors and windows closed, you can still hear sound because of

    (1) ultrasound

    (2) diffraction

    (3) reflection

    (4) the frequency of vibration of the sound

    (5) compression

42. A sound wave is the result of

    (1) compression

    (2) diffraction

    (3) reflection

    (4) rarefactions

    (5) compression and rarefactions

43. Light travels in waves consisting of vibrating electric and magnetic fields. Stronger vibrations cause an increase in brightness. The frequencies of the waves can also be different. Blue light, for example, has a higher frequency than red light, and the distance between its vibrations or wavelength is shorter than the wavelength of red light. Black is the absence of light, and white light is the mixture of all colors. When white light passes through a prism, it is split into a band of colors called the spectrum. A rainbow occurs when drops of water act as a prism because

    (1) the light waves are traveling fast

    (2) a rainbow is made up of white light

    (3) there are a number of frequencies involved

    (4) white light from the sun is dispersed through the drops of water

    (5) the electric and magnetic fields have strong vibrations

Answers

34. **(3)** A mother pushing a baby carriage is an example of Newton's second law. The force the mother uses to push the carriage is proportional to how fast the carriage moves.

35. **(2)** Applying the breaks suddenly to a car would cause the passengers to violently move forward; and as the car stops, they would equally violently move backward causing whiplash.

36. **(4)** The balloon would be propelled into the air by the force of the air escaping. The action of the balloon being propelled into the air is a result of the opposite reaction.

37. **(1)** The compressed air in the diver's jacket protects the diver by forming a bubble of air around him, which acts as a cushion against the pressure of the water allowing him to breathe and expand his chest.

38. **(5)** Because coal and oil take millions of years to produce, conservation is important. If we use more than is produced, these two valuable resources can not be easily replenished.

39. **(1)** Because the water in a solar collector is heated by the sun, the areas of the country that do not receive a great deal of sun or that have generally cool temperatures would find that solar collectors are not an efficient means to provide energy.

40. **(2)** Because fission and fusion are the methods used to produce atomic and hydrogen bombs, many fear that the potential for danger of damaging explosions is great.

41. **(3)** Sound waves generally travel in a straight line, but when waves encounter a surface such as a wall, they are reflected. The sound will not be as loud as it was originally, but in many cases, it can still be heard.

42. **(5)** A sound wave requires both compression of molecules or high pressure and an area of lower pressure or rarefaction where molecules move farther apart.

43. **(4)** The drops of water act as a prism when the white light from the sun is dispersed through the water. The drops split the light into bands of color.

TEST YOURSELF

Choose the *one* best answer to each question.
Items 1–2 refer to the following passage.

Scientific Method is the procedure scientists use to design and conduct an experiment. There are five steps to this procedure: state the problem or ask a question; research the subject; form a hypothesis (based on research, try to predict a solution or answer); plan and conduct an experiment using an experimental group (the test group known as the variable) and a control group (not exposed to the variable); observe, measure, and record the findings; draw conclusions from the findings; repeat the experiment for validity.

1. A scientist wanted to see the effects of sunlight on plants. He developed two groups of plants. Group 1 was exposed to the sun for several hours each day, and Group 2 was only exposed to the sun for two hours each day. In this experiment, Group 2 was the

    (1) hypothesis

    (2) experiment

    (3) variable

    (4) control group

    (5) observation

2. The scientist repeated his experiment on the two groups of plants. The purpose of repeating the experiment was

    (1) to make sure he didn't make any mistakes

    (2) to ensure that the test and his conclusions were accurate

    (3) to ensure that all the plants were growing properly

    (4) to ensure that he could answer any questions

    (5) to make the experiment fit the hypothesis

Choose the *one* best answer to each question.

Items 3–4 refer to the following passage.

Bacteria and viruses are the smallest forms of life, but they have the capacity to survive and adapt to new conditions. All living cells are susceptible to a viral attack that will take control of their activities. Although antibiotics are relatively ineffective against viruses, cells can produce antibodies that give immunity to viral attack. In fact, a vaccination with killed virus can be used against disease. Some synthetic vaccines have been developed that act like a viral antigen. These are injected to stimulate the immune system.

Bacteria are found in cells everywhere, and they can live under almost any conditions. Bacteria can be harmful by producing poisonous stubstances, by clogging vital passages, and by producing allergic reactions. Although antibiotics have been helpful in treating bacterial infections, some bacteria have become resistant to anibiotics. Bacteria are not always harmful, however. In some animals, such as cows and sheep, bacteria helps to break down the indigestible grasses on which they graze. Bacteria are also helpful to humans in making certain food products, such as cheese and butter.

3. Bacteria and viruses are alike in that

    (1) neither is affected by antibiotics

    (2) both can be helpful

    (3) neither can live very long

    (4) both can be killed by vaccines

    (5) both can adapt to their surroundings

4. One can infer from this passage that:

    (1) Scientists need to figure out a way to kill all viruses and bacteria.

    (2) The best scientists can do is to figure out how to treat diseases associated with viruses and bacteria.

    (3) Viruses and bacteria are the same things.

    (4) Vaccinations can be developed to control bacteria.

    (5) Viruses and bacteria are not in all living things.

Choose the *one* best answer to each question.
Item 5 refers to the following passage.

There are three types of rocks on the earth's surface: igneous, metamorphic, and sedimentary. Igneous rocks have been formed by the cooling of molten magma where temperatures are extremely high. Metamorphic rocks have been formed by the compression of older rocks. They are formed below the surface of the earth where both the temperature and pressure are high. Sedimentary rocks are formed by weathering or the remains of living organisms. These are formed on the surface of the earth under low pressures.

5. One can infer from this passage that

    (1) the three types of rocks are all located in different places on the earth

    (2) the three types of rocks can be found anywhere

    (3) the three types of rocks will all look the same

    (4) the three types of rocks are all approximately the same age

    (5) the three types of rocks share common characteristics

Choose the *one* best answer to each question.
Items 6–8 refer to the following passage.

Weather is comprised of air temperature, barometric pressure, wind velocity, humidity, clouds, and precipitation. Weather depends on the movements of large air masses that vary in temperature and humidity according to the land or water surface beneath them, and they shift slowly over the surface of the earth. Static masses account for steady weather conditions. Other masses that are affected by the earth's rotation move rapidly and interact with other air masses. These masses account for changeable weather. Most of North America's weather depends on a west to east movement of air masses and the fronts associated with them.

    The climate of an area is the long-term weather associated with the area. Besides being influenced by the air masses, it is influenced by the relative distribution of land and water, high and low ground, and the presence of major features such as forests and lakes. Tropical climates are hot, temperate climates are variable, and polar climates are cold.

6. The climate of the South Pole would most likely be

    (1) cloudy

    (2) predicted in a west to east movement

    (3) temperate

    (4) polar

    (5) variable

7. Weather depends on

    (1) movement of air masses

    (2) temperature and precipitation

    (3) climate

    (4) distribution of land and water

    (5) a west to east movement

8. North America would most likely have

    (1) A tropical climate

    (2) Static air masses

    (3) A temperate climate

    (4) Long-term weather

    (5) Steady weather conditions

Choose the *one* best answer to each question.

Items 9–11 refer to the following table.

The Major Systems of the Human Body

Skeletal system	More than 200 bones joined by fibrous ligaments
Muscular system	Responsible for internal and external responses to the environment
Digestive system	Digestion and absorption of food's energy giving/body building substances
Circulatory system	Responsible for pumping blood to every part of the body
Skin	Protects tissue, regulates temperature, and helps excrete waste
Nervous system	Receives and responds to all external and internal stimuli

9. According to the table, the process of sweating would involve

    (1) the nervous system

    (2) the muscular and skeletal systems

    (3) the circulatory system

    (4) the muscular system

    (5) the skin

10. Arteries and veins are part of
    (1) the nervous system
    (2) the circulatory system
    (3) the circulatory and nervous systems
    (4) the skeletal system
    (5) the muscular system

11. When Joseph cut his finger and jerked his hand away from the knife, the following systems were involved in the movement
    (1) the skeletal, muscular, and circulatory systems
    (2) the skin and nervous systems
    (3) the digestive and nervous systems
    (4) the nervous, muscular, and skeletal systems
    (5) the nervous and muscular systems

12. Water moves through a natural cycle of evaporation, cloud formation, rainfall, collection, and evaporation. In this cycle, water is self purifying. Smoke from industrial sites is brought to earth by rainfall. This could ultimately interfere with the self purifying cycle because
    (1) the rain can become dangerous
    (2) the pollutants will become part of the continous cycle
    (3) when the pollutants enter the clouds, they stay there
    (4) the pollutants would evaporate into the air
    (5) water cannot evaporate with pollutants in it

13. Atoms are made up of protons and neutrons that are closely packed in the nucleus of the atom. The third component of an atom is the electron. The electrons are spread out more than the protons and neutrons, and much of an atom is comprised of empty space. The electrons are located outside the central nucleus. When two atoms collide, it is most likely that
    (1) the electrons will come into contact with each other
    (2) the nuclei will come into contact with each other
    (3) the protons and neutrons will come into contact with each other
    (4) the electrons and the nuclei will come into contact with each other
    (5) the protons will come into contact with the nuclei

Choose the *one* best answer to each question.

Items 14–15 refer to the following diagram.

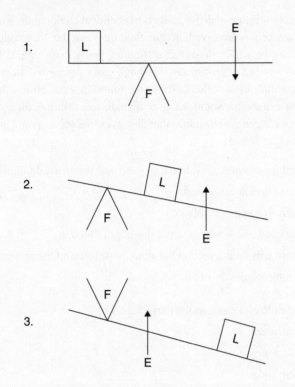

The diagram above illustrates the three types of levers. All three are dependent on the effort (5), load (L), and fulcrum (F). Any lever in which the load and effort balance each other is said to be in equilibrium.

14. A child's seesaw illustrates
    (1) number 1, where the fulcrum is placed between the load and the effort
    (2) number 2, where the fulcrum is at one end, the load is in the middle, and the effort is at the other end
    (3) the use of a fulcrum
    (4) how the effort uses the fulcrum
    (5) number 3, where the effort acts between the fulcrum and the load

15. A wheelbarrow is an example of
    (1) number 3, where the effort acts between the fulcrum and the load
    (2) a lever in equilibrium
    (3) number 2, where the fulcrum is at one end, the load is in the middle, and the effort is at the other end
    (4) the effort pushing downward
    (5) number 1, were the fulcrum is placed between the load and the effort

Choose the *one* best answer to each question.

Items 16–17 refer to the following passage.

A solution is a mixture of different sorts of chemical compounds. Two or more types of molecules involved in the mixture must be thoroughly mixed. Solutions can be solids dissolved in liquids, gases dissolved in liquids, or liquids dissolved in other liquids. Although gases can also dissolve in some solids, and solutions of solids in solids are found in metal alloys, they are not as common as the other solutions. In order to have a solution, there must be an interaction between the substance that dissolves (the solvent) and the material it dissolves (the solute).

16. The inability to make a solution of sand and water would imply that
    (1) the solute doesn't work
    (2) there is too much solvent
    (3) the sand and water were not thoroughly mixed
    (4) there was no interaction between the solute and the solvent
    (5) the molecules do not mix

17. An example of a gas dissolved in a liquid is
    (1) antifreeze
    (2) salt water
    (3) club soda
    (4) liquid plant fertilizer
    (5) gelatin dissolved in boiling water

Choose the *one* best answer to each question.

Items 18–19 refer to the following passage.

The ocean is constantly moving, although in the greatest depths the movement is extremely slow. This movement continually provides oxygen to the water. The surface currents that move the water are caused by prevailing winds, which in turn are related to the density of the water that varies according to temperature and salinity. Heating at the equator causes the water to become less dense while the opposite occurs at the poles through cooling.

18. It was once thought that dangerous radioactive waste could be sealed in a container and dropped to the bottom of the ocean. This would destroy the ecology of the ocean by
    (1) ruining the bottom of the ocean
    (2) taking up valuable space which should be preserved for marine animals
    (3) affecting the surface currents
    (4) causing a difference in the temperature of the ocean
    (5) allowing the waste to mix with the oxygen in the water

19. A high rate of evaporation in the Mediterranean Sea increases the salinity of the water. In turn,

    (1) the water is warmer

    (2) the water is more dense

    (3) there are fewer prevailing winds over the Mediterranean Sea

    (4) there is less oxygen in the water

    (5) the currents move more slowly

20. The human body has two types of glands. Those that release their secretions into a duct are the exocrine glands, and those without ducts release their secretions (hormones) directly into the blood and are known as endocrine glands. The most common endocrine disorder is sugar diabetes. Diabetes occurs when the pancreas fails to produce sufficient amounts of insulin. The best way to treat diabetes would be

    (1) through diet and insulin injections

    (2) surgery to fix the glands

    (3) to increase the activity of the exocrine glands

    (4) increase the amount of hormone released into the blood

    (5) add sugar to the diet

Choose the *one* best answer to each question.

Items 21–22 refer to the following passage.

Most solid matter is composed of crystals. The most obvious crystals we are familiar with are sugar and salt. It is often difficult to identify materials as being composed of crystals since a large number of them have been aggregated to produce the substance. Crystals grow by precipitation out of a solution or a cooling melt. The atoms or ions cluster into small "seeds" and continue to build in layers.

Minerals are naturally occurring inorganic substances made up of one or more elements, and most are crystalline. A mineral is identified by the crystal shape, as well as the cleavage (the way the mineral breaks), the hardness, the color, and the luster (the way in which the light is reflected).

21. You can infer from the passage that

    (1) if you leave a crystal in the rain, it will grow

    (2) sugar is a mineral

    (3) melted crystals form minerals

    (4) not all crystals are minerals

    (5) if a substance does not have a luster, it is not a mineral

22. Which of the following is NOT an identifying factor of a mineral?

    (1) the hardness

    (2) the cleavage

    (3) the solution out of which it grew

    (4) the luster

    (5) the crystal shape

23. A volcano is fed by hot molten rock (magma) that rises from the mantle of the earth. This matter then erupts from the center of the volcano as lava or as ash. As the magma cools, its flow slows down. When ash is released, it is often carried by winds. The greatest damage by a volcano would most likely be

    (1) from the heat of the lava

    (2) from the eruption factor

    (3) from magma exploding from the center of the volcano

    (4) from the wind that carries the ash

    (5) from the ash that is spread over a larger area than the lava is spread

Choose the *one* best answer to each question.

Items 24–26 refer to the following passage.

A comet is made up of small icy particles and gases. There are three main classes of comets. Short period comets whose cycles only amount to a few years and are faint. Long period comets take decades to travel around the sun and are much easier to see because they are fairly bright. Halley's Comet, which is seen every 76 years, is classified as a long period comet. Finally, there are very long period comets whose cycles are so long, they have yet to be accurately measured. Comets are made up of three parts: a nucleus that contains most of the mass; a coma, or head of the comet; and the tail, which is made up of dust and gas. The coma and tail appear when the comet approaches the Sun and solar radiation vaporizes some of the nucleus. Very small comets often do not have tails.

A meteor (or shooting star) is a rapidly moving point of light caused by objects moving at high speeds across the sky. Often a tail is visible on a meteor. A meteor is actually a very small particle that moves around the Sun. Because of its extremely high speed, the meteor creates friction with the air molecules, which causes it to destroy itself before it reaches the earth. The visible streak in the sky is caused by its effect on the atmosphere. A sporatic meteor may appear from any direction at any time. Shower meteors are associated with comets.

24. A comet can be distinguished from a meteor by

    (1) its light

    (2) its cycles

    (3) its size

    (4) its tail

    (5) its speed

25. A meteor

    (1) causes great damage when it falls to Earth

    (2) always has a tail

    (3) never has a tail

    (4) does not cause any damage when it falls to Earth

    (5) has a distinct and recognizable path

26. Comets

    (1) often fall to the earth

    (2) are very small

    (3) are always precisely measured by their cycles

    (4) cannot always be measured by their cycles

    (5) are points of light moving across the sky

Choose the *one* best answer to each question.

Items 27–28 refer to the following passage.

The raw materials that make up all plants are water, carbon dioxide, and sunlight. Plants have no nervous system, and their growth is controlled by the release of hormonal materials. All plants manufacture their own food using oxygen and releasing carbon dioxide. There are two basic groups of plants: seed bearing and non-seed bearing. In the seed bearing group are flowering plants and most trees. An example of non-seed bearing plants are mosses. Among the seed bearing plants are annuals that can have a very rapid life cycle, and perennials that can live to a great age.

27. Trees are considered

    (1) perennials

    (2) annuals

    (3) non-seed bearing

    (4) seed bearing annuals

    (5) flowering plants

28. Because plants do not have a nervous system, they

    (1) are not considered to be living things

    (2) do not grow

    (3) cannot manufacture food

    (4) have their growth controlled by hormonal substances

    (5) need sunlight to grow

Choose the *one* best answer to each question.

Items 29–32 refer to the following passage

The human brain is made up of billions of cells called neurons. At birth, the structure of the brain is almost complete, but it continues to grow until about age 20. The major part of the brain is the cerebrum, and it is divided into two hemispheres that are mainly responsible for movement and sensation of one side of the body. The left hemisphere contols the right side of the body, and the right hemisphere controls the left side. Speech is usually controlled by the left hemisphere.

Inside each of the hemispheres is the cortex. Beneath the cortex are the four lobes of each hemisphere. Each lobe is responsible for a different function. The occipital lobes receive and analyze visual information. The temporal lobes deal wih sound. The frontal lobes regulate voluntary movement and assist in language. The prefrontal lobes located in the frontal lobes are thought to be involved with intelligence and personality. The parietal lobes are associated with our sense of touch and balance.

29. If a right-handed person were to suffer a stoke affecting the left side of his brain, which functions would be involved?

    (1) His right hand

    (2) His left hand

    (3) His right hand and his speech

    (4) His speech

    (5) His whole body

30. The size of the brain of a 30 year old woman is

    (1) the same size it was when she was 25 years old

    (2) the same size it was when she was 12 years old

    (3) different from the size it will be when she is 50 years old

    (4) smaller than it will become when she is older

    (5) smaller than it was when she was 25 years old

31. If the frontal lobe were diseased, it would affect a person's

    (1) intelligence

    (2) sense of touch

    (3) eyesight

    (4) personality

    (5) language

32. The brain is

    (1) one large mass

    (2) divided into two hemispheres

    (3) made up of neurons

    (4) another name for the cortex

    (5) another name for the cerebrum

33. Terms used to measure sound wave frequencies are called hertz and kilohertz. One hertz is equal to one wave per second. One kilohertz is equal to 1,000 waves per second. If you had your radio dial tuned to 89, the 89 would stand for 89 kilohertz. This means that the sound waves are traveling at

    (1) 8,900 waves per second

    (2) 89,000 waves per second

    (3) 1,000 waves each second

    (4) 89,000 hertz

    (5) 89 hertz

Choose the *one* best answer to each question.

Items 34–35 refer to the following passage.

Metabolism is defined as the total of all the chemical activities of the body's cells. The resting metabolism is the rate at which the body uses up energy while it is at rest. The resting metabolism of different people varies according to their age, sex, body size, and shape. There are people who seem to eat a great deal and never gain weight, while there are others who eat very little and seem to gain weight easily. The basal metabolic rate (BMR) is the measure of the rate of metabolism at rest. Those who tend to have a higher BMR also seem to be people who gain little weight. The BMR is also closely related to the amount of lean tissue a person has. Generally, men tend to have more lean tissue than women. The BMR rises with exercise and decreases with age as the body loses lean tissue. The resting metabolism accounts for as much as half of the energy people use.

34. BMR is defined as

    (1) the amount of lean tissue a person has

    (2) the total of all the chemical activities of the body's cells

    (3) the energy used while exercising

    (4) the rate at which people gain weight

    (5) the measure of the rate of metabolism at rest

35. A person who wants to lose weight

    (1) can rest more

    (2) cannot lose weight without changing the amount of lean tissue in his or her body

    (3) eat less

    (4) exercise more to raise the BMR

    (5) increase the activity of the body's cells

Choose the *one* best answer to each question.
Items 36–37 refer to the following passage.

Nearsightedness, or myopia, is the condition of the eye that causes distant objects to appear blurry. In this condition, the light that enters the eye is focusing in front of the retina instead of precisely on the retina. This condition can be corrected with the use of concave lenses.

Farsightedness, or hypermetropia, is the condition of the eye that causes close objects to appear blurry, while distant objects are more clearly focused. In this condition, light rays are focusing behind the retina. This condition can be corrected with the use of convex lenses. The ability to focus on close objects diminishes with age.

36. People who require reading glasses

    (1) have hypermetropia

    (2) are old

    (3) have retinas that do not focus

    (4) have concave lenses in the glasses

    (5) cannot see distant objects

37. Contact lenses would be most appropriate for

    (1) people who suffer from myopia

    (2) people who suffer from hypermetropia

    (3) people who have either hypermetropia or myopia

    (4) people who are old

    (5) anyone with blurry vision

38. Like Earth, Mercury, the smallest planet, revolves around the Sun. It takes nearly 88 days to make one revolution around the Sun. Earth takes 365 to complete one revolution around the Sun. Earth completes one revolution on its own axis in 24 hours, or one day. Mercury, on the other hand, takes 58.5 Earth days to slowly make one turn on its axis. As a result,

    (1) Earth passes it in its revolutions around the Sun

    (2) the surface of Mercury is alternately baked by the Sun and frozen by outer space for long periods.

    (3) Mercury has shorter days than Earth

    (4) As compared to an Earth year, Mercury's year is longer.

    (5) Mercury travels around the Sun at a slower rate than Earh does

Choose the *one* best answer to each question.

Items 39–40 refer to the following passage.

Cholesterol is a substance that is essential for proper function of the cells in humans. It is carried through the body in the bloodstream by lipoproteins. The majority of the cholesterol in the blood is bound to low-density lipoprotein (LDL) and is refered to as LDL cholesterol. This is the major contributor to overall cholesterol levels. The higher this level, the more risk a person has of coronary artery disease. The remaining cholesterol is bound to high-density lipoprotein (HDL). HDL cholesterol actually seems to protect against the risk of coronary artery disease and lowers overall cholesterol. Most of a person's cholesterol is produced by the liver. A great deal of saturated fat in one's diet encourages the liver to produce large amounts of cholesterol.

39. You can infer from this passsage that
    (1) all cholesterol in the blood is bad
    (2) since cholesterol is produced in the liver, no one can control the levels of cholesterol
    (3) all fats are bad for the body
    (4) lowering your intake of saturated fats could help you control your cholesterol level
    (5) coronary artery disease is inescapable

40. People can help to protect themselves from coronary artery disease by
    (1) not eating any fat in their diet
    (2) increasing the amount of LDL cholesterol
    (3) increasing the amount of HDL cholesterol
    (4) only eating saturated fats
    (5) taking injections of high-density cholersterol

41. When rain falls, it will either run downhill over land or be absorbed into the soil. The flow of water on top of the ground forms streams and rivers. Streams and rivers usually begin in mountains or hills, and gravity gives them the energy to continue to flow downward. Erosion occurs as stones and sand are transported downstream to finally be deposited at the mouth of the river. Most erosion occurs during floods because
    (1) the faster the stream flows, the larger and more fragments it can carry
    (2) the water can't be absorbed into the soil
    (3) there is more gravity during a flood
    (4) the mouth of the river becomes enlarged
    (5) there are more streams and rivers during a flood

Choose the *one* best answer to each question.

Items 42–43 refer to the following table.

The animal group that includes spiders, scorpions, and their relatives is known as arachnids. They are classified as arthropods, a group that includes other joint-legged creatures such as crabs, shrimp, and insects.

All Arthropods	Arachnids
External skeleton	External skeleton
Single unit body	Body in two sections
Compound eyes	Simple eyes
Can have wings	No wings
Varying number of legs	Four pair of walking legs
Can have antennae	No antennae

42. According to the table, arthropods and arachnids are only alike in

    (1) the number of eyes they have

    (2) the number of legs they have

    (3) the use of antennae

    (4) the style of body they have

    (5) the skeletal system they have

43. The group known as arthropods

    (1) does not include arachnids

    (2) includes arachnids

    (3) does not include spiders

    (4) includes creatures with an internal skeletal structure

    (5) does not include crabs

44. When gas is compressed, the volume is inversely proportional to the pressure. Compression means that its volume is made to change at a constant termperature. Compressed gas is a store of potential energy. The molecules move continuously at various speeds and directions. Collisions with the walls of the container cause the pressure. Which of the following is NOT an example of compressed air

    (1) an air hose

    (2) a pneumatic drill

    (3) the wind

    (4) a jack hammer

    (5) a spray can

45. Air flowing over the top of a surface has to flow farther than that passing underneath the surface. The upper air speeds up, and its pressure falls. The higher pressure of the slower air below creates "lift." This principle is responsible for all types of aircraft. The lift on a wing depends on a variety of factors. The angle at which the wing meets the air is one factor. Generally, the greater the angle, the greater the lift. Other factors are placement of the wing on the aircraft and the thickness of the wing. A short but wide wing shape can create a great deal of lift. A light plane that provides good lift at low speeds would have

   (1) simple, thick wings

   (2) long, narrow wings

   (3) short wings

   (4) long, thick wings

   (5) narrow wings

Choose the *one* best answer to each question.

Items 46–47 refer to the following passage.

Blood pressure is the measure of the resistance to blood flow in the vessels and can affect the efficiency of the circulatory system. Blood pressure is normally taken in the main artery of the arm by wrapping a cuff around the upper part of the arm. The cuff is then inflated in order to stop the blood flow down the artery. When the cuff is slowly deflated, the return of flow can be measured by feeling for the pulse or by listening with a stethoscope. The pressure reading at this point is the peak, or systolic, pressure in the circulatory system. When the cuff is further deflated, the lowest, or diastolic pressure can be read. This is found in the pause between heartbeats. Generally, a normal reading would be below 140 for the systolic pressure, and below 90 for the diastolic pressure. High blood pressure is often associated with heart disease.

46. The systolic pressure

   (1) is measured in the pause between heartbeats

   (2) is the peak pressure in the circulatory system

   (3) should be below 90

   (4) is taken at the lowest deflation point

   (5) should be the same as the diastolic pressure

47. The diastolic pressure

   (1) should be below 140

   (2) cannot be read with a stethoscope

   (3) is measured in the pause between heartbeats

   (4) is the first, or highest, reading

   (5) is taken when the cuff is fully inflated

Answers

1. **(3)** Group 2 was the variable because it was the test group. This is the group that was only exposed to the sun for 2 hours each day. The scientist exerted more control over the amount of sunlight this group experienced.

2. **(2)** The Scientific Method requires that the hypothesis be tested several times in order to prove that it is supported. To validate a conclusion, an experiment must be repeated to ensure that the same results occur when the procedure is done the same way, under the same conditions.

3. **(5)** Both bacteria and viruses have the ability to adapt to their surroundings. Either has the ability to survive in almost any conditions. Although vaccinations and antibiotics can be helpful in fighting bacteria and viruses, not all strains or varieties are completely killed by treatment.

4. **(2)** Because not all strains of bacteria and viruses respond to treatment, scientists must treat separate diseases with different drugs.

5. **(1)** Because the three types of rocks are all formed differently under different conditions, they cannot all be found in the same locations. Some are formed below the surface of the earth, some come from volcanoes, and some are the result of weathering or the remains of living organisms that have been found in different locations.

6. **(4)** The South Pole would experience a polar climate. Although the temperature at the South Pole can vary, the climate is considered polar.

7. **(1)** The distribution of land and water and high and low ground are the factors that influence the components of weather: air temperature, barometric pressure, wind velocity, humidity, clouds, and precipitation.

8. **(3)** The climate of North America is considered variable because the weather is neither tropical nor polar. The weather changes from hot to cold and is not noted for being either for any great length of time.

9. **(5)** The skin is the system that is responsible for the temperature of the body, and it also excretes perspiration as waste when the body becomes too hot.

10. **(2)** The arteries and veins are part of the circulatory system whose job it is to pump blood to all parts of the body. The blood travels in the arteries and veins.

11. **(5)** The nervous and muscular systems were both involved when Joseph cut his finger and jerked his hand away. The nervous system received and responded to the external stimulus of the knife, and the muscular system responded to the signal from the nervous system and allowed him to move his finger.

12. **(2)** The smoke from industrial sites is brought to earth by rainfall, but then it evaporates with the water to return to the clouds where it becomes part of the cycle.

13. **(1)** Because the electrons are located outside the central nucleus of an atom, and because they are spread out in the surrounding space, they would be more likely to collide than the nuclei that are embedded inside the atom.

14. **(1)** The fulcrum placed between the load and the effort would illustrate the principle used for a child's seesaw since the balance is placed toward the center with the effort to push the load down on one end and the load on the opposite end.

15. **(3)** In a wheelbarrow, the fulcrum is placed at one end with the load in front of it. The effort must be in an upward motion to lift the load.

16. **(4)** In order to have a solution, there must be an interaction between the solute (in this case, sand) and the solvent, which would be water. The types of molecules in sand and water do not thoroughly mix.

17. **(3)** Club soda gets its characteristic bubbles, which identifies any carbonated liquid, from a mixture that includes the gas carbon dioxide.

18. **(5)** If the container dropped into the ocean developed a leak, the radioactive waste would seep out and mix with the oxygen in the water. After this occurs, it would continue to move through the water with the currents.

19. **(2)** Because the evaporation process removes water and leaves behind saline, the water in the Mediterranean Sea would become more dense.

20. **(1)** Although diet might help the pancreas to produce enough insulin, the injection of insulin would ensure that the proper amounts of insulin are continuously produced.

21. **(4)** Although minerals are made up of one or more elements, by definition, not all include crystals.

22. **(3)** The identifying factors of a mineral are its crystal shape, its cleavage, its hardness, its color, and its luster.

23. **(5)** As magma cools, the cooling process stops the flow. Ash, on the other hand, can be carried by winds to cover a much larger area than the lava.

24. **(2)** A meteor can appear from any direction at any time and burns itself out. A comet, however, has a distinct cycle of movement around the Sun.

25. **(4)** A meteor is a very small particle point of light that destroys itself through the process of friction before it falls to the earth, so it does not cause damage.

26. **(4)** Because some comets have very long periods or cycles, sometimes spanning decades, their cycles have not all been accurately identified yet.

27. **(1)** Seed bearing plants can either be annuals or perennials. Because trees continue to grow year after year, they are considered perennials.

28. **(4)** Plants produce their own food and so produce their own hormonal substances, which are responsible for their growth.

29. **(3)** If a right-handed person suffered a stroke that affected the left side of his brain, his right hand and his speech would also be affected because the left hemisphere controls both the right side of the body as well as speech.

30. **(1)** The human brain continues to grow from birth until about age 20. Because of this, there would be no change in the size or development of the brain between the ages of 25 and 30.

31. **(5)** The frontal lobes regulate voluntary movement and assist in language development, so a disease affecting the frontal lobes could affect a person's language functions.

32. **(3)** The cells that make up the brain are called neurons.

33. **(2)** If the radio dial is tuned to 89, this would mean that the waves are traveling at 89,000 waves per second because one kilohertz is equal to 1,000 waves per second. $1,000 \times 89 = 89,000$.

34. **(5)** BMR (basal metabolic rate) is tested and interpreted as the rate of a person's metabolism while at rest.

35. **(4)** BMR rises with exercise, and because metabolism is defined as the rate at which the body burns energy, raising the level of exercise would cause an increase in metabolism causing a person to lose weight more effectively.

36. **(1)** Hypermetropia is the condition of the eye that causes close objects to appear blurry, so those with this condition would have difficulty reading the print in a book. Reading glasses would serve to magnify the print and bring it into focus.

37. **(1)** Because contact lenses use a concave shape, they would be most appropriate for a person who suffers from myopia.

38. **(2)** The surface of Mercury is alternately baked by the Sun and frozen by outer space for long periods of time because it takes 58.5 Earth days to make one turn on its axis. This means that it would be facing either the Sun or outer space for approximately 29 hours at a time. On Earth, we spend significantly less time facing either the Sun or the Moon, the maximum being only approximately 12 hours.

39. **(4)** Because a large amount of saturated fat encourages the liver to produce more cholesterol, lowering your intake of saturated fats would inhibit this process in the liver.

40. **(3)** Because HDL cholesterol actually seems to protect against coronary artery disease, increasing this substance would help to ensure that coronary artery disease would not occur.

41. **(1)** During a flood situation, the flow of water down hills or mountains is significantly increased. Because there is more water and it is flowing faster, it has the potential of transporting more stones and sand.

42. **(5)** Arthropods and arachnids are alike only in that both groups have an external skeletal system.

43. **(2)** Although not all arthropods are arachnids, all arachnids are arthropods. Arachnids are a special group of anthropods with several different characteristics.

44. **(3)** The wind does not represent an example of compressed air because it is not in a container under pressure.

45. **(1)** A thick wing would produce more lift because there would be slower air underneath the thick wing, which would raise the pressure and create greater lift.

46. **(2)** The peak pressure is the systolic pressure and is taken when the cuff is still mostly inflated.

47. **(3)** The diastolic pressure is measured in the pause between heartbeats when the cuff is at its lowest point of deflation.

CHAPTER 6

Math

TEST-TAKING TIPS

Because the majority of the problems on the Math test are word problems, your ability to read and analyze the problem is critical for success. There are several steps to take in doing any math problem.

Make Sure You Read the Problem Carefully

Decide precisely what is being asked in the problem. Frequently, there will be a question at the end of the problem that will let you know exactly what is required for the answer. Reading the problem carefully will keep you from making careless mistakes. Although there will frequently be a question at the end of the problem, sometimes the question will be embedded within the problem. If you have not read carefully, you may miss what would have been an easy problem for you to solve simply because you didn't answer the right question about the problem. Try to solve the following problem:

> During a bake sale, Sally and her daughter sold a total of 50 pies. Sally sold 18 more pies than her daughter. How many pies did Sally sell?
>
> (1) 32
>
> (2) 16
>
> (3) 34
>
> (4) 13
>
> (5) 30

What was your answer? Did you choose (2)? If you did, you did not read the problem carefully. Sally's daughter sold 16 pies, but the problem stated that Sally sold 18 more pies than her daughter, so the correct answer would be (3). Let $x =$ the number of pies Sally's daughter sold, and $x + 18 =$ the number of pies Sally sold.

$$x + x + 18 = 50 \text{ (the total number of pies sold)}$$
$$2x + 18 = 50$$
$$\underline{-18 \quad -18}$$
$$2x = 32$$
$$x = 16$$
$$16 + 18 = 34$$

Decide What Procedures Will Be Required to Solve the Problem

Devise a plan of action for solving the problem. This will require that you decide how many operations the solution will need and in what order you will perform the operations.

Work Through the Problem Following the Steps You Outlined

Use your scratch paper to draw diagrams of geometry problems if they are not supplied within the text of the problem. Taking the time to draw a diagram is important to help you visualize the problem.

As with the other multiple-choice questions on the GED, you will be given a choice of 5 possible answers. With some of the problems, you will find that you can use the process of elimination to strike 1 or 2 answers immediately.

Use Your Knowledge of Estimation

When you are working on a problem, there will be times when you will be able to estimate the answer. This can be particularly helpful when time is at a premium. As you proceed through the problem, review the answers. You may have completed the problem sufficiently to estimate the correct answer without completing all the operations.

BASIC MATH

Whole numbers

Adding, subtracting, multiplying, and dividing are the four basic operations you will need to know to work with whole numbers.

Adding Whole Numbers

When you are adding whole numbers, make sure you set the numbers into a column so you will add them correctly. The numbers should be lined up so that the ones column (the column to the extreme right) is aligned. On your scratch paper, set up the following list of numbers: 36, 4, 182, 45, and 3720.

$$
\begin{array}{r}
4 \\
36 \\
45 \\
182 \\
+ 3720 \\
\end{array}
$$

You are now ready to add the columns. Always start the process by adding the numbers in the right-hand column. You will then work your way to the left for the final answer. Because you can only put one number in each column in your answer until you reach the extreme left, you might have to **carry** numbers to the next column and add them in with that column. When you add the first column of numbers in the above problem (4, 6, 5, 2, and 0), your answer is 17. This means that you will place the 7 under that column and add the 1 to the next column to the left.

$$
\begin{array}{r}
{}^{1}4 \\
36 \\
45 \\
182 \\
+\ 3720 \\
\hline
7
\end{array}
$$

You are now ready to move to the next column to the left in which you added the 1 and add those numbers (1, 3, 4, 8, and 2). Because the answer is 18 and you can only write the 8 in the appropriate column, you must once again carry the 1 to the next column to the left.

$$
\begin{array}{r}
{}^{1}4 \\
36 \\
{}^{1}45 \\
182 \\
+\ 3720 \\
\hline
87
\end{array}
$$

Adding the third column from the right, the answer is 9, and you can place the number in this answer column without having to carry a number.

$$
\begin{array}{r}
{}^{1}4 \\
36 \\
{}^{1}45 \\
182 \\
+\ 3720 \\
\hline
3987
\end{array}
$$

Because the fourth column from the right has only one number in it, that number 3 can simply be dropped into its proper column in the answer. The correct answer to this problem then is 3,987.

Practice

Write the following problems in columns and then add them.

1. 38 + 64   6. 60 + 183

2. 162 + 11   7. 5,874 + 79

3. 342 + 86   8. 97 + 149

4. 4,947 + 1,290   9. 9,672 + 6,328

5. 22 + 87   10. 74,132 + 4,278

Answers

1. 102	4. 6,237	7. 5,953	10. 78,410
2. 173	5. 109	8. 246	
3. 428	6. 243	9. 16,000	

Subtracting Whole Numbers

When you are subtracting, you are taking one number away from another. It is the opposite of adding. For example, $7 - 4 = 3$, or 7 take away 4 is 3. The numbers are aligned in columns just as they are in addition. Look at the following problem: $148 - 26$. Written in columns, the problem would appear as follows:

$$\begin{array}{r} 148 \\ -26 \\ \hline 122 \end{array}$$

In the above problem, you can easily take 6 away from 8 and 2 away from 4, but in some problems, you will be required to **borrow** from the next column in order to complete the problem. In the following problem, we will look at how to borrow to find the correct answer.

$$\begin{array}{r} 853 \\ -64 \\ \hline \end{array}$$

Because you cannot take 4 away from 3 or 6 away from 5, you must borrow 1 from each column to the left of those numbers. Now the problem looks like this:

$$\begin{array}{r} {}^{7}\cancel{8}\,{}^{14}\cancel{5}\,{}^{1}3 \\ -\quad 6\;4 \\ \hline 789 \end{array}$$

The 1 that was borrowed from the 5 is placed in front of the 3, making it 13 and leaving 4 in the next column to the left. Now, you can subtract 4 from 13 and the answer (9) is placed in the proper column below the line. Because you can't take 6 away from the 4 that is left, you must borrow again, this time from the 8 to the left. When you take the 1 from the 8, 7 remains, and the 1 that you borrowed is placed next to the 4 making it 14. Now you can complete the problem by subtracting 6 from 14 and placing the 8 in the proper column, and dropping the 7 to its proper place.

> **HINT:** A good way to check your subtraction is to ADD the numbers starting from the answer to the problem and working to the top. The sum of the bottom two numbers should be the same as the top number of the original subtraction problem.

789   (the bottom number or answer)

+ 64   (the middle number)

853   (the top number)

Practice

Write the following problems in columns and then subtract them checking your work as you proceed.

1. 87 – 62

2. 93 – 23

3. 648 – 44

4. 52 – 24

5. 73 – 29

6. 145 – 63

7. 4,822 – 638

8. 703 – 51

9. 860 – 482

10. 6,983 – 2,741

Answers

1. 25	4. 28	7. 4,184	10. 4,242
2. 70	5. 44	8. 652	
3. 604	6. 82	9. 378	

Multiplying Whole Numbers

The answer to a multiplication problem is called its **product**. Essentially, the process of multiplication is a simple way to add numbers a specified number of times. For example, the **product** of $6 \times 3 = 18$. You could have added 6 three times and the answer would be correct, but it is easier, especially for longer problems, to simply multiply 6 and 3. When you are multiplying, you will be required to use your knowledge of addition to complete the problems. Look at the problem below.

$$
\begin{array}{r}
\overset{2}{8}\overset{1}{3}6 \\
\times\ \ 72 \\
\hline
1672 \\
5852\quad \\
\hline
60192
\end{array}
$$

Note that this group of numbers is aligned with the second column.

Starting with the numbers on the extreme right, multiply 6×2. The product of this is 12. Because you can only write one number in this column, you must carry the 1 to the next column on the left. Then, multiply 3×2 and add the carried 1. This gives you 7, which is written in the next column. Finally, multiply 2×8. The product is 16, and because there are no more numbers to multiply in the top figure, simply align the 16 in the proper columns.

You are now ready to multiply the next number, which is 7. Again, because the product of 7×6 is 42, and because you must align the numbers in the correct columns, there is only space for the 2, and the 4 must be carried to the next column. Next, multiply 7×3, which gives you 21. You must now add the carried 4 to this number, making the new number 25. The 5 will be written in its line, and the 2 must be carried to the next column to the left. Finally, multiply 7×8 (equals 56) and add the carried 2 to make the final number 58. This is again written in columns.

Finally, to complete the problem, you will add the products, applying the technique of carrying when necessary.

> **HINT:** If you are multiplying by a number that ends with one or more zeros, you only have to multiply by the other numbers and add the correct number of zeros to the final answer.

Example: Find the product of 832×500.
Answer:

$$
\begin{array}{r}
8\overset{1}{3}2 \\
\times\ \ 5 \\
\hline
4160
\end{array}
$$

Because 500 has two zeros, simply add them to the answer. The correct answer to the problem then is 416,000.

Practice

Write the following problems, correctly aligning the columns, and find the product of each.

1. 28×5
2. 36×9
3. 48×62
4. 95×13
5. 367×17

6. 749×86
7. 40×15
8. 409×48
9. 567×231
10. 890×420

Answers

1. 140
2. 324
3. 2,976

4. 1,235
5. 6,239
6. 64,414

7. 600
8. 19,632
9. 130,977

10. 373,800

Dividing Whole Numbers

The opposite of multiplication is division. If $2 \times 5 = 10$, then $10 \div 2 = 5$. $10 \div 2 = 5$ can also be written

$$2\overline{)10} \quad \text{with } 5 \text{ on top}$$

There are several steps to completing a long division problem. Pay careful attention to each step in solving the example problem.

Find $324 \div 6$

$$\begin{array}{r} 5 \\ 6\overline{)324} \\ 30 \end{array}$$

Because 3 cannot be divided by 6, you must go to the next number and look at both numbers together. This means you will be looking at 32. 6 will divide into 32, 5 times ($6 \times 5 = 30$), so the 5 is written above the 2.

$$\begin{array}{r} 5 \\ 6\overline{)324} \\ \underline{30} \\ 24 \end{array}$$

Subtract 30 from 32 and bring the 4 straight down.

$$\begin{array}{r} 54 \\ 6\overline{)324} \\ \underline{30} \\ 24 \\ \underline{24} \\ 0 \end{array}$$

6 will divide into 24 ($6 \times 4 = 24$), so the 4 is written in its column. When you subtract 24 from 24, nothing is left, so you have completed the problem.

HINT: Check your work by multiplying the divisor (the number on the outside of the division symbol) times your answer. That number should be the same as the number inside the division symbol. In our example, $54 \times 6 = 324$, so we know the answer is correct.

As you work through the practice division problems, make sure you are following each step. Carefully check your multiplication and subtraction as you proceed.

Practice

1.	$176 \div 8$	6.	$836 \div 22$
2.	$336 \div 6$	7.	$2,128 \div 38$
3.	$328 \div 4$	8.	$364 \div 14$
4.	$434 \div 7$	9.	$2,992 \div 44$
5.	$520 \div 13$	10.	$1,860 \div 62$

Answers

1. 22	4. 62	7. 56	10. 30
2. 56	5. 40	8. 26	
3. 82	6. 38	9. 68	

Decimals

You use decimals in your daily life every time you make a purchase at a store. Most of us are familiar with decimals in terms of money. When you have $5.87, you have 5 whole dollars, 8 dimes (or 8 tenths of a dollar), and 7 cents (or 7 hundredths of a dollar).

When a number is written in decimal form, everything to the **left** of the decimal point is a whole number, and everything written to the **right** of the decimal point represents a part of the whole (a tenth, hundredth, thousandth, and so on).

Adding and Subtracting Decimals

The same procedure is used for setting up an addition or a subtraction problem using decimals. The numbers are placed in columns with the decimal points lined up. It is sometimes useful to add zeros to the ends of some numbers as place markers. Keep in mind that adding zeros to the end of a number does not change its value when you are working with decimals, but it will change the value of the number if the zero is placed in front of the number. For example, in terms of working with decimals, .5 is the same as .50 or .5000. A zero placed in front of a number, however, does change its meaning. .05 means five hundredths, and .5 means five tenths. Look at the following examples.

Add 3.4, 28.06, 6, and .2

```
03.40
28.06     Notice how the decimal points are lined
06.00     up throughout the problem and how zeros
00.20     were added as place markers.
37.66
```

Subtract 3.6 from 28.38

```
28.38     Notice that a zero was added to the
-3.60     second number as a place marker and
24.78     that the decimal points were lined up.
```

Practice

Solve the following problems, making sure that you have lined up the decimals and that you have used zeros as place markers if necessary.

Add:

1. 3.6 + 7.2
2. 0.83 + 0.6
3. 34.8 + .16
4. 4.98 + 2.78
5. 3.846 + 20.05

6. 3.040 + .74
7. 546.9 + .82
8. 6.954 + 30.71 + .630
9. 5.9 + .721 + 8
10. $4.67 + $22.00 + $1.20

Answers

1. 10.8	4. 7.76	7. 547.72	10. $27.87
2. 1.43	5. 23.896	8. 38.294	
3. 34.96	6. 3.78	9. 14.621	

Practice

Subtract:

1. 76.4 - 22.3
2. 87.39 - 38.52
3. 93.6 - 4.3
4. 56.2 - .623
5. 6.146 - 2.38

6. 80.50 - 30
7. 48.4 - 3.6
8. $35.00 - $.64
9. $43.89 - $1.98
10. $5.34 - $2.56

Answers

1. 54.1	4. 55.577	7. 44.8	10. $2.78
2. 48.87	5. 3.766	8. $34.36	
3. 89.3	6. 50.50	9. $41.91	

Multiplying Decimals

A multiplication problem dealing with decimals is set up and worked through in the same manner as a whole number problem. The only difference is that at the end of the problem, you must place the decimal point in the correct place in your answer. Keep in mind that a misplaced decimal point will render your answer wrong, so it is important to count off spaces carefully. The example below will show you how to decide where to place the decimal point in your answer.

$$
\begin{array}{r}
65.12 \\
\times\ 2.4 \\
\hline
26048 \\
13024\ \\
\hline
156.288
\end{array}
$$

Starting with the top number of the problem, count off the number of places **to the right** of the decimal point. In our example, there are two places. Then count off the number of places **to the right** of the decimal point in the second number. In our example, there is one place. Add the total number of places. There are three places in the example. This is the number of places that must be marked off in the answer. The correct answer for the example, then, is 156.288. If there are fewer numbers in the answer than the total number of places to be marked off, add zeros **to the left** of the last number. This is shown in the example below.

$$
\begin{array}{r}
6.19\ \ \text{(2 places)} \\
\times\ .002\ \ \text{(3 places)} \\
\hline
1238
\end{array}
$$

Because there must be five places in the final answer, a zero must be added before the 1. The correct answer, then would be .01238.

Set up and solve the following multiplication problems.

Practice

1. 25.6×6

2. 3.64×8

3. 49.1×2.3

4. 90.45×1.07

5. $6.094 \times .003$

6. $0.004 \times .45$

7. $3.821 \times .05$

8. $500 \times .005$

9. 0.982×0.15

10. 38×3.946

Answers

1. 153.6
2. 29.12
3. 112.93
4. 96.7815
5. .018282
6. .0018
7. .19105
8. 2.5
9. .1473
10. 149.948

Dividing Decimals by Whole Numbers

If you can divide whole numbers, you can divide decimals. The procedure is the same except for making sure that you correctly place the decimal point in your final answer. So that you don't forget this important step, it is helpful to place the decimal point before you even begin dividing. The decimal point will be placed directly above its place in the problem as in the example below.

246.4 ÷ 35

$$\begin{array}{r} 7.04 \\ 35\overline{)246.40} \\ \underline{245} \\ 1\ 40 \\ \underline{1\ 40} \end{array}$$

Note that because this problem would have had a remainder and because you can add a zero to the right of the last number, the division was carried out one step further to eliminate the remainder.

Dividing Whole Numbers by Decimals

In order to divide by a decimal, the decimal must be renamed as a whole number by moving the decimal point to the far right of the number. When you do this, you must also add a decimal point to the whole number and add as many zeros as places you moved the decimal point. Then you must move the decimal point to the far right of the last zero. Study the following example.

124 ÷ .62

$$.62\overline{)124}$$

$$.62\overline{)124.00}$$

$$\begin{array}{r} 200. \\ 62\overline{)12400.} \\ \underline{124} \\ 0\ 0 \\ \underline{0\ 0} \\ 0 \end{array}$$

Note that the decimal point in the answer is still lined up directly above the decimal in the body of the problem.

Practice

1. 7.60 ÷ 38
2. 545.4 ÷ 25
3. 306 ÷ 1.02
4. 288 ÷ .36
5. 128.57 ÷ 43
6. 3.00 ÷ 4
7. 1.20 ÷ 48
8. 36 ÷ .06
9. 36 ÷ .006
10. 672 ÷ .56

Answers

1. .2	4. 800	7. .025	10. 1,200
2. 21.816	5. 2.99	8. 600	
3. 300	6. .75	9. 6,000	

To divide a decimal by another decimal, move the decimal point in the number you are dividing by to rename it as a whole number. Then, move the decimal point in the number that is being divided the same number of places to the right.

Fractions

A fraction is a part of a whole. There are 10 dimes in each dollar, so one dime is one-tenth of a dollar. The fraction to represent one-tenth is written $\frac{1}{10}$. The top number of a fraction is called the **numerator**, and the bottom number is called the **denominator**. $\frac{1}{10}$ is a **proper fraction** or one in which the numerator is less than the denominator. An **improper fraction** is one in which the numerator is the same as or greater than the denominator. $\frac{12}{10}$ is an improper fraction. Sometimes you will see a whole number and a fraction together. This is called a **mixed number**. $4\frac{3}{5}$ is a mixed number. **Simplifying fractions** is the procedure you will use to bring the fraction to its simplest form. To reduce a fraction, you must divide the numerator *and* the denominator by the *same number*. The division must be done evenly with no remainders. Look at the following fraction:

$$\frac{10}{25}$$

The first step in simplifying this fraction is to figure out by which number the numerator and the denominator are divisible. Both can be divided by 5

$$\frac{10 \div 5 = 2}{25 \div 5 = 5}$$

HINT: Sometimes, you will be able to easily see by which number the numerator and the denominator can be divided, but always review your work to make sure the answer is in the lowest term. Look at the example below

$$\frac{12}{36}$$

In this problem, you may decide that the numerator and the denominator can both be divided evenly by 2.

$$\frac{12 \div 2 = 6}{36 \div 2 = 18}$$

When you look at the answer, you will note that $\frac{6}{18}$ has not been simplified to its simplest form, so you must repeat the division process. Now, it is easy to see that both numbers can be divided by 6.

$$\frac{6 \div 6 = 1}{18 \div 6 = 3}$$

Practice

Simplify the following fractions to their simplest form.

1. $\dfrac{5}{15}$

2. $\dfrac{8}{24}$

3. $\dfrac{16}{64}$

4. $\dfrac{12}{32}$

5. $\dfrac{6}{16}$

6. $\dfrac{9}{36}$

7. $\dfrac{22}{66}$

8. $\dfrac{7}{35}$

9. $\dfrac{36}{88}$

10. $\dfrac{42}{63}$

Answers

1. $\dfrac{1}{3}$

2. $\dfrac{1}{3}$

3. $\dfrac{1}{4}$

4. $\dfrac{3}{8}$

5. $\dfrac{3}{8}$

6. $\dfrac{1}{4}$

7. $\dfrac{1}{3}$

8. $\dfrac{1}{5}$

9. $\dfrac{9}{22}$

10. $\dfrac{2}{3}$

Renaming Improper Fractions as Whole or Mixed Numbers

An improper fraction is renamed as a whole or mixed number by dividing the numerator by the denominator. If there is a remainder when you divide, it is expressed as a fraction with the remainder as the numerator. The denominator remains the same as in the original fraction unless it needs to be simplified to simplest form.

$$\frac{125}{10}$$

$$
\begin{array}{r}
12 \\
10\overline{)125} \\
\underline{10} \\
25 \\
\underline{20} \\
5
\end{array}
$$

$\frac{125}{10}$ expressed as an improper fraction is $12\frac{5}{10}$. When the fraction is simplified to its simplest form, the answer is $12\frac{1}{2}$.

Practice

Rename the following improper fractions as whole or mixed numbers. Remember to simplify fractions to the simplest form.

1. $\frac{18}{8}$

2. $\frac{82}{7}$

3. $\frac{22}{11}$

4. $\frac{25}{4}$

5. $\frac{86}{10}$

6. $\frac{38}{4}$

7. $\frac{100}{20}$

8. $\frac{74}{32}$

9. $\frac{169}{13}$

10. $\frac{64}{5}$

Answers

1. $2\frac{1}{4}$

2. $11\frac{5}{7}$

3. 2

4. $6\frac{1}{4}$

5. $8\frac{3}{5}$

6. $9\frac{1}{2}$

7. 5

8. $2\frac{5}{16}$

9. 13

10. $12\frac{4}{5}$

Adding and Subtracting Fractions

In order to add or subtract fractions, they must have the **same** or a **common** denominator. The addition or subtraction process is done only with the numerator, and the denominator stays the same throughout the problem. This is illustrated in the following examples. The answer is then simplified to the simplest form.

Adding fractions with the same denominator

$$\frac{3}{7} + \frac{6}{7} = \frac{9}{7} = 1\frac{2}{7}$$

Subtracting fractions with the same denominator

$$\frac{5}{8} - \frac{1}{8} = \frac{4}{8} = \frac{1}{2}$$

Practice

Add or subtract the following fractions. Simplify your answer to the simplest term.

1. $\dfrac{5}{8} - \dfrac{3}{8}$

2. $\dfrac{3}{10} + \dfrac{9}{10}$

3. $\dfrac{2}{9} + \dfrac{4}{9}$

4. $\dfrac{9}{32} - \dfrac{3}{32}$

5. $\dfrac{3}{16} + \dfrac{5}{16}$

6. $\dfrac{3}{5} + \dfrac{4}{5}$

7. $\dfrac{23}{32} - \dfrac{10}{32}$

8. $\dfrac{7}{12} - \dfrac{5}{12}$

9. $\dfrac{13}{14} - \dfrac{3}{14}$

10. $\dfrac{3}{7} + \dfrac{6}{7}$

Answers

1. $\dfrac{1}{4}$

2. $1\dfrac{1}{5}$

3. $\dfrac{2}{3}$

4. $\dfrac{3}{16}$

5. $\dfrac{1}{2}$

6. $1\dfrac{2}{5}$

7. $\dfrac{13}{32}$

8. $\dfrac{1}{6}$

9. $\dfrac{5}{7}$

10. $1\dfrac{2}{7}$

Adding and Subtracting Mixed Numbers

When you must add or subtract mixed numbers and the fractions have common denominators, simply work with the whole numbers first and then proceed by adding or subtracting the fraction as in the examples below.

$$3\dfrac{1}{4} + 2\dfrac{1}{4}$$

Adding the whole numbers gives you 5.
Adding the fractions gives you $\dfrac{2}{4}$, which can be simplified to $\dfrac{1}{2}$.
The answer is $5\dfrac{1}{2}$.

$$8\dfrac{4}{5} - 4\dfrac{1}{5}$$

Subtracting the whole numbers gives you 4.
Subtracting the fractions gives you $\dfrac{3}{5}$.
The fraction cannot be simplified, so the answer is $4\dfrac{3}{5}$.

Practice

Add or subtract the following mixed numbers. Remember to simplify the fractions to the simplest form if necessary.

1. $6\frac{3}{8} + 2\frac{1}{8}$

5. $7\frac{7}{12} - 3\frac{5}{12}$

2. $8\frac{4}{5} + 3\frac{3}{5}$

6. $26\frac{7}{8} - 13\frac{1}{8}$

3. $14\frac{5}{16} - 4\frac{1}{16}$

7. $432\frac{3}{4} - 120\frac{1}{4}$

4. $9\frac{1}{2} + 8\frac{1}{2}$

8. $38\frac{5}{22} + 42\frac{3}{22}$

Answers

1. $8\frac{1}{2}$ 3. $10\frac{1}{4}$ 5. $4\frac{1}{6}$ 7. $312\frac{1}{2}$

2. $12\frac{2}{5}$ 4. 18 6. $13\frac{3}{4}$ 8. $80\frac{4}{11}$

Finding Common Denominators

Often you will find that you must rename one or both fractions in order to find the common denominator before you can proceed with solving the problem. For example, if you are asked to add $\frac{3}{4}$ and $\frac{1}{8}$, you would first have to change one denominator in order to make them the same. At a glance, you can see that 8 can be divided by 4, so your first step to solving the problem is to rename $\frac{3}{4}$ as a fraction that has 8 as the denominator. The first step is to ask yourself how many times 4 will go into 8. The answer is 2, so now you must *multiply* both the numerator **and** the denominator of the fraction by 2 as illustrated below.

$$\frac{3}{4} \times \frac{2}{2}$$
$$3 \times 2 = 6$$
$$4 \times 2 = 8$$

Your new fraction is $\frac{6}{8}$

To complete the problem, add $\frac{6}{8}$ and $\frac{1}{8}$. The answer to this problem is $\frac{7}{8}$.

Sometimes, you will need to rename both fractions in order to solve the problem. For example, if you were asked to add $\frac{1}{4}$ and $\frac{1}{3}$, you would have to rename both fractions because neither denominator can be divided evenly by the same number. You must find the **least common denominator** or the least number that both can be divided by evenly. In order to do this, first list the multiples of each denominator. In our example, the multiples of 4 are 4, 8, 12, 16, and so on. The multiples of 3 are 3, 6, 9, 12, 15, 18, and so on. The smallest multiple of each is 12, so that will become our new denominator. This will be the **least common denominator** of both fractions. Both fractions must now be renamed as fractions using 12 as the denominators.

$$\frac{1}{4} \times \frac{3}{3} = \frac{3}{12}$$ (Since 12 ÷ 4 = 3, the fraction is multiplied by $\frac{3}{3}$)

$$\frac{1}{3} \times \frac{4}{4} = \frac{4}{12}$$ (Since 12 ÷ 3 = 4, the fraction is multiplied by $\frac{4}{4}$)

Now, the two fractions, $\frac{3}{12}$ and $\frac{4}{12}$ can be added because they have the same denominator, and the answer is $\frac{7}{12}$.

Practice

Solve each problem by first finding the least common denominator.

1. $1\frac{1}{4} + \frac{2}{3}$

2. $\frac{2}{3} - \frac{1}{2}$

3. $\frac{1}{6} + \frac{3}{8}$

4. $2\frac{3}{4} + \frac{5}{6}$

5. $8\frac{2}{3} - \frac{4}{15}$

6. $7\frac{2}{3} - 2\frac{3}{8}$

7. $16\frac{1}{4} + 8\frac{2}{3}$

8. $12\frac{5}{6} - 3\frac{1}{18}$

9. $\frac{4}{7} - \frac{2}{10}$

10. $9\frac{1}{2} + 6\frac{3}{7}$

Answers

1. $1\frac{11}{12}$

2. $\frac{1}{6}$

3. $\frac{13}{24}$

4. $3\frac{7}{12}$

5. $8\frac{2}{5}$

6. $5\frac{7}{24}$

7. $24\frac{11}{12}$

8. $9\frac{7}{9}$

9. $\frac{13}{35}$

10. $15\frac{13}{14}$

Borrowing from Whole Numbers

Just as with some whole number subtraction problems, there are times when you will have to borrow to complete a fraction subtraction problem. Look at the following example.

$$20 - 3\frac{1}{3}$$

Because there is no fraction from which to subtract $\frac{1}{3}$, you must create a fraction by borrowing from 20. To do this, simply rename the 20 as $19\frac{3}{3}$. You have now borrowed from the whole number and renamed it as a fraction so you have something from which to subtract. The answer to this problem is $16\frac{2}{3}$.

Sometimes, your problem will be more complicated. In the following example, you must borrow from the whole number and add to the numerator in order to solve the problem.

$$5\frac{1}{3} - 2\frac{5}{12}$$

Your first step is to find the least common denominator, which in this case is 12.

$$\frac{1}{3} = \frac{4}{12}$$
$$5\frac{4}{12} - 2\frac{5}{12}$$

Because you can't subtract $\frac{5}{12}$ from $\frac{4}{12}$, you must borrow from the whole number 5 and add $\frac{12}{12}$ to the $\frac{4}{12}$ making the new number $4\frac{16}{12}$. Now you can easily solve your problem.

$$4\frac{16}{12} - 2\frac{5}{12} = 2\frac{11}{12}$$

Practice

Borrow where necessary to solve the following problems.

1. $4\frac{1}{3} - \frac{2}{3}$

2. $3\frac{1}{6} - \frac{1}{3}$

3. $30\frac{1}{2} - 4\frac{5}{8}$

4. $7 - 2\frac{3}{8}$

5. $12 - 4\frac{1}{4}$

6. $10 - 3\frac{4}{5}$

7. $18\frac{3}{4} - 4\frac{15}{16}$

8. $6\frac{1}{4} - 3\frac{7}{8}$

Answers

1. $3\frac{2}{3}$ 3. $25\frac{7}{8}$ 5. $7\frac{3}{4}$ 7. $13\frac{13}{16}$

2. $2\frac{5}{6}$ 4. $4\frac{5}{8}$ 6. $6\frac{1}{5}$ 8. $2\frac{3}{8}$

Renaming Fractions as Decimals

To rename a fraction as a decimal, divide the numerator by the denominator. Because the denominator is larger than the numerator, a decimal point and zeros must be added. In the example below, the fraction $\frac{3}{4}$ has been renamed as a decimal.

$$
\begin{array}{r}
.75 \\
4\overline{)3.00} \\
\underline{28} \\
20 \\
\underline{20} \\
0
\end{array}
$$

Note that the decimal point in the division has simply been moved in a straight line to the top of the problem.

Practice

Change the following fractions into decimals.

1. $\frac{4}{5}$

2. $\frac{1}{2}$

3. $\frac{7}{8}$

4. $\frac{1}{10}$

5. $\frac{2}{3}$

6. $\frac{3}{5}$

Answers

1. .80   3. .875   5. $.66\overline{6}$

2. .5   4. .1   6. .6

To multiply a fraction by a fraction, simply multiply the numerators, then multiply the denominators and finally, simplify the resulting fraction to the simplest form.

To multiply a fraction by a whole number, simply write the whole number as a fraction by using 1 as the denominator and proceed as if you were multiplying a fraction by a fraction.

To multiply a fraction by a mixed number, or to multiply two mixed numbers, rename the mixed numbers as improper fractions and proceed as if you were multiplying a fraction by a fraction.

Dividing common factors To make multiplying fractions easier, there are times when it is possible to divide common factors. Divide any numerator and any denominator *by the same number*. The division must come out evenly with no remainders. In the example below, you will see how this works.

$$\frac{5}{6} \times \frac{3}{10}$$

The numerator from the first fraction (5) and the denominator from the second fraction (10) can both be divided by 5, and the denominator from the first fraction (6) and the numerator from the second fraction (3) can both be divided by 3.

Our new multiplication problem now looks like this:

$$\frac{1}{2} \times \frac{1}{2} = \frac{1}{4}$$

Practice

Solve the following multiplication problems. Remember to divide common factors wherever possible to make the process easier. Simplify your answer to its simplest form.

1. $12 \times \frac{4}{9}$

2. $8 \times 3\frac{2}{3}$

3. $18 \times \frac{1}{3}$

4. $\frac{4}{5} \times \frac{3}{8}$

5. $2\frac{8}{9} \times 1\frac{5}{16}$

6. $6\frac{3}{4} \times \frac{30}{31}$

7. $\frac{5}{6} \times \frac{4}{5}$

8. $3\frac{3}{5} \times 2\frac{1}{10}$

9. $\frac{2}{3} \times \frac{5}{7}$

10. $4\frac{1}{2} \times 16$

Answers

1. $5\frac{1}{3}$

2. $29\frac{1}{3}$

3. 6

4. $\frac{3}{10}$

5. $3\frac{19}{24}$

6. $6\frac{33}{62}$

7. $\frac{2}{3}$

8. $7\frac{14}{25}$

9. $\frac{10}{21}$

10. 72

Dividing Fractions

If you can multiply fractions, you can divide fractions. To divide two fractions, multiply by the reciprocal of the divisor. The reciprocal of a fraction means to turn it upside down. This means that the denominator, now becomes the numerator. If you were to write the reciprocal of the fraction $\frac{4}{5}$, the new fraction would be $\frac{5}{4}$.

If you were dividing mixed numbers, first convert them to improper fractions and then follow the procedure.

To divide a fraction by a whole number, first rename the whole number as a fraction and use its reciprocal. For example, if you were dividing by the number 6, you would rename it as the fraction $\frac{6}{1}$ and then use its reciprocal, $\frac{1}{6}$.

Practice

Solve the following division problems. Simplify your answer to the simplest form.

1. $\frac{1}{2} \div \frac{1}{4}$

2. $4 \div \frac{1}{5}$

3. $\frac{2}{3} \div 6$

4. $8\frac{1}{4} \div \frac{3}{4}$

5. $1\frac{3}{5} \div 3\frac{9}{10}$

6. $5\frac{2}{5} \div 3\frac{1}{5}$

7. $8 \div \frac{8}{9}$

8. $\frac{1}{3} \div \frac{5}{6}$

9. $4\frac{1}{3} \div 2\frac{2}{7}$

10. $6\frac{1}{5} \div \frac{1}{15}$

Answers

1. 2

2. 20

3. $\frac{1}{9}$

4. 11

5. $\frac{16}{39}$

6. $1\frac{11}{16}$

7. 9

8. $\frac{2}{5}$

9. $1\frac{43}{48}$

10. 93

Percents

A percent is a fraction or a decimal in a different form. A percent expressed as a fraction is the number divided by 100. For example, 25% written as a fraction is $\frac{25}{100}$ or $\frac{1}{4}$. 25% written as a decimal is .25. The number before the percent sign is the numerator of the fraction. The denominator *is always 100*. To rename a fraction as a percent, first rename it as a decimal by dividing the numerator by the denominator. Remember that this is done by adding a decimal point and two zeros to the numerator. Using our example from above, the problem would look like this

$$
\begin{array}{r}
.25 \\
4{\overline{\smash{\big)}\,1.00}} \\
\underline{8} \\
20 \\
\underline{20} \\
0
\end{array}
$$

To rename a percent as a decimal, simply remove the percent sign (%) and insert the decimal point two places *to the left*. For example, 45% written as a decimal is .45. If there is a fraction with the percent as in $45\frac{1}{2}\%$, rename the fraction as a decimal first and then move the decimal point two places to the left. $45\frac{1}{2}\%$ becomes 45.5% and then .455. If the number in the percent has only one digit, a zero is "added" to the left of the number so that there are enough spaces to insert the decimal point. For example, if you were to rename 4% as a decimal, you would need to "add" a zero to the left of the 4 so that you could insert the decimal point two spaces. 4% expressed as a decimal, is .04.

To rename a decimal as a percent, simply reverse the process moving the decimal point two places *to the right*. If there are not two places to the right, as in 2.3, you must "add" a zero to make two spaces. 2.3 becomes 230% when renamed as a percent.

Practice

Rename the percents to decimals and the decimals to percents.

1. .87

2. $24\frac{1}{2}\%$

3. 18%

4. 364%

5. .623

6. 3.8

7. 6%

8. 22%

Answers

1. 87%	3. .18	5. 62.3%	7. .06
2. .245	4. 3.64	6. 380%	8. .22

Practice

Rename the percents to fractions and the fractions to percents.

1. 62%

2. 8%

3. $\frac{4}{5}$

4. 13%

5. $\frac{1}{10}$

6. $\frac{2}{5}$

7. $\frac{1}{8}$

8. 50%

Answers

1. $\frac{31}{50}$

2. $\frac{2}{25}$

3. 80%

4. $\frac{13}{100}$

5. 10%

6. 40%

7. $12\frac{1}{2}\%$

8. $\frac{1}{2}$

Every percent problem is made up of four parts: the **part**, the **whole**, the **percent**, and **100**. The problem will give you information on three of the four parts, and you will have to solve the problem by finding the fourth part. An easy way to deal with percent problems is to set up a grid for yourself to decide which part is missing and then to solve for that missing part. The grid should be arranged as in the example below.

The arrangement of the sections of a percent problem will always remain the same.

part	percent
whole	100

The 100 will *always* be in the lower right-hand corner. The percent is the number with the percent sign (%) after it, but it is written in its place without the percent sign. In order to find the whole, **look for the word "of"** in the problem. The figure representing the part is often **near the word "is."**

Once you have set up your problem in the proper order, solve the problem by multiplying the diagonals that have been filled in. Finally, you will divide by the remaining number in your grid. Look at the examples below.

Finding the Percent

30 is what percent of 50?

30	?
50	100

Notice that the word "of" is by the 50, so that is the whole, and the word "is" is by the 30, so that is the part. There is no percent sign in the problem, so that is what you are looking for.

Multiply the numbers that fill in the grid diagonally.

100
× 30
3000

Now, divide by the leftover number.

3000 ÷ 50 = 60

30 is 60% of 50

Finding the Whole

25% of what number is 80?

80	25
?	100

Notice that the percent is the number with the %, and the part (80) has the word "is" near it. The whole, or the number near the word "of," is missing.

Multiply the numbers that fill in the grid diagonally.

100
× 80
8000

Divide by the leftover number in the grid.

8000 ÷ 25 = 320

25% of 320 is 80

Finding the Part

75% of 200 is what number?

?	75
200	100

The percent (75) is the number with % by it, and the whole (200) is the number near the word "of." The part, or the number near the word "is" missing.

Multiply the numbers that fill in the grid diagonally.

200
×75
15,000

Divide by the leftover number in the grid.

15,000 ÷ 100 = 150

75% of 200 is 150

Practice

Set up a grid and solve each of the following percent problems.

1. 30% of 300 is what number?

2. What % of 60 is 12?

3. 15 is 25% of what number?

4. 15% of 240 is what number?

5. What % of 125 is 25?

6. What % of 300 is 15?

7. 20% of 75 is what number?

8. 48 is 20% of what number?

9. 60 is 10% of what number?

10. What % of 250 is 25?

Answers

1. 90	4. 36	7. 15	10. 10%
2. 20%	5. 20%	8. 240	
3. 60	6. 5%	9. 600	

Test Yourself

The majority of problems you will encounter will be word problems. Each problem will give you a choice of 5 possible answers, and your job is to decide which is the **best** answer. Sometimes, there will be no correct answer. If, however, one of the answer selections is "Not enough information is given," don't assume that this will be the correct answer.

There will also be times when you are given more information than needed to solve the problem. One of your tasks is to decide what information is necessary and what information can be ignored when solving the problem.

Reading each problem carefully is the best way to ensure that you will answer the question correctly. Certain key words will often be included in the body of the problem, and these words will give you a clue as to which basic math operation you will use to solve the problem.

- **sum, total**—addition
- **difference**—subtraction
- **product, of**—multiplication
- **quotient, average, each**—division

For each word problem below, choose the *one best answer*. Remember to read carefully and to decide which operations are necessary to solve the problems. In a multistep problem, you may have to choose more than one operation to complete the problem.

1. If Susan earns $6 an hour, how much does she earn in a 40-hour work week?

    (1) $240

    (2) $360

    (3) $200

    (4) $180

    (5) $64

2. A bolt of fabric contains 165 yards of material. If 38 yards were cut off, how much is left over?

    (1) 130 yards

    (2) 120 yards

    (3) 127 yards

    (4) 117 yards

    (5) 107 yards

3. When Ms. Gomez checked out at the grocery store, she had purchased a frozen dinner at $2.49, a bag of apples at $1.99, a dozen eggs at $.79, and a gallon of milk at $1.39. If she gave the clerk $20.00, how much change should she receive?

    (1) $15.00

    (2) $13.50

    (3) $11.34

    (4) $13.34

    (5) $12.89

4. Mr. Johnson bought 24 feet of pvc pipe at the hardware store for a total of $96.00. How much did he pay for each foot of pipe?

    (1) $3.00

    (2) $6.50

    (3) $4.00

    (4) $12.00

    (5) $8.75

5. If potatoes are on sale at $.75 a pound, how much would 6.8 pounds of potatoes cost?

    (1) $6.20

    (2) $5.10

    (3) $4.80

    (4) $5.75

    (5) Insufficient data is given to solve the problem

6. Joe earns $7.50 an hour when he works on weekdays and time-and-a-half an hour when he works on the weekend. Last week, he worked 40 hours Monday through Friday and 6 hours on Saturday. How much did he earn for the week?

    (1) $400.75

    (2) $350.00

    (3) $367.50

    (4) $300.00

    (5) $364.50

7. Jason ate $\frac{1}{3}$ of a pizza for dinner and his brother ate $\frac{1}{6}$ of the pizza. How much of the pizza was left over for their sister?

    (1) $\frac{1}{3}$

    (2) $\frac{1}{6}$

    (3) $\frac{2}{3}$

    (4) $\frac{1}{2}$

    (5) $\frac{5}{6}$

8. Cathy bought $5\frac{1}{2}$ pounds of chicken for $1.99 a pound and $3\frac{2}{3}$ pounds of pork chops. How much more chicken did she purchase than pork chops?

    (1) $1\frac{5}{6}$

    (2) $2\frac{1}{3}$

    (3) $2\frac{1}{6}$

    (4) $1\frac{2}{3}$

    (5) $2\frac{1}{2}$

9. Zachary rode his bike $23\frac{3}{10}$ miles the first week in September and $12\frac{1}{8}$ miles the second week. How many miles did he ride during these two weeks?

    (1) $35\frac{17}{40}$

    (2) $35\frac{1}{2}$

    (3) $35\frac{2}{9}$

    (4) $35\frac{3}{8}$

    (5) $35\frac{5}{16}$

10. The gas tank of a large truck holds a total of 64 gallons of gas. If the tank is $\frac{5}{8}$ full, how many gallons of gas would be in the tank?

   (1) $32\frac{1}{2}$

   (2) 40

   (3) $38\frac{1}{8}$

   (4) $63\frac{1}{2}$

   (5) $40\frac{1}{2}$

11. A professional baseball player attempted to hit 88 pitches during one practice session. Of those, he hit only 22 of those pitches. What percent of the practice pitches did he hit?

   (1) 22%

   (2) 28%

   (3) 25%

   (4) 30%

   (5) 46%

12. Gretchen was shopping for a new coat. At one department store, the original price of a coat was $79.00, and it was on sale for 30% off the original price. At another store, the same coat was originally $65.00, and it was on sale for 10% off the original price. After taking the discounts, what was the price of the least expensive coat?

   (1) $58.50

   (2) $58.30

   (3) $55.50

   (4) $55.30

   (5) Insufficient data is given to solve the problem

13. The value of a new computer decreases 20% each year. If Mr. Wiley originally purchased his computer for $1,500.00, what would be its value at the end of the second year he owned it?

   (1) $1,200

   (2) $900

   (3) $960

   (4) $950

   (5) $1,000

14. Dr. Martinez spends $\frac{1}{2}$ of his time seeing patients in his office and $\frac{2}{5}$ of his time at the hospital. How much time is left for him to complete his paperwork?

   (1) $\frac{1}{10}$

   (2) $\frac{2}{5}$

   (3) $\frac{1}{5}$

   (4) $\frac{3}{5}$

   (5) $\frac{3}{10}$

15. A 25-pound bag of fertilizer costs $28.30. How much does each pound cost? (Round your answer to the nearest penny.)

   (1) $1.14

   (2) $1.25

   (3) $1.30

   (4) $1.12

   (5) $1.13

16. Marlene and Rose own a florist shop. In 1997, their profits totaled $16,873.00. In 1998, they made $18,728.90; and in 1999, the profits totaled $20,159.30. If the profits are split evenly, how much did each make over the three-year period?

   (1) $17,832.45

   (2) $27,880.60

   (3) $20,780.60

   (4) $22,562.45

   (5) $21,808.60

17. Jennifer is planning on making a new dress. She will need $3\frac{3}{4}$ yards of fabric, which is on sale for $2.50 a yard. She will also need a zipper that costs $1.99, 2 packs of buttons that cost $1.49 each, and a spool of thread that costs $0.89. How much will the dress cost her to make?

   (1) $13.75

   (2) $15.24

   (3) $14.35

   (4) $14.00

   (5) $13.25

18. A recipe for chocolate cake calls for $3\frac{2}{3}$ cups of flour and $1\frac{1}{2}$ cups of sugar. If Ann wanted to triple the recipe, how much flour would she need?

    (1) $4\frac{1}{2}$

    (2) $9\frac{2}{3}$

    (3) 11

    (4) 8

    (5) 9

19. Paul wants to make birdhouses to sell at a craft show. How many birdhouses can he make from $26\frac{3}{4}$ feet of lumber if each birdhouse takes $3\frac{1}{2}$ feet?

    (1) 4

    (2) 8

    (3) 6

    (4) 7

    (5) 9

20. Maria is making bows for party favors. She has $13\frac{1}{3}$ yards of ribbon to make the bows. If she wants to make 40 bows, how many yards of ribbon will each bow use?

    (1) 3

    (2) $\frac{1}{3}$

    (3) $3\frac{1}{3}$

    (4) $2\frac{2}{3}$

    (5) Insufficient data is given to solve the problem

Answers

1. **(1)** Multiply $6 \times 40 = \$240$.

2. **(3)** Subtract $165 - 38 = 127$.

3. **(4)** Add each item then subtract the total from $20.00.

   $$\begin{array}{r} \$2.49 \\ 1.99 \\ .79 \\ +\,1.39 \\ \hline \$6.66 \end{array} \qquad \begin{array}{r} \$20.00 \\ -\,6.66 \\ \hline \$13.34 \end{array}$$

4. **(3)** Divide $96.00 by 24.

   $$\begin{array}{r} 4.00 \\ 24\overline{)96.00} \\ \underline{96} \\ 0 \end{array}$$

5. **(2)** Multiply 6.8 times \$0.75. Count off three places to the left for the decimal point.

   $$\begin{array}{r} 6.8 \\ \times.75 \\ \hline 340 \\ \underline{476} \\ 5.100 \end{array}$$

6. **(3)** To determine Joe's time and a half pay, divide \$7.50 by 2 (\$3.75) and add to the \$7.50 he usually makes an hour. His time and a half rate is \$11.25. Multiply \$7.50 times 40, then multiply \$11.25 times 6. Finally, add these two figures together.

   $$\begin{array}{r} 7.50 \\ \times 40 \\ \hline 300.00 \end{array} \qquad \begin{array}{r} 11.25 \\ \times \quad 6 \\ \hline 67.50 \end{array} \qquad \begin{array}{r} \$300.00 \\ +\,67.50 \\ \hline \$367.50 \end{array}$$

7. **(4)** Add the fractions, then subtract the total from the whole.

   $$\begin{array}{r} \frac{1}{3} = \frac{2}{6} \\ +\,\frac{1}{6} = \frac{1}{6} \\ \hline \frac{3}{6} = \frac{1}{2} \end{array} \qquad \begin{array}{r} \frac{2}{2} \\ -\,\frac{1}{2} \\ \hline \frac{1}{2} \end{array}$$

8. **(1)** Subtract $3\frac{2}{3}$ from $5\frac{1}{2}$.

   $$\begin{array}{r} 5\frac{1}{2} = \\ -\,3\frac{2}{3} = \\ \hline \end{array} \qquad \begin{array}{r} 5\frac{3}{6} = \\ -\,3\frac{4}{6} = \\ \hline \end{array} \qquad \begin{array}{r} 4\frac{9}{6} \\ -\,3\frac{4}{6} \\ \hline 1\frac{5}{6} \end{array}$$

9. **(1)** Add the fractions.

$$23\frac{3}{10}= \qquad 23\frac{12}{40}$$

$$+12\frac{1}{8}= \qquad +12\frac{5}{40}$$

$$\overline{\qquad\qquad} \qquad \overline{35\frac{17}{40}}$$

10. **(2)** Multiply 64 times $\frac{5}{8}$.

$$\frac{64}{1}\times\frac{5}{8}=\frac{8}{1}\times\frac{5}{1}=\frac{40}{1}=40$$

11. **(3)** Multiply the part (22) times 100, then divide by the whole (88).

22	?
88	100

12. **(4)** Multiply $79.00 times 30% and subtract the answer from $79.00. Then multiply $65.00 times 10% and subtract the answer from $65.00

$79.00	$79.00	$65.00	$65.00
× .30	−23.70	× .10	− 6.50
$23.70	$55.30	$ 6.50	$58.50

13. **(3)** Multiply $1,500.00 times 20%. Subtract your answer from $1,500.00. Multiply that answer times 20% and subtract your answer again.

$1,500.00	$1,500.00	$1,200.00	$1,200.00
× .20	− 300.00	× .20	− 240.00
$ 300.00	$ 1,200.0	$ 240.00	$ 960.00

14. **(1)** Add the fractions, then subtract from the whole.

$$\frac{1}{2}= \qquad \frac{5}{10} \qquad \frac{10}{10}$$

$$+\frac{2}{5}= \qquad +\frac{4}{10} \qquad -\frac{9}{10}$$

$$\overline{\qquad\qquad} \qquad \overline{\frac{9}{10}} \qquad \overline{\frac{1}{10}}$$

15. **(5)** Divide $28.30 by 25.

$$\begin{array}{r} 1.13 \\ 25\overline{)28.30} \\ \underline{25} \\ 3\,3 \\ \underline{2\,5} \\ 80 \\ \underline{75} \\ 5 \end{array}$$

16. **(2)** Add the three figures, then divide by 2.

$16,873.00 $55,761.20 ÷ 2 = $27,880.60
 18,728.90
+ 20,159.30
$55,761.20

17. **(2)** Rename $3\frac{3}{4}$ as the decimal 3.75. Multiply 3.75 times $2.50, multiply $1.49 times 2, then add the totals to the other figures.

3.75	$1.49	$9.38
× 2.50	× 2	1.99
18750	$2.98	2.98
750		.89
9.3750		$15.24

18. **(3)** Multiply

$$3\frac{2}{3} \times 3 = \frac{11}{3} \times \frac{3}{1} = \frac{33}{3} = 11$$

19. **(4)** Divide $26\frac{3}{4}$ by $3\frac{1}{2}$

$$26\frac{3}{4} \div 3\frac{1}{2} = \frac{107}{14} \times \frac{2}{7} = \frac{107}{14} = 7.64$$

20. **(2)** Divide $13\frac{1}{3}$ by 40

$$\frac{40}{3} \div \frac{40}{1} = \frac{40}{3} \times \frac{1}{40} = \frac{1}{3}$$

ANALYZING DATA

Graphs, Tables, and Charts

You will find graphs, tables, and charts in the Math section of the GED, but they might also appear in the Science and Social Studies sections. Always read the title of the graph before you begin. The title will give you the information concerning the graph that will enable you to decide what is being compared or shown. It is important to know how to analyze the information in bar graphs, line graphs, and picture and circle graphs.

Bar Graphs

Bar graphs will appear as single, double, or combination illustrations, but they are basically read the same way.

Look at the graph below:

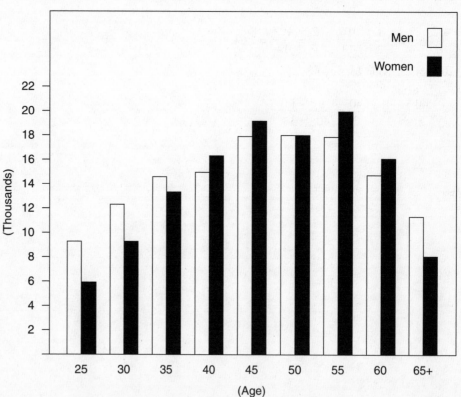

Dentists in Kansas by Age and Sex, 1983

At what age were the number of male and female dentists equal? Look at the graph and see where the white and black bars are the same, then look at the figures at the bottom of the chart to see the age. The number of male and female dentists were equal at age 50.

How many female dentists were there in Kansas who were 40 years old? Look at the black bar representing age 40, then look horizontally to the left to see how many thousands of female dentists there were. The bar stops approximately at 16, so there were approximately 16 thousand female dentists who were 40 years old.

How many more male dentists were there at age 30 than female dentists? The bar for male dentists at age 30 reaches approximately 12,000, and the bar for female dentists reaches approximately 9,000, so there were approximately 3,000 more male than female dentists.

Line Graphs

Line graphs are used to show changes in terms of trends. If more than one line is on a graph, it shows a comparison of two changing amounts. Look at the line graph below.

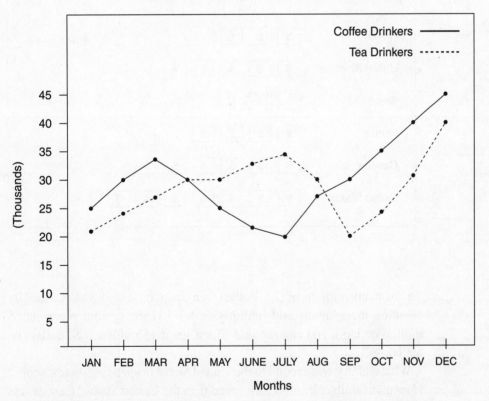

Number of Coffee and Tea Drinkers over 12 months

What was the month showing the most consumption of coffee? Look at the solid line and follow it to the highest point on the graph then look to the bottom of the graph to see the month. The month with the highest consumption of coffee is December.

At what month was the consumption of coffee and tea the same? Look at the graph to see at what point the solid and broken lines intersect with a dot, then look to the bottom of the graph to identify the month. April is the month with identical consumption of coffee and tea.

Which months show the lowest point of coffee and tea consumption? How many thousands were drinking coffee and tea during these months? The lowest point for coffee consumption was in July, and the lowest for tea was in September. Both reflect approximately 20,000 drinkers.

Picture Graphs

A picture graph uses appropriate symbols to represent information. Counting the number of pictures or the partial pictures gives you the information needed. Look at the picture graph below.

Amount Spent on Textbooks at College Level, 1996

$	5 Million U.S. Dollars

China	$ $ $
United Kingdom	$ $ $ $ $
Italy	$ $
France	$ $ $ $
Canada	$ $ $ $ $ $
United States	$ $ $ $ $ $ $ $

How many millions of U.S. dollars were spent on textbooks in China? By counting the symbols and multiplying by 5 (each symbol represents 5 million dollars), you can see that China spent 15 million U.S. dollars on textbooks.

What country was second to the United States in spending on textbooks? How many dollars less did they spend than the United States? Canada was second to the United States, spending 30 million dollars, while the United States spent 35.5 million. Canada spent 5.5 million dollars less than the United States.

Which country spent the least amount on textbooks? Italy has only two symbols, so they spent the least amount.

Circle Graphs

Circle graphs are sometimes referred to as pie charts. They show the parts or pieces of a whole. Most often, the parts are percents of the whole. The pieces or parts of the pie or circle add up to 100%. Look at the circle graph below.

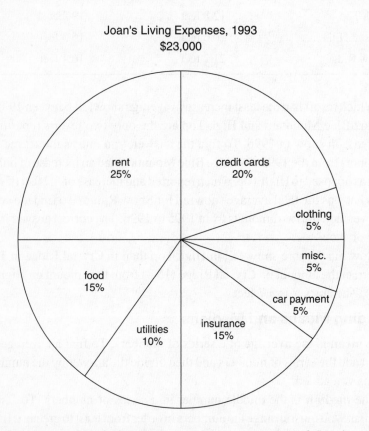

Joan's Living Expenses, 1993
$23,000

Each item on the circle graph represents a percent of Joan's salary ($23,000) for 1993. To find out how much Joan spent on each item, multiply the percent, renamed as a decimal, and her total salary. For example, to find how much money Joan spent on rent, multiply $23,000 and .25. She spent $5,750 on rent.

What was the difference between the percent Joan spent on clothing and food? Subtract 5% from 15%. Joan spent 10% more on food than she did on clothing.

What fraction of Joan's salary was spent on credit cards? Change 20% into a fraction by using 20 as the numerator and 100 (the total amount) as the denominator. She spent $\frac{20}{100}$ or $\frac{1}{5}$ of her salary on credit cards.

Tables

Generally, a table will have rows and columns that represent specific information. If you take public transportation, you are already familiar with time tables.

Look at the table below.

Average Yearly Snowfall for Ski Resorts

Resort	1995	1996
Blue Mountain	14.8 feet	18.6 feet
High Top	12.8 feet	19 feet
Crystal Hill	20.6 feet	15.3 feet
Snow Ridge	21.2 feet	16.4 feet

Which resort had the least increase in average snowfall between 1995 and 1996? Blue Mountain and High Top are the only two resorts reporting an increase in snow in 1996. To find the answer, you must subtract the 1996 amounts from the 1995 amounts. Blue Mountain had an increase of only 3.8 feet as opposed to High Top, which reported and increase of 6.2 feet of snow.

What was the total average snowfall for Snow Ridge? To find the correct answer, add the two amounts from 1995 to 1996. The correct answer is 37.6 feet of snow.

How much more snow fell in High Top than in Crystal Ridge in 1996? Subtract the amount on Crystal Ridge (15.3) from the amount on High Top (19). The answer is 3.7 feet.

Finding Means and Medians

The **mean** is the **average** of a series of numbers. To find an average, you must add the series of numbers and then divide the answer by the number of items you added.

The **median** is the middle number in a series of numbers. To find the median, you must arrange the numbers in order from least to greatest. If there is an odd number of items, the number in the middle is the median. If there is an even number, the two middle numbers are averaged together to find the median.

Find the average price per pound of the following varieties of apples.

McIntosh—$.89 per pound

Winesap—$.96 per pound

Granny Smith—$.79 per pound

Delicious—$.85

Johnathan—$.89

Add the prices.

```
$ .89
  .96
  .79
  .85
+ .89
$ 4.38
```

Now, because there are five varieties in the list, divide the answer by 5.

$4.38 \div 5 = .876$

The average price of the apples is $.88 (money is always rounded up to the nearest penny).

Joseph received the following scores on his social studies tests last year: 86, 92, 88, 76, 94, 78, 80, 90. What was his median score?

First, arrange the numbers in order with the least score first.

76, 78, 80, 86, 88, 90, 92, 94

Because there is an even number of scores (8), you must average the two middle scores to find the median.

$86 + 88 = 174$
$174 \div 2 = 87$

87 is Joseph's median score.

Ratio and Proportion

A **ratio** is a way of comparing two numbers. The win/loss record of a football team is usually expressed as a ratio. For example, if a team won 4 games and lost 5 games, their record would be expressed as 4 to 5. This ratio can also be written 4:5 or $\frac{4}{5}$. When setting up a ratio, the first number expressed is the first number written in the ratio. Because ratios are really fractions, they should be simplified to their simplest form. If the team in the above example won 5 games and lost 10, the ratio would be written 1:2 or $\frac{1}{2}$ because the fraction $\frac{5}{10}$ can be simplified.

A **proportion** is also a comparison. It is a comparison of two equal ratios. Look at the proportion below.

$$\frac{6}{8} = \frac{3}{4} \qquad 6:8 = 3:4$$

These ratios are proportions because they are equal in their relationships. Six is $\frac{3}{4}$ of eight and three is $\frac{3}{4}$ of four. An easy way to deal with proportions is to draw a grid similar to the one you used for figuring percents.

6	3
8	4

If you multiply the numbers that are diagonally placed from each other, they will be the same. $6 \times 4 = 24$ and $8 \times 3 = 24$.

If one part of the proportion were missing, you would solve the missing part in the same manner that you solved a missing part in a percent problem.

6	?
8	4

To solve for the missing number, first multiply diagonally, then divide by the remaining number. $6 \times 4 = 24$. $24 \div 8 = 3$.

Practice

Express the following items as ratios. Make sure you simplify them to their simplest form. Write each ratio three ways.

1. 3 men to 12 women

2. 100 apples to 50 oranges

3. 4 feet to 6 feet

4. 24 winners to 8 losers

Find the unknown values in each of the following proportions.

5. 11:12 = ?:36

6. 12:8 = 3:?

7. 3:? = 24:32

8. ?:15 = 64:40

Answers

1. 1 to 4, 1:4, $\frac{1}{4}$

2. 2 to 1, 2:1, $\frac{2}{1}$

3. 2 to 3, 2:3, $\frac{2}{3}$

4. 3 to 1, 3:1, $\frac{3}{1}$

5. 33

6. 2

7. 4

8. 24

Test Yourself

Questions 1–4 refer to the following graph.

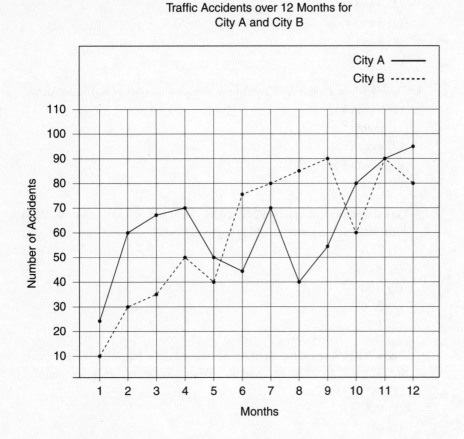

Traffic Accidents over 12 Months for
City A and City B

1. In which month did City A and City B have the same number of traffic accidents?

    (1) month 3

    (2) month 8

    (3) month 11

    (4) month 5

    (5) month 2

2. What is the *difference* in the number of traffic accidents between City A and City B in the second month?

    (1) 30

    (2) 25

    (3) 10

    (4) 15

    (5) 20

3. Between which months did City B have the greatest increase in the number of traffic accidents?
   (1) 10 and 11
   (2) 5 and 6
   (3) 3 and 4
   (4) 9 and 10
   (5) 1 and 2

4. During which month did City A have the least number of traffic accidents?
   (1) month 8
   (2) month 5
   (3) month 6
   (4) month 1
   (5) month 9

5. On a science test, Manuel got 24 questions right and missed 6 questions. What is the ratio of the number right to the total?
   (1) 24:6
   (2) 30:24
   (3) 6:30
   (4) 24:6
   (5) 4:5

6. One week in August, the thermometer recorded the following temperatures: 96°, 87°, 92°, 91°, 88°, 86°, and 98°. What was the median temperature?
   (1) 88°
   (2) 87°
   (3) 94°
   (4) 98°
   (5) 91°

Questions 7–11 refer to the following table.

Average Rainfall in Three Cities

	March	April	May
City 1	2.4 inches	3 inches	.03 inches
City 2	4 inches	1.6 inches	1.02 inches
City 3	3.1 inches	2.3 inches	3.4 inches

7. What was the average rainfall for the three cities in the month of April?
   (1) 3.2
   (2) 2
   (3) 2.3
   (4) 3.0
   (5) 2.1

8. What was the difference in rainfall amounts in April and May for City 1?

    (1) 2.97

    (2) .6

    (3) 1.4

    (4) 2.1

    (5) 2.9

9. What is the median rainfall for the three cities in the month of March?

    (1) 3.2

    (2) 3.1

    (3) 4

    (4) 2.4

    (5) 2.3

10. What is the ratio of rainfall in City 3 for the months of April to May?

    (1) 3:.03

    (2) 2.3:3.4

    (3) 3.1:2.3

    (4) 2.4:4

    (5) 3:4

11. What is the median rainfall for City 2?

    (1) 3.31

    (2) 1.02

    (3) 4

    (4) 1.06

    (5) 1.6

12. David packed a total of 40 boxes in 5 hours. How many boxes would Samuel have to pack in 3 hours in order to pack the same number of boxes?

    (1) 45

    (2) 25

    (3) 24

    (4) 15

    (5) 30

13. If 24 pencils cost $4.82, how much would 4 pencils cost?

    (1) $2.40

    (2) $1.20

    (3) $.60

    (4) $.81

    (5) $1.40

Questions 14–17 refer to the following circle chart.

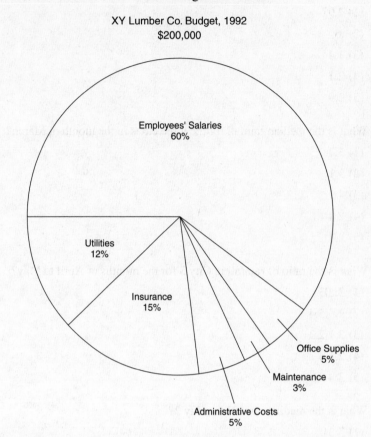

XY Lumber Co. Budget, 1992
$200,000

Employees' Salaries
60%

Utilities
12%

Insurance
15%

Office Supplies
5%

Maintenance
3%

Administrative Costs
5%

14. What is the percent difference between the cost of employees' salaries and administrative costs and insurance combined?

    (1) 50%

    (2) 45%

    (3) 40%

    (4) 25%

    (5) 20%

15. What fraction of the total budget was spent on utilities and office supplies combined?

    (1) $\dfrac{17}{100}$

    (2) $\dfrac{3}{25}$

    (3) $\dfrac{1}{20}$

    (4) $\dfrac{1}{4}$

    (5) $\dfrac{2}{3}$

16. How much money was budgeted for administrative costs?

    (1) $1,000.00

    (2) $10,000.00

    (3) $100.00

    (4) $100,000.00

    (5) Insufficient data given to solve the problem

17. Employees' salaries and maintenance costs represent how much of the total budget for XY Lumber Co.?

    (1) $110,000.00

    (2) $150,000.00

    (3) $100,000.00

    (4) $125,000.00

    (5) $126,000.00

18. Sandra is 3 years old, and her older sister, Julie, is 8 years old. Express Julie's age to Sandra's age in ratio form.

    (1) 3:8

    (2) 8:11

    (3) 8:3

    (4) 11:3

    (5) 11:8

19. There were only 8 inches of snowfall in 1993 in Laketown and 24 inches the following year. What is the ratio of snowfall from 1993 to 1994? (Be sure to express the ratio in simplest form.)

    (1) 8:24

    (2) 24:8

    (3) 3:1

    (4) 1:3

    (5) 8:32

20. The prices of a gallon of milk at different grocery stores are $1.39, $1.22, $1.29, and $1.30. What is the average price of a gallon of milk?

    (1) $1.32

    (2) $1.30

    (3) $1.25

    (4) $1.29

    (5) $1.31

Answers

1. **(3)** In month 11, the lines intersect.

2. **(1)** In the second month, City A had 60 traffic accidents and City B had 30 traffic accidents. $60 - 30 = 30$

3. **(2)** Between the 5th and 6th months, City B had an increase of approximately 35 accidents.

4. **(4)** In the first month, City B had 10 accidents.

5. **(5)** Add 24 and 6 to find the total number of questions. The number right is 24, so the ratio is 24:30. This should be simplified to the simplest form, so the answer is 4:5.

6. **(5)** The numbers in order from least to greatest are 86°, 87°, 88°, 91°, 92°, 96°, and 98°. The middle number is 91°.

7. **(3)** Add the 3 amounts of rainfall for April, then divide by 3.

$$
\begin{array}{r}
3.0 \\
1.6 \\
+2.3 \\
\hline
6.9
\end{array}
$$

$6.9 \div 3 = 2.3$

8. **(1)** $3 - .03 = 2.97$

9. **(2)** The numbers in order for the month of March are 2.4, 3.1, and 4. The median, or middle number, is 3.1.

10. **(2)** 2.3:3.4

11. **(5)** The three amounts of rainfall for City 2 in order are 1.02, 1.6, and 4. The middle number is 1.6.

12. **(3)** Set up a grid to solve the problem. Multiply diagonally with known numbers, and then divide by the third known number.

boxes 40	?
hours 5	3

$40 \times 3 = 120$
$120 \div 5 = 24$

13. **(4)** Set up a grid to solve the problem. Multiply diagonally with known numbers, and then divide by the third known number.

pencils 24	4
cost $4.82	?

$\$4.82 \times 4 = \$19.28$
$\$19.28 \div 24 = \$.81$

HINT: Money is always rounded up to the nearest penny.

14. **(3)** Add the insurance cost and the administrative costs, then subtract the total from 60%.

$$
\begin{array}{rr}
15 & 60 \\
+5 & -20 \\
\hline
20 & 40
\end{array}
$$

15. **(1)** Add the utilities and the office supplies, then rename your answer as a fraction.

$12 + 5 = 17\dfrac{17}{100}$ (The denominator is the whole, or 100.)

16. **(2)** $5\% \times \$200,000.00 = \$10,000.00$

17. **(5)** Add 60% and 3%, then multiply by the total budget.

   $63\% \times \$200,000.00 = \$126,000.00.$

18. **(3)** The instructions said to compare Julie's age to Sandra's age, so Julie's age is expressed first.

   8:3

19. **(4)** The ratio of snowfall from 1993 to 1994 is 8:24. Simplified to the simplest form, the ratio is 1:3.

20. **(2)** Add $1.39, $1.22, $1.29, and $1.30, then divide by 4 (the number of items you added).

   $\$1.39$ $\$5.20 \div 4 = \$1.30$
   1.22
   1.29
   $\underline{+1.30}$
   $\$5.20$

RELATIONSHIPS OF NUMBERS

Positives and Negatives

A **positive** is any number *greater than zero*, and a **negative** number is any number *less than zero*.

Adding Two Positives or Two Negatives

When the signs are the same, adding two positives or two negatives is an easy procedure. You simply add the two numbers together and give the answer either a positive or a negative sign. Adding $4 + 7$, the 4 and the 7 are both positives, the answer is +11. Adding $-4 + -7$ uses the same procedure. Because the sum of the two numbers is 11, the number in the answer is 11, but because both numbers were preceded by the negative sign, the answer is –11.

Adding Positive and Negative Numbers

Look at the following problem.

   $(+4) + (-7) = -3$

The parentheses around the numbers separate them from the math procedure. The sign within the parentheses tells you that the sign goes with the number and not the procedure. The sign that will go with the number in the answer is the sign from the number with the greater absolute value, the "larger" number, in the problem. To solve the problem, you must **subtract** 4 from 7 even though this is an addition problem, and then give the answer the sign of the number with the greater absolute value, the larger number. In this case, the answer is –3. Thinking of this problem in terms of money may make it easier for you to visualize the procedure. If you owe someone $7, you are in debt or –7. If you pay back $4, you still owe $3, so you are still –3.

Subtracting Positive and Negative Numbers

When you subtract positive and negative numbers, you will change the sign of the number being subtracted and then **add**. Look at the following problem.

$$(-4) - (+7) = -11$$

To solve this problem, you must change the sign of the 7 from a positive to a negative and then add the numbers together. The answer will be given a minus sign. Look at this problem in terms of money. If you owe someone $4, you are in debt or –4. If you borrow another $7, you must add this amount to your debt, now you owe $11, so you are –11.

To subtract $(-4) - (-7)$, follow the same procedure outlined above. Change the sign of the 7 from a negative to a positive, and then add the numbers together. Your answer is 3.

$$(-4) - (-7) = (-4) + (+7) = 3$$

If you borrow $4 from someone, you are $4 in debt, or –4. If you mistakenly pay them back $7, you will take that 7 away from the 4 you owed originally, but now you are actually $3 ahead or +3.

Working with Several Numbers

You can add or subtract groups of positive and negative numbers by solving the problem in steps. Look at the problems below.

$$(+3) + (-5) + (-6) + (+5) =$$

Add the positive numbers $(+3) + (+5) = +8$
Add the negative numbers for a negative total $(-5) + (-6) = -11$
Subtract the number with the least absolute value from the number with the greater absolute value $11 - 8 = 3$

Because the number with the greater absolute value had the negative sign, your answer should also have a negative sign. The answer to the problem, then, is –3.

$$(-4) - (+3) + (-6) - (+11) =$$

Change the signs of the numbers to be subtracted, and then add.

$$(-4) + (-3) + (-6) + (-11) = -24$$

Multiplying and Dividing with Signed Numbers

Whether your problem involves multiplying or dividing using signed numbers, the rules are the same.

If both numbers are positive or both are negative, the answer is always positive.

If the numbers have different signs, the answer is always negative.

Look at the example below.

$(+3)(+4) = 12$

(When numbers appear in parentheses with no sign between them telling you what operation to perform, you multiply.)

$(-3)(-4) = 12$

$(-3)(+4) = -12$

$(-12) \div (+4) = -3$

Practice

Solve the following problems

1. $(-4) - (+10) + (-2) =$

2. $(-12) + (-8) =$

3. $(-8)(10) =$

4. $(3) + (18) - (-6) =$

5. $(-44) \div (+11) =$

6. $(+5) + (-6) - (+8) =$

7. $(-9) - (-8) + (-12) - (+6) =$

8. $(-62)(-5) =$

9. $(+10) + (-18) + (+10) - (-12) =$

10. $(+72) \div (-6) =$

11. $(-2) + (-22) - (+15) - (-30) =$

12. $(-8) + (+8) - (-16) =$

13. $(-288) \div (-48) =$

Answers

1. –16
2. –20
3. –80
4. +27
5. –4
6. –9
7. –19
8. 310
9. +14
10. –12
11. –9
12. +16
13. +6

Exponents and Scientific Notation

The mathematical expression 6^3 means 6 to the third power. The 3 is the **exponent** or the **power**. Simply, this means that you must multiply 6 by itself 3 times. $6^3 = 6 \times 6 \times 6 = 216$. **It does not mean 6×3**.

   Scientific notation is a system for writing an extremely large number. Basically, it is a number between 1 and 10 written to the power of 10. For example, the number 380,000,000,000 can be written as 3.8×10^{11}. The number between 1 and 10 that you are working with is 3.8. When you count the number of zeros plus the number to the right of the decimal point, you can see that there are 11 digits. That means that the exponent is 11.

Practice

1. $4^4 =$

2. $3^2 =$

3. $8^3 =$

4. $2^5 =$

Write each of the following in scientific notation

5. 620,000,000

6. 752,000,000,000

7. 87,000,000,000,000

8. 839,000,000,000,000

Answers

1. 256	3. 512	5. 6.2×10^8	7. 8.7×10^{13}
2. 9	4. 32	6. 7.52×10^{11}	8. 8.39×10^{14}

Squares and Square Roots

A **square** is a number that has the exponent of 2. Five squared is expressed as 5^2. A **square root** is the number that, when multiplied by itself is the same as the number inside the symbol for square root. For example, when you see $\sqrt{25}$, you know that the square root is 5 because $5 \times 5 = 25$. A perfect square is any whole number that, when multiplied by itself, is the same as the number inside the square root symbol. On the GED test, you will generally be working with perfect squares.

Test Yourself

1. Melissa had $500.00 in her checking account. She wrote checks in the amounts of $35.75, $120.50, $98.25, and $350.00. She then deposited $375.00. How much money did she have in her account after her deposit?

   (1) $375.00

   (2) $604.50

   (3) $270.50

   (4) $200.00

   (5) Insufficient data is given to solve the problem

2. A high school football team carried the ball 5 times in one quarter. During those 5 times, they gained 4 yards, lost 6 yards, lost 4 yards, gained 8 yards, and lost 5 yards. How many yards did they lose in all?

   (1) 11

   (2) 10

   (3) 5

   (4) 3

   (5) 15

3. During one year, the federal government loaned a total of $783,000,000,000 to other countries. What is the scientific notation to express this figure?

   (1) 7.83×10^{11}

   (2) 78.3×10^{11}

   (3) 78.3×10^{10}

   (4) 7.83×10^{10}

   (5) $.783 \times 10^{12}$

4. Sam returned a pair of shoes and was credited with $54.99 in his account. At the same store, he bought a shirt for $22.50, a tie for $14.95, and sox for $3.98. How much credit was remaining in his account?

    (1) $15.99

    (2) $13.00

    (3) $11.43

    (4) $12.50

    (5) $13.56

5. 4.62×10^8 can be written as which of the following numbers?

    (1) 462,000

    (2) 46.2,000

    (3) 4.620,000,000

    (4) 462,000,000

    (5) 4620.000,000

6. Angelique has been in business for 6 years. In her first year, her profit was $7,560.00. Her second year profit was $5,300.00. During her third and fourth years, she suffered a loss of $8,450.00. Her fifth year saw a profit of $4,000.00. What is her total profit for the time she has been in business?

    (1) $11,560.00

    (2) $16,860.00

    (3) $8,410.00

    (4) $8,300.00

    (5) Insufficient data is given to solve the problem

7. At midnight, the temperature was –15°. By dawn, the temperature had risen 25°. What was the temperature at dawn?

    (1) 25°

    (2) 10°

    (3) –5°

    (4) –10°

    (5) Insufficient data is given to solve the problem

8. Over a six-month period, a certain stock rose 6 points, fell 4 points, fell another 8 points, rose 5 points for each of the next two months and ended the period by rising another 3 points. What was the total gain for this stock?

    (1) 7 points

    (2) 2 points

    (3) 19 points

    (4) 4 points

    (5) 6 points

9. $12^2 =$

   (1) 24

   (2) 6

   (3) 144

   (4) 2.4

   (5) 1,444

10. $\sqrt{64} + 16 =$

   (1) 80

   (2) 24

   (3) 48

   (4) 32

   (5) 26

Answers

1. **(3)** Add the amounts of the checks written ($604.50), subtract that number from the original $500.00 in the account (– $104.50), then add the deposit ($375.00).

2. **(4)** Add the yardage gained $4 + 8 = 12$. Add the yardage lost $(-6)+(-4)+(-5) = -15$. Subtract the gain from the loss. Because the lost yardage is the greatest number, the answer is –3.

3. **(1)** The number that falls between 1 and 10 that you are working with is 7.83. Count the number of places to the right of the decimal point. This number is the exponent. 7.83×10^{11}

4. **(5)** Add the amounts he spent. $22.50 + $14.95 + $3.98 = 41.43. Subtract this amount from the total credit. $54.99 – $41.43 = 13.56.

5. **(4)** Because the number you are writing is to the 8th power, there must be 8 places to the right of the decimal point.

6. **(5)** Insufficient data is given to solve this problem since no figure is given for the 6th year.

7. **(2)** Add +25 (the amount the temperature rose) to –15 (the temperature at midnight).

8. **(1)** $6 + 5 + 5 + 3 = 19$ These four figures represent the months in which the stock rose. $(-4) + (-8) = -12$. These two figures represent the months in which the stock fell. $(+19) + (-12) = +7$

9. **(3)** $12 \times 12 = 144$

10. **(2)** $\sqrt{64} = 8$

   $8 + 16 = 24$

MEASUREMENT

You will need to know how to solve problems that include measurement. For most problems dealing with **length**, you will need to know that *12 inches (in) = 1 foot (ft)* and that *3 feet = 1 yard (yd)*.

The **time** measurements that you must know are: *60 seconds (sec) = 1 minute (min), 60 minutes = 1 hour (hr), 24 hours = 1 day, 7 days (4) = 1 week (wk), 12 months (mo) = 1 year (yr), and 365 days = 1 year*.

When you are working on a problem dealing with **weight**, you should know that *16 ounces (oz) = 1 pound (lb), and 2,000 pounds = 1 ton (T)*.

Frequently used **liquid measures** are: 8 ounces (oz) = 1 cup (3), 2 cups = 1 pint (pt), 2 pints = 1 quart (qt), and 4 quarts = 1 gallon (gal).

Generally, when you are working with measurements, you will work with the different units of measurement separately. There will also be times when you will be required to convert measurements in order to solve a problem. Look at the problems below.

Adding Measurements

```
        6 feet 2 inches
        2 feet 8 inches
     +  3 feet 4 inches
       11 feet 14 inches
```

First add the feet (6 + 2 + 3 = 11)
Now add the inches (2 + 8 + 4 = 14)

Because there are 12 inches in each foot and the total number of inches added is 14, we can convert the inches to 1 foot 2 inches (14 ÷ 12 = 1 and a remainder of 2)

Now add the converted foot to the original 11 feet and the answer to the problem is 12 feet 2 inches. The answer to this problem is 12 feet 2 inches.

Subtracting Measurements

```
        6 hours 30 minutes
     -  3 hours 45 minutes
```

Because you cannot subtract 45 minutes from 30 minutes, you must convert one hour from the 6 hours into minutes then add those 60 minutes to the 30 minutes. The problem now looks like this:

```
        5 hours 90 minutes
     -  3 hours 45 minutes
        2 hours 45 minutes
```

Multiplying Measurements

Multiply 8 lbs 10 oz by 6

Multiply the pounds and ounces separately.

8 lbs × 6 = 48 lbs

10 oz × 6 = 60 oz

Convert the ounces to pounds.

60 ÷ 16 = 3 lbs 12 oz

Add the converted ounces to the pounds.

8 lbs 10 oz × 6 = 51 lbs 12 oz

Dividing Measurements

Divide 10 cups 7 ounces by 3.

Divide the 10 cups by 3.

10 ÷ 3 = 3 with a remainder of 1 cup

Convert the remaining cup into ounces.

1 cup = 8 ounces

Add the converted ounces to the 7 ounces.

8 + 7 = 15

Divide the 15 ounces by 3.

15 ÷ 3 = 5

The answer is 3 cups 5 ounces.

Practice

1. 10 lbs 5 oz ÷ 5
2. 12 hrs 16 min + 4 hrs 50 min
3. 4 ft 5 in – 1 ft 6 in
4. 4 gal 3 qts × 6
5. $13\frac{1}{2}$ ft 2 in ÷ 4
6. 7 hrs 14 min + 3 hrs 8 min + 1 hr 45 min
7. 4 c 6 oz – 1 c 7 oz
8. 2 yds 2 ft × 8

Answers

1. 33 oz
2. 17 hrs 6 min
3. 2 ft 11 in
4. 28 gal 2 qts
5. 3 ft 5 in
6. 12 hrs 7 min
7. 2 c 7 oz
8. 21 yd 1 ft

Test Yourself

1. Juanita walked 1 hour 20 minutes every day for one full week. At the end of the week, how many hours did she walk altogether?

   (1) 7 hr 20 min

   (2) 9 hr 20 min

   (3) 8 hr

   (4) 10 hr 10 min

   (5) Insufficient data is given to solve the problem

2. Mona bought 2 packages of ground beef, each weighing 3 pounds 4 ounces, and a package of pork chops weighing 2 pounds 9 ounces. How many pounds of meat did she buy?

   (1) 5 pounds 13 ounces

   (2) 9 pounds

   (3) 8 pounds 9 ounces

   (4) 6 pounds 9 ounces

   (5) 9 pounds 1 ounce

3. Lili bought 3 quarts of soda to make punch for a party. If she had 3 pints left over, how much did she use?

   (1) 3 pints

   (2) 2 quarts

   (3) 1 quart

   (4) 2 pints

   (5) 1 pint

4. If Deborah had a piece of fabric 15 yds 9 in long, and she wanted to cut it into 3 equal lengths for 3 dresses, how much fabric will be in each length?

   (1) 3 yd 5 in

   (2) 4 yd 6 in

   (3) 5 yd 3 in

   (4) 6 yd 2 in

   (5) 4 yd 3 in

5. Michael planned to spend $3\frac{1}{4}$ hours working in his garden. If he has already worked 45 minutes, how much time does he have left to work?

   (1) 2 hr 30 min

   (2) 2 hr 45 min

   (3) 1 hr 15 min

   (4) 2 hr 15 min

   (5) 1 hr 30 min

6. Thomas purchased 1 lb 4 oz bananas, 2 lb 8 oz apples, 3 lb peaches, and 3 lb 6 oz plums. How much fruit did he buy in all?

    (1) 10 lb 2 oz

    (2) 12 lb 8 oz

    (3) 9 lb 8 oz

    (4) 10 lb 8 oz

    (5) 9 lb 2 oz

7. Michelle has $4\frac{1}{2}$ pounds of fish to prepare for dinner. If she has 8 guests to feed, how many ounces of fish will each receive?

    (1) 6 oz

    (2) 2 oz

    (3) 8 oz

    (4) 9 oz

    (5) 4 oz

8. Mr. Jackson has a pine board measuring 8 ft 5 in and a redwood board measuring 6 ft 8 in. How much larger is the pine board than the redwood board?

    (1) 2 ft 3 in

    (2) 1 ft 9 in

    (3) 2 ft 9 in

    (4) 2 ft

    (5) 1 ft 3 in

9. Janine has a piece of ribbon $\frac{3}{4}$ yd in length. If she cuts 23 in from the ribbon, how many inches does she have left?

    (1) 14 in

    (2) 1 in

    (3) 3 in

    (4) 4 in

    (5) 12 in

10. Jackie is leaving from New York on a flight to Los Angeles at 1:30 PM. The flight takes 4 hours 30 minutes, and she will lose 3 hours of time by traveling to the West Coast. What time will she arrive in Los Angeles?

    (1) 2:30 PM

    (2) 6:00 PM

    (3) 5:00 PM

    (4) 5:30 PM

    (5) 3:00 PM

Answers

1. **(2)** Multiply 1 hour 20 minutes by 7 = 7 hours 140 minutes. Convert 140 minutes into hours. $140 \div 60 = 2$ hours 20 minutes. Add the converted hours to the answer = 9 hours 20 minutes.

2. **(5)** Add 3 lb 4 oz, 3 lb 4 oz, 2 lb 9 oz = 8 lb 17 oz. Convert the 17 oz to pounds and add to the answer = 9 lb 1 oz.

3. **(1)** Convert 3 quarts to 6 pints, then subtract 3 pints = 3 pints.

4. **(3)** 15 yd 9 in $\div$ 3 = 5 yd 3 in.

5. **(1)** Subtract 45 min from 3 hr 15 min. First convert 3 hr 15 min to 2 hr 75 min.

   2 hr 75 min -45 min = 2 hr 30 min

6. **(1)** 1 lb 4 oz + 2 lb 8 oz + 3 lb + 3 lb 6 oz = 9 lb 18 oz. Convert to 10 lb 2 oz.

7. **(4)** Convert $4\frac{1}{2}$ lb to ounces ($4\frac{1}{2} \times 16 = 72$).

   $72 \div 8 = 9$

8. **(2)** Convert 8 ft 5 in to 7 ft 17 in.

   7 ft 17 in $-$ 6 ft 8 in = 1 ft 9 in

9. **(4)** Convert $\frac{3}{4}$ yd to inches.

   (1 yd = 3 ft) (1 ft = 12 in) (3 $\times$12 = 36)

   $\frac{3}{4}$ of 36 = 27

   $27 - 23 = 4$

10. **(5)** 1:30 + 4 hr 30 min = 6:00. Subtract 3 hours for the time difference.

    6:00 $-$ 3 hr = 3:00

GEOMETRY

When you take the GED, you will be provided with a page of formulas that you will need to complete the geometry and algebra questions on the test. You do not need to memorize formulas since they will be given to you, but you need to be familiar with the process for using formulas.

Geometric Concepts

Angles

Angles are indicated by the symbol $\angle$. They are measured in degrees (°). The letter "m" is used to indicate the measure of an angle. The lines that form an angle are called **rays.** The rays of an angle meet at a point called the **vertex**. Angles are named by letters. Look at the angle on the following page.

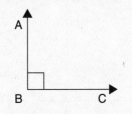

The name of this angle is $\angle$ABC. This angle is called a **right angle** and it measures 90°. The small square drawn in the angle indicates that it is a right angle. The two lines that meet to form a right angle are **perpendicular** to each other.

An angle that measures *less than 90°* is called an **acute angle**. $\angle$VWX below is an acute angle.

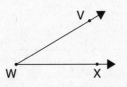

An angle that measures *more than 90°* is called an **obtuse angle**. $\angle$EFG below is an obtuse angle.

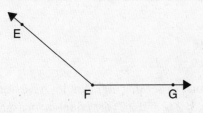

A **straight angle** measures *180°*. $\angle$XYZ is a straight angle.

Two angles whose measurements add up to 180° are called **supplementary angles**. The diagram below shows how ∠DEF and ∠FEG are supplementary angles.

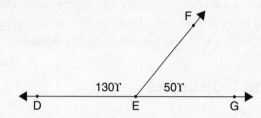

Two angles are called **complementary angles** when their measurement adds up to 90°. In the diagram below, m ∠ABC = 90°.   ∠ABE and ∠CBE are complementary because they add up to 90°.

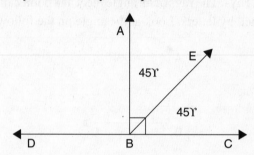

In geometry, when a set of points makes up a flat surface, it is referred to as a **plane**. When two lines in the same plane never meet, no matter how far they are extended, they are considered to be **parallel lines**. Because parallel lines never meet, they cannot form angles. If those two lines are intersected by a third line, however, eight angles are formed. The line that intersects two parallel lines is called the **transversal**. Look at the diagram below.

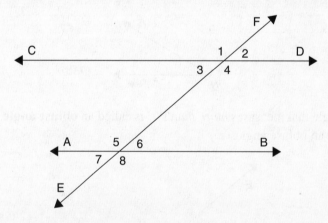

In the diagram, you can see that eight angles have been formed. The four acute angles (∠2, ∠3, ∠6, and ∠7) are equal in measurement, and the four obtuse angles (∠1, ∠4, ∠5, and ∠8) are also equal in measurement.

The sum of any acute angle plus any obtuse angle, in this picture, equals 180°.

If the transversal intersects two parallel lines perpendicularly, all eight angles that are formed are right angles.

Triangles

A triangle is a shape that is made up of three angles. The sum of the three angles that make up a triangle is 180° no matter how large or what the shape the triangle is. The diagram below shows the three types of triangles with which you will be working.

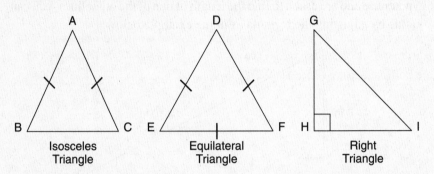

Isosceles
Triangle

Equilateral
Triangle

Right
Triangle

The **isosceles triangle** has two sides of equal length. $\angle B$ and $\angle C$ have the same measurement. $\overline{AB}$ and $\overline{AC}$ are the same length. In the **equilateral triangle**, all three angles have the same measurement, and all three sides are the same length. In the **right triangle**, one angle is a right angle, and the other two angles are acute angles. The longest side of a right triangle (in this case, $\overline{GI}$) is called the **hypotenuse**.

The Pythagorean Theorem

The Pythagorean Theorem is a very important concept in working with right triangles, and you will no doubt be asked to use it in solving problems on the GED. The formula for the Pythagorean Theorem is $c^2 = a^2 + b^2$. You do not have to memorize this formula because it will be on the formula page you will be given with the GED test, but you should be familiar with how to use it. Look at the example below.

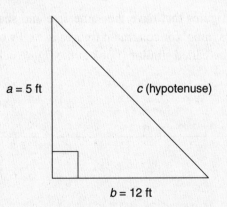

$a = 5$ ft

c (hypotenuse)

$b = 12$ ft

In our diagram, we are given the length of line a and line b, but we need to find the length of line c. To do this, we will use the Pythagorean Theorem.

$$c^2 = a^2 + b^2$$
$$c^2 = 5^2 + 12^2$$
$$c^2 = 25 + 144$$
$$c^2 = 169$$
$$c = \sqrt{169}$$
$$c = 13 \text{ feet}$$

If you are working with a problem where you are given the length of the hypotenuse and are asked to find the length of one of the other lines, you can do this by adjusting the formula as in the example below.

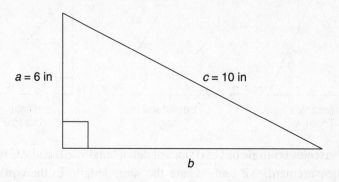

The order in which the formula is set up is changed slightly to solve this problem. The unknown line (in this case, line b) starts the formula and, instead of adding the two squared numbers, you must subtract them.

$$b^2 = c^2 - a^2$$
$$b^2 = 10^2 - 6^2$$
$$b^2 = 100 - 36$$
$$b^2 = 64$$
$$b = \sqrt{64}$$
$$b = 8 \text{ inches}$$

Congruent and Similar Triangles

Two geometric figures that have the same size and shape are said to be **congruent**. The symbol for congruent figures is $\cong$. Two figures that have the same shape are called **similar**. Look at the figure below.

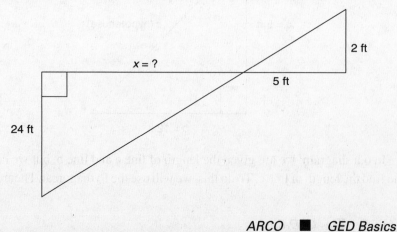

In order to find the length of the corresponding side of the larger triangle, you must set up a proportion. Because the triangles are similar, their sides are in proportion.

$$\frac{x}{5} = \frac{24}{2}$$

To solve the proportion, cross multiply.

$2x = 120$

Now, to find x, divide 120 by 2.

$120 \div 2 = 60$

The unknown side is 60 feet long.

Perimeter and Area of Triangles

The perimeter of a triangle is the sum of the lengths of the three sides of the triangle. The formula for the perimeter of a triangle is P = a + b + c.

The area of a triangle means the space inside the figure. It is equal to one-half the length of any side times the height. The formula for the area of a triangle is $A = \frac{1}{2}bh$. This means that you would multiply the base times the height, then divide that number by two.

Practice

1. If two angles of a triangle measure 72° and 60°, what is the measure of the third angle?

2. Find the area of the triangle below.

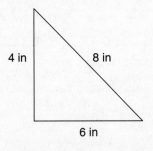

4 in   8 in

6 in

3. A right angle measures how many degrees?

4. What is the measurement of ∠A in the diagram below?

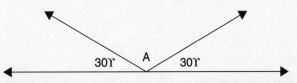

30Ƴ   A   30Ƴ

5. What is the perimeter of a triangle whose sides measure 8 feet, 6 feet, and 5 feet?

6. Two angles whose sum is 180° are called what?

7. Find the length of the unknown side of the triangle below.

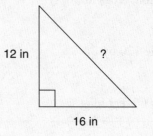

8. One acute angle of a right triangle measures 60°. What does the other acute angle measure?

9. If the vertex angle of an isosceles triangle measures 98°, what is the measure of each base angle?

10. If the two triangles below are similar, what is the length of the unknown side?

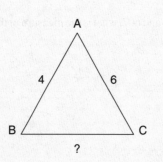
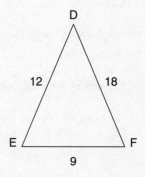

Answers

1. 48°   4. 120°   7. 20 in   10. 3

2. 12 sq in   5. 19 ft   8. 30°

3. 90°   6. supplementary 9. 41°

Circles

There are several terms relating to circles that you will need to know to solve some of the geometry problems on the GED. The **diameter** of a circle is the distance through the center of the circle. The **radius** is one-half of the diameter. The **circumference** is the distance around a circle, and the **area** is the amount of space inside the circle. The diameter and radius are shown in the diagram below.

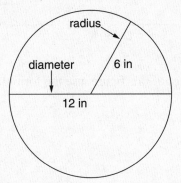

If the diameter of our example circle is 12 inches, then the radius is 6 inches.

To find the circumference of our circle, we must follow a formula. The formula for finding the circumference is $C = \pi d$. C stands for the circumference, π stands for the Greek letter *pi*, and *d* stands for the diameter. Unless you are told to do otherwise, use the number 3.14 as the value of π. Below is the solution to finding the circumference of our example circle.

$C = \pi d$

$C = 3.14 \times 12$

$C = 37.68$

The formula for finding the area of a circle is $A = \pi r^2$. This means that you will multiply π times the radius squared.

$A = \pi r^2$

$A = 3.14 \times 6 \times 6$

$A = 113.04$

Other Geometric Shapes

Besides triangles and circles, you should be familiar with rectangles and squares. A rectangle is a figure whose length and width are not the same size, while a square has all sides the same. To find the perimeter of a rectangle, multiply the length by two, multiply the width by two, then add the figures together. Because a square has all four sides equal, you simply have to multiply one side times four. Remember that the perimeter is the distance around the outside of the figure. Look at the diagram below.

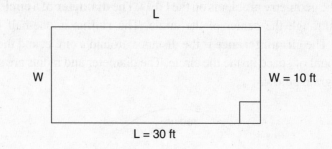

To find the perimeter of this figure, use the formula $P = 2l + 2w$

$P = 2l + 2w$

$P = (2 \times 30) + (2 \times 10)$

$P = 60 + 20$

$P = 80$ ft

The area of a square or a rectangle is the space inside the perimeter of a figure. To find the area, simply multiply the length times the width. The formula for finding the area is $A = l \times w$. The area of the figure above is $10 \times 30 = 300$ sq. feet.

Volume is the amount of space a solid or three dimensional figure occupies. Volume is measured in cubic measurement. Look at the diagram below of a rectangular solid.

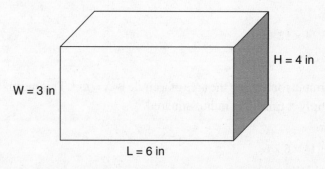

To find the volume, or how much space the rectangular solid occupies, the formula is $V = lwh$. This means that we must multiply the length times the width times the height.

$V = lwh$

$V = 6 \times 3 \times 4$

$V = 72$ cubic inches

To find the volume of a cube, because the length, width, and height are equal, the formula is $V = s^3$. s is the side, so we would multiply that figure by itself three times.

To find the area of the surface of the solid rectangle, the formula is A = 2*lw* + 2*wh* + 2*lh*. The area of our example can be expressed as follows:

A = 2*lw* + 2*wh* + 2*lh*

A = 2 × 18 + 2 × 12 + 2 × 24

A = 36 + 24 + 48

A = 108 in

A cylinder is another geometric figure you might be asked to work with. In a cylinder, the top and bottom bases are circles that lie in parallel planes. Look at the diagram below.

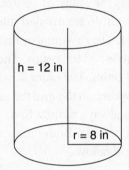

To find the volume of a cylinder, you must multiply the area of one base by the height. The formula for finding the volume of a cylinder is V = π*r²h*.

V = π*r²*h

V = 3.14 × 8² × 12

V = 3.14 × 64 × 12

V = 2,411.52 cu in

Practice

1. Find the area of the floor of a room that is 6 ft long and 8 ft wide.

2. If the diameter of a circle is 46 inches, what is its radius?

3. What is the area of a circle that has a diameter of 6 feet?

4. A rectangular solid measures 8 in wide by 6 in long by 12 in high. What is its surface area?

5. What is the volume of the rectangular solid described above?

6. What is the volume of a cylinder that measures 18 inches high and has a diameter of 9 inches?

7. What is the volume of a cube with sides that measure 4 feet?

8. If a circle has a diameter of 16 inches, what is its circumference?

9. What is the perimeter of a rectangle whose length is twice its width and whose width is 8 feet?

10. If the circumference of a circle is 25.12 feet, what is its diameter?

Answers

1. 48 sq ft	4. 432 sq in	7. 64 cu ft	10. 8 ft
2. 23 in	5. 576 cu in	8. 50.24 in	
3. 28.26 sq ft	6. 1144.53 cu in	9. 48 ft	

COORDINATE GEOMETRY (DISTANCE AND SLOPE)

Finding points on a plane is the study of coordinate geometry. A grid is commonly used to do this. Grids are divided into four sections, and each section is called a **quadrant**. The two number lines that divide the grid into quadrants are called the *x*-**axis** and the *y*-**axis**. The points that are drawn on the grid are called **ordered pairs**. The order in which the pairs of numbers are written will determine where on the grid the numbers are placed. The *x*, or horizontal coordinate, is always written first. This number is separated from the *y* coordinate by a comma. Both numbers in a pair are written in parentheses. Look at the grid below.

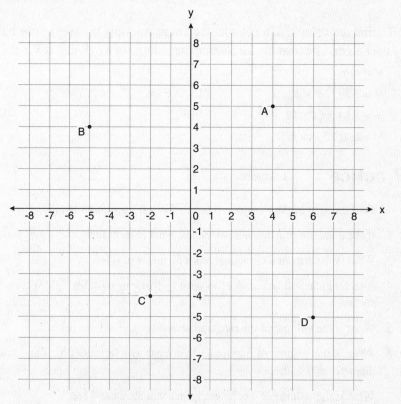

The ordered pair for point *A* is (4,5). Starting at the zero in the middle of the grid, count over four squares to the right on the *x*-axis. This gives you the coordinate for the first number of the pair. Now, count up 5 squares on the *y*-axis.

Look at point *C* on the grid. What is the ordered pair to express point *C*'s location? Because you must count two squares to the left of the zero and four squares below the zero, the ordered pair is (–2,–4).

Distance

Finding the distance between two points that are directly horizontal or vertical from each other is simply a matter of counting the number of squares that separate the points or subtracting the lesser number from the greater number.

If you are asked to find the distance between two points, you use the Pythagorean theorem. Look at the grid below.

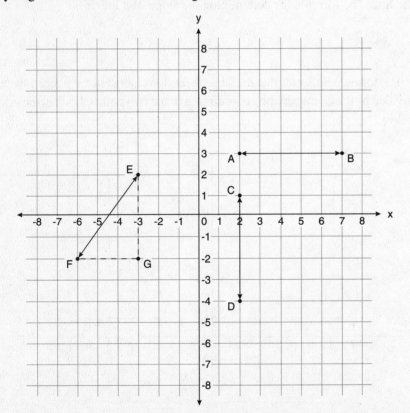

The distance between points *A* and *B* is 5. The distance between points *D* and *C* is also 5. To find the distance between points *E* and *F*, first determine the distance between *E* and *G*. Then figure the distance between *F* and *G*. The distance between *E* and *G* is 4, and the distance between *F* and *G* is 3.

When you set up the formula for the Pythagorean theorem, c will be the distance between E and F. The solution for finding the distance between E and F is shown below.

$c^2 = a^2 + b^2$

$c^2 = 4^2 + 3^2$

$c^2 = 16 + 9$

$c^2 = 25$

$c = \sqrt{25}$

$c = 5$

The distance between points E and F is 5.

Slope

The **slope** of a line is the distance that the line rises between two points on the line. The formula for determining the slope of a line is

$$m = \frac{y_2 - y_1}{x_2 - x_1}$$

The formula indicates that the slope (m) is the change in the y coordinates divided by the change in the x coordinates of the two points. Look at the grid below.

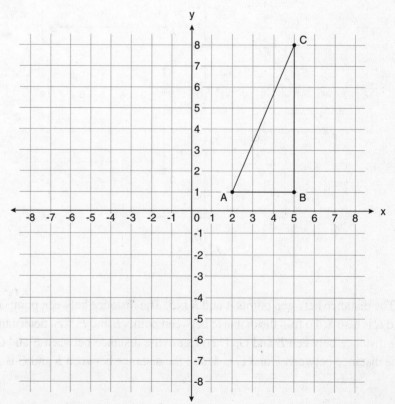

The coordinates of point A are (2,1), the coordinates of point B are (5,1), and the coordinates of point C are (5,8). The solution to finding the slope of $\overleftrightarrow{AC}$ is below.

$$m = \frac{y_2 - y_1}{x_2 - x_1}$$

$$m = \frac{8 - 1}{5 - 2}$$

$$m = \frac{7}{3}$$

Practice

Using the grid below, answer the following questions.

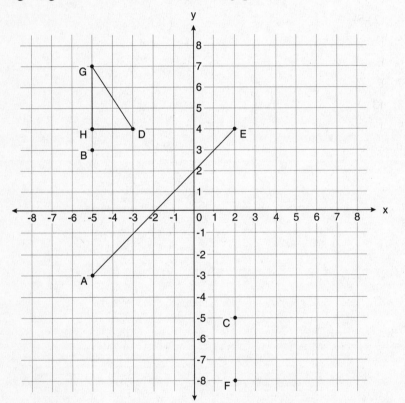

1. What are the coordinates for point *A*?

2. The coordinates for point *B* are?

3. What is the distance between points *A* and *B*?

4. What are the coordinates for point *C*?

5. (–3,4) are the coordinates for what point?

6. (2,4) are the coordinates for what point?

7. (2,–8) are the coordinates for what point?

8. What is the distance between points *D* and *F*?

9. What is the slope of $\overleftrightarrow{AE}$?

10. What is the distance between points *G* and *D*?

Answers

1. (–5,–3)
2. (–5,3)
3. 6
4. (2,–5)
5. D
6. E
7. F
8. 13
9. 1
10. $\sqrt{13}$

Test Yourself

Questions 1–2 refer to the following diagram.

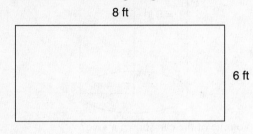

1. Janine is planning a vegetable garden measuring 8 ft long by 6 ft wide. How many square feet will her garden cover?

    (1) 14 sq ft

    (2) 48 sq ft

    (3) 64 sq ft

    (4) 36 sq ft

    (5) 28 sq ft

2. If Janine wants to put a fence around the garden, how many feet of fencing will she need?

    (1) 48 ft

    (2) 96 ft

    (3) 14 ft

    (4) 38 ft

    (5) 28 ft

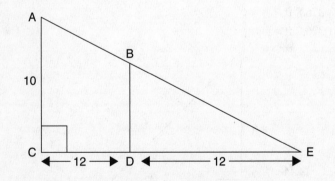

3. Find the length of $\overline{BD}$ in the above triangle.

    (1) 6

    (2) 8

    (3) 5

    (4) 20

    (5) 12

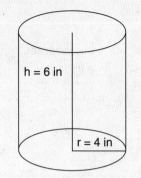

4. What is the volume of the can shown above?
   (1) 24 cu in
   (2) 301.44 cu in
   (3) 204.24 cu in
   (4) 48 cu in
   (5) 192,902 cu in

5. A box is 10 inches long, 5 inches wide, and 3 inches high. What is the area of surface of the box?
   (1) 18 cu in
   (2) 150 cu in
   (3) 36 cu in
   (4) 190 cu in
   (5) 140 cu in

6. The diameter of a circular playground is 60 feet. If Anthony walks around the playground twice, how many feet will he have walked?
   (1) 188.4 ft
   (2) 120 ft
   (3) 300.8 ft
   (4) 376.8 ft
   (5) 326.7 ft

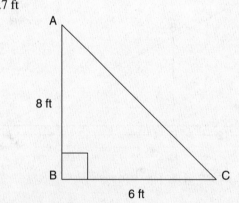

7. What is the length of $\overline{AC}$ in the triangle above?
   (1) 10 ft
   (2) 14 ft
   (3) 12 ft
   (4) 48 ft
   (5) Insufficient data is given to solve the problem

Items 8–10 refer to the diagram below. Lines *a* and *b* are parallel.

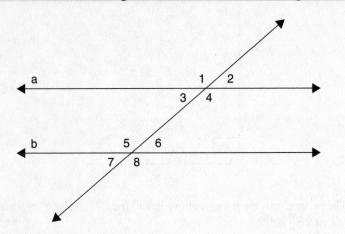

8. If ∠5 measures 140°, what is the measurement of ∠6?

   (1) 80°

   (2) 40°

   (3) 60°

   (4) 45°

   (5) 90°

9. Which angle is equal to ∠1, ∠4, and ∠5?

   (1) ∠3

   (2) ∠2

   (3) ∠6

   (4) ∠7

   (5) ∠8

10. What is the sum of ∠6 and ∠8?

    (1) 140°

    (2) 120°

    (3) 180°

    (4) 260°

    (5) 160°

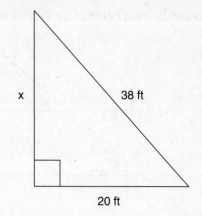

11. The perimeter of the triangle above is 130 feet. What is the length in feet of the missing side?

    (1) 58

    (2) 72

    (3) 55

    (4) 62

    (5) 80

Items 12–13 refer to the following diagram.

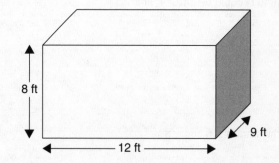

12. The room diagramed above will be carpeted with wall-to-wall carpeting. In square *yards*, how much will be needed?

    (1) 12

    (2) 108

    (3) 21

    (4) 29

    (5) 120

13. Two adjacent walls in the room are to be wallpapered. What is the area in square *yards* of the two walls?

    (1) 108

    (2) 204

    (3) 21.6

    (4) 18.9

    (5) Insufficient data is given to solve the problem

Items 14–17 refer to the following diagram.

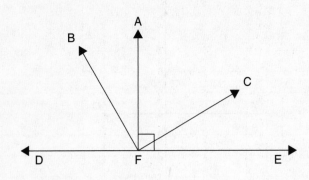

14. What is the measurement of ∠AFE?

    (1) 10°

    (2) 60°

    (3) 180°

    (4) 45°

    (5) 90°

15. Which two angles are supplementary angles?

    (1) ∠AFD and ∠AFE

    (2) ∠BFD and ∠AFE

    (3) ∠BFC and ∠AFC

    (4) ∠AFE and ∠BFE

    (5) ∠CFE and ∠BFE

16. What is the measurement of ∠DFE?

    (1) 90°

    (2) 360°

    (3) 180°

    (4) 45°

    (5) 120°

17. If m∠AFB = 45°, what is the measurement of ∠BFE?

    (1) 160°

    (2) 135°

    (3) 145°

    (4) 120°

    (5) 85°

Items 18–20 refer to the following grid.

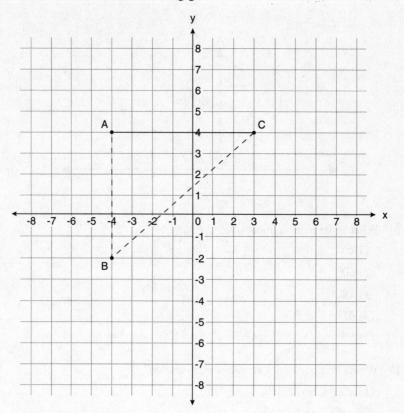

18. What are the coordinates of point *A*?

    (1) (5,4)

    (2) (4,5)

    (3) (–4,4)

    (4) (–5,–4)

    (5) (4,–5)

19. What is the distance between points *A* and *C*?

    (1) 7

    (2) 6

    (3) 4

    (4) 8

    (5) 5

20. What is the distance between points *B* and *C*?

    (1) 8

    (2) $\sqrt{85}$

    (3) $\sqrt{68}$

    (4) 16

    (5) Insufficient data is given to solve this problem.

Answers

1. **(2)** Use the formula $A = l \times w$

   $8 \times 6 = 48$ sq ft

2. **(5)** Use the formula $P = 2l + 2w$

   $P = 2 \times 8 + 2 \times 6 = 16 + 12 = 28$ ft

3. **(3)** Set up a proportion for similar triangles

   $\frac{12}{24} = \frac{x}{10}$ $24x = 120$; $x = 120 \div 24 = 5$

4. **(2)** Use the formula $V = \pi r^2 h$

   $V = 3.14 \times 4^2 \times 6$

   $V = 3.14 \times 16 \times 6$

   $V = 301.44$ cu in

5. **(4)** Use the formula $A = 2lw + 2wh + 2lh$

   $A = 2 \times 10 \times 5 + 2 \times 5 \times 3 + 2 \times 10 \times 3$

   $A = 100 + 30 + 60$

   $A = 190$ cu in

6. **(4)** $C = \pi d$

   $C = 3.14 \times 60$

   $C = 188.4$

   Because he walked twice around the playground, you must multiply 188.4 by 2 = 376.8.

7. **(1)** $c^2 = a^2 + b^2$

   $c^2 = 8^2 + 6^2$

   $c^2 = 64 + 36$

   $c^2 = 100$

   $c = \sqrt{100}$

   $c = 10$ ft

8. **(2)** $180° - 140° = 40°$

9. **(5)** $\angle 8$

10. **(3)** $180°$

11. **(2)** Use the formula $P = a + b + c$ but use x for the unknown because you know the perimeter.

    $130 = 38 + 20 + x$

    $130 = 58 + x$

    $130 - 58 = 72$

12. **(1)** First convert the feet to yards

    9 ft = 3 yds (width)

    12 ft = 4 yds (length)

    Use the formula $A = l \times w$

    $3 \times 4 = 12$

13. **(4)** Convert the feet to yards

    $h \approx 2.7$ yd

    $l = 4$ yd

    $w = 3$ yd

    Use $A = l \times w$ to find the area of each wall

    $2.7 \times 4 = 10.8$

    $2.7 \times 3 = 8.1$

    $10.8 + 8.1 = 18.9$

14. **(5)** A right angle measures 90°

15. **(1)** $\angle AFD$ and $\angle AFE$. The sum of supplementary angles is 180°

16. **(3)** 180°

17. **(2)** $45° + 90° = 135°$

18. **(3)** (−4,4)

19. **(1)** 7

20. **(2)** Use the formula $c^2 = a^2 + b^2$

    $c^2 = 6^2 + 7^2$ (the distance between A and B is 6 and the distance between A and C is 7)

    $c^2 = 36 + 49$

    $c^2 = 85$

    $c = \sqrt{85}$

ALGEBRA

In algebra, numbers are sometimes replaced by letters. These letters are called **variables.** You have already worked with variables in some of the problems you solved in previous sections when you were working with basic math. For example, when you were asked to solve the problem $6 + ? = 13$, the variable was the question mark. To write that problem as an algebraic expression, you would write $6 + x = 13$. In the expression $5x$, the x is the variable and the 5 is called the **coefficient**. Look at the term below:

$4a + 6a + 2b + 2a - x$

The first thing to do is to **simplify** the problem. There are 3 a combinations, 1 b, and 1 x. To simplify, you combine all the same letter terms. After simplifying, the problem looks like this:

$12a + 2b - x$

A division problem in algebra is usually expressed using the fraction symbol. For example, instead of writing $12 \div x = 6$, the problem would be written $\frac{12}{x} = 6$.

The multiplication symbol is not used in algebra. Instead, a multiplication problem would be written in one of three ways:

- The numbers and variables are written with nothing between them: $12xy$

- The numbers are written with a raised dot between them: $12 \cdot x \cdot y$

- Each number, variable, or group of numbers and letters are written in parentheses: $(12)(x)(y)$

Parentheses are also used in algebraic expressions to indicate the order of the procedure to follow to solve the problem. Look at the problem below:

$5(6 + 10)$

In this problem, you would first add the numbers that are in parentheses, then multiply the sum by 5.

$5(16) = 80$

To combine like terms when there are exponents and you are multiplying, the exponents are added together. In the term $(3x^2)(4x^2)$, the solution would be $12x^4$.

To combine like terms where there are exponents and you are dividing, the exponents are subtracted. In the term $\frac{15x^3y^2}{3x^2y^2}$, the solution would be $5x$. $15 \div 3 = 5$ and when x^3 is divided by x^2, the answer would be x^1, which is simply written as x. $y^2 \div y^2 = 1$, so that variable is eliminated from the equation.

Factoring is the process by which you divide common elements out of an expression and rewrite the expression in a simplified way. Look at the expression below:

$3a^2b - 2a^2c$

In this expression, the common element on either side of the minus sign is a^2, so that is simplified by only writing it one time as follows:

$a^2(3b - 2c)$

Practice

Factor the following expressions

1. $6a + 6b$ 3. $x^2 - xy$

2. $4x^2 + 4y^2$ 4. $2xy + 6ab$

Simplify the following terms

5. $4a - 2a + -3a + 3b$ 6. $4x^3 - x + 3b$

7. $\dfrac{6a^3xy}{2a^2xy}$ 8. $(6x^3)(3x^2)$

Answers

1. $6(a + b)$ 3. $x(x - y)$ 5. $-a + 3b$ 7. $3a$
2. $4(x^2 + y^2)$ 4. $2(xy + 3ab)$ 6. $4x^3 - x + 3b$ 8. $18x^5$

Solving Equations

An equation is an algebraic expression that says two values are equal. To solve an equation, all the numbers need to be on one side of the equation and the variables need to be on the other side. To accomplish this, remember, **whatever you do to one side of the equation, you must do to the other side.** The process you will use to separate the numbers from the variables is called **inverse operations**. An inverse operation is the opposite of the original operation in the equation. Instead of adding, you will subtract; instead of multiplying, you will divide. Look at the equation below:

$x + 23 = 52$

To solve this equation, you must first look at the addition sign and the number to be added. Since the equation tells you to add, you would do the opposite, or subtract, 23 from both sides of the equation. $x + 23 - 23 = x$, and $52 - 23 = 29$, so the solution is $x = 29$.

Solving Equations with Variables on Both Sides of the Equal Sign

An equation that has variables on both sides of the equal sign is solved in much the same manner as one in which there is a variable on only one side.

It will, however, take three steps to solve this type of equation. Look at the example below:

$6x + 2 = 5x + 5$

First, use the inverse to get all the unknowns on one side of the equation.

$6x + 2 - 5x = 5x - 5x + 5$

$x + 2 = 5$

Now, use the inverse again to move the 2 to the other side of the equation.

$x + 2 - 2 = 5 - 2$

$x = 3$

Practice

Solve the following equations

1. $18 = 6 + x$
2. $y - 22 = 68$
3. $3c = 36$
4. $\dfrac{w}{7} = 84$
5. $3x + 2 = 20$

6. $3a + 4 = 40$
7. $\dfrac{a}{2} = 12$
8. $3y + 7 = 37$
9. $2(x + 5) = 3(x - 1)$
10. $\dfrac{2}{3}x = 12$

Answers

1. 12
2. 90
3. 12
4. 588
5. 6
6. 12
7. 24
8. 10
9. 13
10. 18

Test Yourself

1. Simplify $6x - x + 8x$
   (1) $2x$
   (2) $3x$
   (3) $13x$
   (4) $5x$
   (5) $-13x$

2. Simplify $6xy^3 + xy^3$
   (1) $7xy^6$
   (2) $7x3y^3$
   (3) $7xy^3$
   (4) $7x^2y^6$
   (5) $7x^2y^6$

3. $(-2x^2)(-3x^3) =$
   (1) $6x^5$
   (2) $-6x^5$
   (3) $6x^6$
   (4) $6x$
   (5) $-6x^6$

4. $\dfrac{-18a^3b^2}{3a^2b^2} =$
   (1) $6ab$
   (2) $-6a$
   (3) $-6ab$
   (4) $6a^2b$
   (5) $-6a^5b^4$

5. Find the value of $3y^2 + 2y - 2(y + 3)$ if $y = 5$
   (1) 60
   (2) 72
   (3) 62
   (4) 69
   (5) 81

6. Find the value of $-6a + a^2 + 3(a + 6)$ if $a = 3$
   (1) -18
   (2) 27
   (3) 28
   (4) 9
   (5) 18

7. Solve for x: $3(x + 6) = 2(x - 1)$
   (1) -20
   (2) 16
   (3) 7
   (4) 8
   (5) -16

8. Solve for y: $\dfrac{y}{4} + 1 = 3$
    (1) 8
    (2) 16
    (3) 4
    (4) 7
    (5) 3

9. Solve for w: $3w + 5w = 40$
    (1) 8
    (2) 10
    (3) 5
    (4) 6
    (5) 9

10. After picking berries, Susan had 6 more pints of berries than Jan. Together they had 28 pints. How many pints did Jan have?
    (1) 28
    (2) 16
    (3) 12
    (4) 21
    (5) 11

11. $x + y + 3z + 2x - z =$
    (1) $x + 3y + z$
    (2) $3x + y + 2z$
    (3) $2x + 3z + y$
    (4) $2x + 3y + z$
    (5) $2x + y + z$

12. Manuel earns x dollars in one day. His brother earns y dollars in one day. Which expression shows how much they earn together in 15 days?
    (1) $x + y$
    (2) $15x + y$
    (3) $15(x + 2y)$
    (4) $15x + 15y$
    (5) $15x - y$

13. Find the value of $\dfrac{1}{2}y^3$ if $y = 4$
    (1) 64
    (2) 12
    (3) 18
    (4) 62
    (5) 32

14. Solve for x: $5x - 16 = 2 - 7x$
    (1) 2
    (2) $3\dfrac{1}{2}$
    (3) $1\dfrac{1}{2}$
    (4) 4
    (5) $2\dfrac{1}{2}$

15. Solve for y: $\dfrac{4y}{2} = 8y - 12$

    (1) −2
    (2) 2
    (3) 12
    (4) −12
    (5) 6

16. Find the value of x in the equation $x + 3x + (x + 3) = 18$

    (1) 4
    (2) 6
    (3) 2
    (4) 5
    (5) 3

17. A ribbon was cut into 8 pieces. Each piece was 3 inches long. Which expression shows how long the ribbon was before it was cut?

    (1) $L = 8(3)$
    (2) $L = \dfrac{8}{3}$
    (3) $3L = 8$
    (4) $L = \dfrac{3}{8}$
    (5) $L = 8 + 3$

18. After a purchase of 35 dollars, Joseph had 75 dollars left. Which equation shows how much money Joseph had originally?

    (1) $35 + d = 75$
    (2) $75 - 35 = d$
    (3) $75 + 35 = d$
    (4) $75 - d = 35$
    (5) $35 - d + 75$

19. Sarah has 25 dollars. She buys 2 books that cost 7 dollars and 50 cents each. How much money does she have left? Which expression represents this problem?

    (1) $x = 25 - 2(7.50)$
    (2) $x = 25 - 7.50$
    (3) $x = 2(7.50) - 25$
    (4) $2x = 25 - 7.50$
    (5) Insufficient data to solve this problem

20. A dressmaker must cut a length of fabric 100 inches long into two pieces so that one piece will be 34 inches longer than the other piece. Find the length of the shorter piece.

    HINT: Let x = the shorter piece and $x + 34$ = the longer piece.

    (1) 66 inches
    (2) 33 inches
    (3) 56 inches
    (4) 53 inches
    (5) 43 inches